AF413284

THEY TAUGHT ME *HOW* TO BE THE MAN I AM

MENTORS AND MENTEES

DR. JOHN L. SMITH, JR.

THEY TAUGHT ME *HOW* TO BE THE MAN I AM

MENTORS AND MENTEES

DR. JOHN L. SMITH, JR.

A Smith Junior Literary Works Publication

THEY TAUGHT ME HOW TO BE THE MAN I AM

Mentors and Mentees

Written by
Dr. John L. Smith Jr.

Presented by
Smith Junior Literary Works

The fonts are Avenir 10pt., 12pt., and Charter. Dr. Smith shares stories from his life as he celebrates the nurturing heroes in his life: His mentors.

Copyright 2024 © Dr. John L. Smith, Jr.
Cover Photo by Smith Family
Cover Photo Features "The Smith Brothers: Jake, David, John Lee Sr. (the author's father) and Garland."
The photo collage seen throughout features the mentors and the mentee.

Smith Junior Literary Works
P.O. Box 48035
16350 Bruce B. Downs Blvd.
Tampa, Florida 33647
info@smithjuniorliteraryworks.com

ISBN 979-8-218-41627-0

Library of Congress
1. Mentoring 2. Education 3. Social Sciences 4. American Black History

Hard Cover

Printed in the United States

$24.99

THE BEGINNING

Believing that we pull ourselves up by our own bootstraps is indeed self-empowering. However, a careful examination most often reveals that there were other people who were crucial to our fate and destiny. They often appeared as relatives, or intervening teachers, preachers and advisers, ordinary human encounters, all with magical sway. And, by fully acknowledging their powerful influence in our lives, we make ourselves whole.

DEDICATION

For the generous human hearts who unselfishly lift up others to help make them whole; and for my loving wife, Juel and family, who grounded me in faith, humility and purpose.

I am forever grateful for the caring individuals who encouraged and supported me as University of South Florida Fine Arts Dean and Fisk University President by sending personal notes and cards and attending my Fisk inauguration—gracious actions never forgotten.

ACKNOWLEDGEMENTS

My heartfelt thanks to all the generous contributors for this humble effort. Gwendolyn J. Jackson (Publisher), Myra C. Harris (Editor), Susan Ingram (Editor), Angela Preston (Editor), Rev. Sister Erma Coburn (Prayers), Patricia Russell McCloud (Friendship and Introductions), Rohan Preston, Stuart Hinds (UMKC Libraries), Juel Smith, Jue-L Consultants, Deborah Hofmann, Becky Briggs Becker (UMKC Archivist), Dr. Julie Sullivan, Dr. William Alexander, William "Bill" Miller, Myrtle Scott, Barbara Terry, Grace Reese, Gertrude Batiste, Amy Batiste, Emily Williamson Literary Agency, Angelica Spicer Johnson, Dr. Vernetta K. Williams, Shirley Toland-Dix.

TABLE OF CONTENTS

INTRODUCTION

This book is a hybrid. What I wanted to say and how I wanted to say it couldn't fit neatly into a single traditional publishing category. It encompasses biography, autobiography (memoir), history, race, education, music, sociology, spiritual, relationships, inspiration, and of course, mentoring. It is also a metaphor of my own personal traits which reflect multiple dimensions including African and Jewish ancestry, and introvert and private, but extrovert and gregarious as the situation dictates. Further, this is not an instructional manual on mentorship, or a narrative about the singular influence of a high-profile person. Although, the stories demonstrate creative approaches for nurturing lives.

THEY TAUGHT ME HOW TO BE THE MAN I AM is a collection of independent, but related stories about common, ordinary relationships that nurtured and significantly influenced my life, each revealing close bonding between an individual and me. Musical references serve as an interweaving bridge for the different short stories. The powerful, natural relationships shaped me and dramatically swayed my life's successful journey. And, although not a memoir exclusively, my identity, along with my mentors, is revealed through our intermingled lives that occur within interesting and informative contexts.

My mentors came into my life by fate, and happen to be all men, except for my mother whose powerful presence deserves separate exploration. However, instances of her nurturing role are often referenced, particularly in the book's early chapters.

This book began with a simple list of names compiled while reflecting on my life during the early days of retirement, attempting to answer the nagging question: How did I become who I am and manage to accomplish the things that I did? It unexpectedly evolved from there, much like my life. The names were of people critical to my legacy, each having a dedicated chapter. Developing the narrative led to further researching their identities and lives, and exploring the transformative relationships we shared. This, unavoidably, meant confronting and writing about my own evolving-self.

Our entangled lives portray my mentor's intense interest in me, and their compassion and encouragement shaped by the historical times and places in which we lived; stories that deserve to be shared for the joy and benefit of others. It is also my way of honoring and expressing my gratitude for the individuals who shared so much of themselves with me. I'm truly pieces of all of them. They mattered greatly.

PART I

Nurturing Village

Chapter 1

Apple Tree

The apple fell, slowly rolled uphill
protected and nurtured to weather storms
and claim its purpose.

"You tellin' me you lost your driver's license, boy?!" the police officer shouted.

"Yessum," the old Black man said softly, head lowered, his eyes cast down, sweat stained straw hat held chest-high in both hands.

"Well, what am I gon' do with you, boy? I can't keep givin' you another license if you keep losin' em, can I?"

"No-um," the sad figure responded, standing in front of an olive-green army desk that separated him from the seated abusive uniformed officer. Fresh sweat stains punctuated his blue coveralls and gray long-sleeve shirt as he stood there dejected waiting his punishment.

"Get on out're here now. Come back tomorrow, I'll see what I can do," the officer ordered finally.

Dipping his head even farther, the old man turned, legs shuffling left the room without lifting his eyes or looking left or right.

Sitting alone in a chair against the room's back wall, I could not believe what I had just witnessed, an updated scene from a 1930s Stepin Fetchit movie I recall seeing that stereotyped Black Americans as submissive and uncouth. But this was 1957. How could this be happening now?

Suddenly I heard, "Next!" "Next!" The only person left in the room, that was me.

Still in shock, I stood slowly, walked to the desk, and sat down in the chair next to where the old man had stood. The policeman stared at me with a sneer. For a moment I wondered why, finally realizing I sat down without his invitation. But after a long silence, during which I did not stood up, he proceeded, his eyes still slicing through me.

"Give me your driver's license," he snapped.

I managed to comply, though still not clear-headed.

"Is the permanent address on the license still the same?" he asked, examining my license.

"Yes," I said.

He glared at me. "What did you say?"

"Yes," I repeated, thinking he didn't hear me the first time.

"What. Did. You. *Say?*"

"Yes, the permanent address is correct," I said a bit louder.

Then it hit me. He wanted me to say, "Yessum," just like the old man had. Adrenaline shot through me, my anger rising. A long moment passed when neither of us said a word.

"Well, I don't have to issue you no license, boy!" the officer shouted finally, looking somehow even whiter.

"And I don't need a license from you either!" I responded while snatching my license out of his hand, surprising him and myself. Standing up abruptly, I turned and stomped out of the office.

"John L., what's going on?" was the next voice I heard as my mother met me at the door, responding to the shouting. Concerned about the officer following me and others showing up, we hurried out of the courthouse, jumped into our car and anxiously drove home under the speed limit, obeying every stop sign and traffic signal, making sure not to draw attention.

This was near the end of my 1957 college Christmas break, happily home in Bastrop, Louisiana. Me and my mother had driven to the Morehouse Parish Courthouse to renew my driver's license, while she took care of personal business in the same building. Now safely back home, my mother worried that I would become one of the rapidly growing number of young Black men missing or found dead in the Deep South.

After all, only two years earlier in the summer of 1955, 14-year-old Emmett Till's horribly mutilated body was discovered in the Tallahatchie River in Mississippi, just 140 miles northeast of Bastrop. Till, a middle-class young Black teenager from Chicago, was visiting relatives in Money, Mississippi, when he was kidnapped, brutally beaten, and shot, allegedly for whistling at a white woman. The two white men who kidnapped and murdered him were acquitted by an all-white, all-male jury.

Since my birth, my parents worked diligently to protect me from such evil white hands and did not intend now to lose that battle. And after my courthouse confrontation, I hoped I hadn't damaged the respected reputations they had worked so hard to establish among

Bastrop's white citizens in order to safely pursue their dreams. It was not uncommon for Black residents of southern towns to suddenly find themselves losing their jobs and livelihoods, sometimes without provocation. My mother, a public-school teacher, was the most vulnerable. Until that day, she and my father had somehow managed to steer clear of targeted racial hostilities, while maintaining their dignity and pursuing racial justice.

"Well, no one followed you home and it appears everything is alright," my father said calmly after hearing our story. "I am really proud of you son for standing up for yourself," he continued, "and I don't believe we have anything to worry about. But since you are due back at Lincoln University next week, I think you should leave tomorrow."

The next day, after driving twenty-five miles to the State Police office in Monroe and acquiring a renewed driver's license without incident, my parents put me on the train to Jefferson City, Missouri, Lincoln's college town.

Though my reaction to what had happened in the Parish Courthouse demonstrated my parents' influence, and the historically Black college's Black empowerment effect, they didn't want me expressing those learned lessons at that particular time in my hometown of Bastrop. So, it was Daddy's calmness and wisdom that expedited my return to Lincoln and saved the day.

And, quite possibly my life.

My father, my first and most profound mentor from birth, continued protecting and nurturing his son until his death at age 97. Affected immensely those years by his patience, courage and disciplined work ethic, his presence mattered greatly; the powerful confluence of both innate inheritance and intimate nurturing. My soul and character embody his significant influence as gene contributor, teacher, counselor and role model, passing on introvert and shyness to me.

Daddy was so shy that when the time came to explain sex to me, traditionally a father's role for a son, he was uncomfortable. He did attempt a few subtle approaches, including teaching me how to repair an electrical plug for an end-table lamp by explaining that the plug's two prongs were "male," which go into the "female" socket.

"Got it, son?"

"Huh?" I missed that.

And then one day in my early teens, condoms mysteriously appeared in my sock drawer.

Before settling down with my mother in Bastrop, his birthplace, my father told me about his adventuresome life traveling the country, not explaining why he left home at the age of 23. But he must have been inspired by the "Great Migration" of southern African Americans who sought a better life north and west—away from the horrific Old South racist ethos and customs. [See Isabel Wilkerson's *The Warmth of Other Suns.*] In her book, Ms. Wilkerson references the Foster family in Monroe, Louisiana who we knew socially and professionally. Black people, she explains, living in Louisiana and Mississippi typically headed to the urban communities of Chicago, Milwaukee, Kansas City, St. Louis, Oakland, and Los Angeles, through train routes. Daddy and two of his brothers, Garland and David, followed those hopeful paths to explore the world beyond Bastrop with the brothers finally settling in Kansas City and Oakland, respectively.

Curious and courageous, my father explored north and west of Louisiana, enjoying his youthful independence. Without financial resources and only a fourth-grade education, he worked his way across the rapidly developing western plains and rugged Rocky Mountains to the placid Pacific Coast, then back again to Bastrop, surviving sometimes by talking himself into jobs that were completely alien to him.

Arriving in Kansas City, the Midwest's railroad and cattle stockyard center, my father described his response from a desperate need for money: "I saw a *cook wanted* sign in a Chinese restaurant window, so I applied. They asked if I could cook Chinese food? I said yes. They hired me, so with a little advice, I quickly learned, and got pretty good at it."

In Los Angeles he described another scenario: An automobile dealership sign read 'Porter Wanted.' Not really sure what it meant, I applied and convinced them I could handle the job. It included moving cars around the lot. So, I closely watched others drive, and little-by-little learned to drive the cars." Lighting up with a bright smile, he continued, "I came close to hitting another car a few times, but I did alright."

Driving a car was a very advanced and useful skill in those days and for the future, particularly if you were Black.

Eventually, an unbearable longing for home and family sent him heading back to Bastrop, again, working various jobs during travel, including several months as chief cook at an Arkansas logging camp that cut, tied and floated logs down Bayou Bartholomew to Arkansas and Louisiana to the awaiting saw and paper mills. They also laid new pipes for interstate transport of natural gas for a southern Arkansas company.

"Whenever I could I got a newspaper to read when I was traveling. It helped me get better at reading and understand what's going on around me for jobs and for protecting myself," he responded one day when I asked about his fondness for the Bastrop and Monroe newspapers. And apparently those years of negotiating and calculating his wages and expenses provided the financial knowledge and skills for a future business venture he had not anticipated.

However, settling back into his hometown was not easy. The liberal and more accepting culture he was exposed to outside the Deep South altered his self-perception as a Black man and human being that he could no longer be the complacent, subservient person (in which that part of the country demanded). He knew he had to somehow find a way to live in his Southern hometown on his own terms as a liberated, confident and self-respecting man. There were enormous risks, but home was home, family was family—his parents and several siblings still lived there—and he was going to find a way to reconcile his changed persona with the hostile, racist environment that existed. This is my home, he must have thought determinedly, and I'm gonna make it work. He fully intended to survive and thrive, even under those circumstances.

Surprising me one day in a late-life conversation, my father revealed that he secretly married while in California; his wife later joining him in Bastrop to establish temporary residence in his parents' house. "Unfortunately," he explained, "she didn't like living here in the South, the way Black people were treated. And my parent's house was a bit tight, not giving her enough space and privacy." Pausing, showing some discomfort with the subject, he went on. "I lived in California and understood her unhappiness. This wasn't a good marriage, and it wasn't much I could do about it. So, I arranged for a quick divorce and bought her train ticket back to California." Sadly adding, "I never heard from her again. Hope she got there okay."

Soon after that traumatic episode, Daddy decided to use some of his hard-earned savings to purchase a car. He was bitten by the driving bug and the mobility and freedom it represented. Not to mention, owning an automobile might help in attracting the next Mrs. Smith.

He went to the only local dealership, Chevrolet, and after convincing the owner he could drive and had cash for the deposit and purchase, he was allowed to place his name on a "first come, first served waiting list," due to the Depression. "I waited, and I waited for months," his modest anger spewing out to me, "and I decided to go back and see where my name was on the list. They didn't want me to, but after a while they allowed me to see the list. What they were doing was moving my name down the list so the white folks got the cars as they came in. I told them I wanted my deposit back and take me off the list. They didn't want to, but they finally did." A few days later Daddy went to the Chevrolet dealership in Monroe, placed his name on a similar waiting list after proving his financial capability, and in a short duration, "I finally got my car," he said with a big grin on his radiant face that also shows up in a cherished photo taken when he was courting my mother, with the two of them poised on the front bumper of his stylish new black 1933 Chevy two-door sedan. He was handsome, sharply attired head to foot, proud and full of youthful cockiness.

As an African American it was risky to pursue or acquire something that whites believed you didn't deserve, simply because you were Black. Lives were at stake for stepping out of line. Though the anguish and stress he experienced while purchasing the car was daunting, he never for one moment wavered. And except for the last car he purchased during his lifetime, a Buick, all of his cars were purchased and serviced in Monroe.

Over the years, the Bastrop Chevrolet dealership's owner and ancestors tried convincing my father to patronize their business. I witnessed, and was appalled by, some of their unscrupulous behavior: "I just dropped by Johnnie just to see if you could come on up and let me sell you a new car," said with insistence. "This is where you should be getting your cars, nowhere else," getting more intimidating. "So let me see you soon! I won't take no for an answer." Sometimes they threatened economic reprisals and an occasional hint of violence. What the dealership owner was really reacting to was the impact Daddy's boycott was having on sales to other African Americans. His personal boycott became known and was affecting the car-buying decisions of Black individuals throughout the region, who were taking their business to other dealerships. Since Daddy owned his house and grocery business free and clear, paid cash for all purchases and relied on African American customers, economic threats from white's were meaningless.

It wasn't long after buying his car that Daddy, an ambitious, handsome bachelor with eye-catching four-wheel mobility, acquired another bride. But it took a bit of persuasion. It seems that Julia Mae Scott, the very attractive, equally ambitious hometown lady who was to become my mother, initially felt that the twenty-year age difference was more than she could accept in marriage. And after-all, she had completed high school with college in mind.

"Why would I want to marry an old man with just a fourth-grade education?" she protested to relatives and close friends, and later confessed to me.

However, they saw it differently. "That man is so handsome, and has a house, small business and car. Age don't matter much in this situation," they argued. Eventually she was convinced. Julia Mae finally succumbed to my father's proposal, but for all the right reasons. Both of them had extraordinarily ambitious dreams that included a family and economic stability, and as husband and wife they could possibly make their dreams reality, together. They married April 22, 1934, fell deeply in love, and were greatly devoted to each other for the duration of my father's life. A perfect arrangement for my later entrance into the world.

Daddy's father, Armstead David Smith II, had awarded him a share of the family's property, which he did for each child that settled in Bastrop. Armstead had done well as a successful blacksmith. He purchased a one-acre lot and built a sizable house near its center. Daddy, the eighth born of twelve children, was one of four that received thirty-by-fifty-foot lots on the property. His brothers, Jake, Guy, and Archie were the others. Ralph, an older brother, died early, the victim of drowning that Daddy had witnessed. I could tell this deeply affected him when he told me about it, a sense of self-blame, not able to save him.

My father selected the southwest corner section of the property facing Haynes Avenue, and his father quickly deeded it to him. Haynes Avenue was the main east/west thoroughfare for one of two developing black residential communities in Bastrop. Robert Street, on the west side of the property, dead ended at Haynes creating a busy intersection. The site was significant for my father's yet-to-be-determined entrepreneurial venture.

Using money saved from his financially lucrative travels, Daddy built a three-room shotgun house with front porch facing Haynes, set back neatly on a small hill above the street. The first room served as a sitting room, the second a bedroom (after marriage also a sewing parlor for my mother to sew and repair garments for Black and white clients), and a back-room kitchen/bathing room. They purchased a foot-pedal-powered Singer sewing machine for her, my mother's initial contribution to their dream of economic sufficiency and raising a family.

As he completed the house, my father needed to figure out how to make a living. The money he had saved from his earlier ventures was running out – fast. He was not interested in continuing to work with his father in the blacksmith business. Nor was he interested in working anymore for racist whites. But it was early 1928, and the Great Depression had begun to make its ugly presence known.

"I watched people walking pass our house often because they didn't have ice boxes, several times each week, going uptown to the white store for food. They needed something closer to home," explaining to me the thoughts behind his initial vision. "It was a real struggle for Black people just to eat, and to face disrespect and racist treatment on each trip." He started to visualize a small place on his father's property not knowing where he would get food to sell. "I went to the bank and the local wholesale dealer and they wouldn't help. Then I went to the nearby farms. They weren't interested either. But I kept trying until one day Mr. Robertson (later the owner of Robertson Fruit and Produce), who had a farm on the Crossett Road just outside of Bastrop, allowed me to pick a tub full of vegetables from alongside the road for $5.00 cash."

Daddy proudly tells this remarkable story as the beginning of his famous and successful "everything-you-need" *Mr. Johnnie's Grocery Store*, starting with $5.00 cash because loans and credit were denied him by white financial institutions and wholesale outlets. It developed into a popular consumer-responsive business, a commercial pillar for the Black community, and Bastrop's second largest general store. This was the source for me and my sister's unusual economic security as we experienced the growing Black middle-class family lifestyle in the Deep South.

There was no precedence in Bastrop for Black businesses that competed directly with white-owned establishments, except the juke joints, barbershops, cafés, and mortuaries, small businesses that catered to specific cultural needs. My father knew he would be wading into uncharted territory in a harshly racist environment, where white wealth largely depended on cheap or free labor by Black people desperately needing any type of work to survive. Free self-employed Blacks could be considered a threat to the South's social order.

"When I got home with my $5.00 worth of vegetables," Daddy, continuing his story, "I arranged them on the front porch with a 'For Sale' sign and charged what people could pay. It didn't take long before they were bought up. The next morning, I went back to Mr. Robinson and asked to buy $8.00s worth. He said okay. And I kept going back for more and more, adding fruit to my requests. He was really nice about this, and I have used his business ever since." Indeed, as a car-driving teen, I sometimes picked up Daddy's orders, and was treated with courtesy and respect as his son.

The increased revenue from the fruits and vegetables allowed him to make cash purchases of other grocery items from local wholesale dealers who would not provide credit. The additional inventory quickly overwhelmed the small front porch, so he confiscated the front room to display items. Mr. Johnnie's Grocery Store was well on its way.

At five foot, nine inches, the same as my mature height, with proportional physique and weight, our metabolism allowed us to eat whatever and how much we wanted, though in moderation, usually without major weight variances. His light-chocolate skin color, never varying whether in the intense summer sun or during frigid overcast winters, was as constant as his temperament.

A well-trimmed whiff of mustache slightly less than the width of his nose graced his upper lip. His face, featuring perfectly spaced light brown eyes, slightly pronounced nose, and thin lips, was topped by hair that was as straight as it was curly, which became white, long, and wild during his "mature" years. My mother said "those church women loved that hair, so I had to watch them closely while Johnny was at church," teasing him. My father wore rimless glasses during midlife but later did not need them. And then he completely lost his sight altogether during his ninth decade.

Daddy's physical movements were smooth and deliberate with little or no wasted effort. Except in playing baseball, where he, and I, never learned to use our wrists when throwing the ball, we were all arm motion. I imitated him when we played catch. I still have that flaw: fast arm, slow ball. While growing up, my close pals thought I was rather peculiar when we played baseball. They joked about it. (Well, I threw the way my father did, so go suck on a lemon, I thought).

My father was also very perceptive, resourceful, and courageous in efforts to provide a protected social incubator for his family without inhibiting the development of me and my big sister, Barbara's self-esteem, self-confidence and independence. Those attributes describe me, particularly independence. His fierce financial independence provided a social and economic firewall that protected us from the most egregious hostilities, including limiting shopping at white businesses. Three of the major clothing stores in town were Jewish-owned and more welcoming. We felt secure playing and roaming around the one-acre property with him and mama encouraging our growth and development, both exemplary role models for us. Daddy replaced part of the orchard at the stores new location with a basketball half-court-playground that attracted neighborhood boys compelling my sports interest and social growth. As we grew into teens, the close-knit Black village, church and public school fervently extended the secure parameter. Of course, when in town and other general public spaces, we knew to observe the southern "color" Jim Crow codes and traditions, though we were taught to maintain our dignity.

As inventory rapidly outgrew the sitting room in the shotgun house, Daddy considered expansion. He noticed a one-acre corner lot for sale a block west on the opposite side of Haynes Avenue at another busy intersection, Pruett and Haynes. Again, using cash, he purchased the property, a portion of which contained a fragile fruit-tree orchard with mature pear, peach, fig, and plum trees. He later added a grapevine that produced a modest yield. After saving enough cash, he hired skilled Black carpenters to construct a free-standing building on the property, large enough to offer a general-store variety and quantity.

Using the white-owned store as his model, my father meticulously designed the building, daily overseeing its construction to assure that his vision was executed properly. When completed, he oversaw the interior layout according to appropriate food and household-item zones and the anticipated customer flow. It amazes me how perceptive he was in determining human behavior patterns.

The store was positioned midway on the new lot, facing Haynes, and set back on a slight incline from the street. The gabled building included a thick, reinforced concrete-slab floor, wood siding, a corrugated tin roof and a lean-to in back. The sound of rain falling on the roof was mesmerizing and calming, however, not the best thing when I had chores to complete. Two large, framed picture-windows adorned the front of the building next to the covered main entrance, and a ground level small, dysfunctional meat refrigerator with a window was installed to display school supplies. The rear asphalt-roofed lean-to enclosed the meat market and small storage area, with screened half-windows on three sides for air circulation.

Daddy stocked the store with every conceivable item he thought people needed for survival and delight. Two large used refrigeration units were stocked with fruit, vegetables, dairy products, soft drinks and butchered and processed meats. He taught me how to put oil into small caps on the refrigerator motors to make sure they stayed lubricated. Behind the meat refrigerator was a meat-cutting block (part of a tree trunk on three legs), a scale, hand-turned meat slicer, electric "Big Red" meat grinder, double-tub utility sink, and a two-burner gas grill. All items were previously owned.

The check-out counter and four-flavor, hand-dipped ice cream freezer was positioned next to the front entrance; dipping cones for other kids was one of my favorite jobs. Tobacco products were placed behind the checkout counter on top of the school supply display unit. Additionally, other display cases were stationed throughout the store for dry goods, cosmetics, dishware, kitchen utensils, toys, and candy. On top of one display case near the checkout were large two-gallon glass containers of dill pickles and pickled pigs' feet, and a plastic container with sugar cookies. Nearby, a banana bunch hung from the ceiling. Open floor-to-ceiling shelves for canned foods, baking products, seasonings, cereal, toiletries, laundry products and medications lined the walls.

Hardware occupied one corner, with two wooden kegs of numbers 6 and 8 nails, sold by weight, just beneath the potato bin. Washtubs sat on the fruit and vegetable refrigerator. The building was warmed with a large gas heater that sat across from the checkout counter next to a strategically placed studio stool, useful for his elder customers, customers interested in conversation, and salesmen.

Underneath the store's covered entrance, next to the door, stood a hand-pumped, coal-oil tank to provide fuel for lamps and wood-burning stoves that were needed to cook, heat bath water and warm homes. It was sold by the gallon in customer-owned gallon glass or metal containers. When I was old enough to manage the job, this became one of my responsibilities.

Usually attired in a white or beige shirt with sleeves rolled up just above the elbow, casual wool slacks, white cotton socks and dark thick sole shoes; Daddy managed the store six and a half days a week, closed half-days on Sundays. But when the occasion dictated, he donned a three-piece suit, stiffly starched white shirt, cuff links, tie, Stetson hat, thin-sole dress shoes, and wool overcoat with leather gloves for winter months. He was dressed that way for a weekend father-son, fall vacation car trip for a visit with his relatives in Arkansas, sitting proudly behind the wheel with me, a young boy, happily at his side.

Daddy shaved daily, no exceptions, exemplifying the discipline I acquired from him. I witnessed him occasionally with suds on his face, using a double-edge metal razor, moving it up and down and across, and carefully shaping the whiff of mustache under his nose. And, he regularly visited the barbershop located on Madison Street in the Black business district, which was next to his brother Jake's café. Mr. Jackson, the barbershop's owner, also owned the lone Black dry cleaners within the same building. When Daddy took me there for my first haircuts, I got an early introduction to the unique communal Black-barbershop culture where customers came early and stayed late—long after being served. Barbershops were centers of loud and vigorous, but jubilant, male discourse on human relationships and community and social matters, highbrow and grapevine—a vibrant dialogue-scenario that continues today, a historical Black cultural expression.

However, the barbers were respectful of young customers' ears and steered the energetic conversations toward appropriate topics like sports, church, and local politics. As I grew older, the issues I learned about varied widely, but the respectful vulgar-free language never did. This held true for my father, from whom I never heard a curse word or vulgar expression even when hitting his thumb with a hammer.

"Shoot!" he would shout.

As a result, my vocabulary remains relatively untarnished, even after serving in the Navy.

As the business continued to grow, white wholesalers and banks began offering credit. But out of principle, and perhaps anger, which he never overtly expressed, my father continued to operate on a cash-only basis, taking most of his business to companies that had not previously denied him credit. And most of the wholesale companies were in Monroe, the major northeast Louisiana business, banking, and industrial center.

Initially, white salesmen did not come to the store to take merchandise orders for later delivery as occurred for white businesses, forcing Daddy to travel to the wholesale businesses to purchase and transport the items himself. However, later, as the store's wholesale cash-only purchase volume continued to increase, salesmen began coming to the store to take orders for delivery and solidify Daddy's business. I observed them to be respectful, for now they were competing for his sizable cash purchases, demonstrating once again, that green often overpowered racist tradition. Daddy sometimes took me with him to the wholesalers to make the purchases, always interesting ventures when I was preadolescent.

I recall Swift's Meat Packing Company's huge walk-in refrigerated lockers with big, thick heavy doors, and walking inside to confront grisly cow and pig carcasses hanging from the ceiling within its dark confines. Stacked along the walls were crates of assorted butchered and processed meats, all of which made the experience foreboding, intriguing, and cold. Swift was Daddy's source for chickens, bacon slabs, whole hams, beef liver, smoked pork link sausages, bologna and salami tubes, neck-bones, and frankfurters.

For fresh cuts of meat, Daddy bought slaughtered cow- and pig-halves from a Bastrop wholesale dairy and cattle farm located on Madison Avenue, a few miles east of town. Often with me, his preadolescent or adolescent son in tow, he would drive to the white-fenced complex and personally select the meat-halves from carcasses hanging in the large, refrigerated storage unit for next-day delivery. Again, I found myself looking up at those strange, dissected animals while making sure not to bump into one of them, wary of a frightening encounter that might leave me and my clothes smeared with blood. As a preadolescent standing close, holding on to Daddy's reassuring leg, kept my fear in check and my skinny body warm.

After the next day's delivery, we returned to Daddy's store after dinner to begin the laborious butchering process that lasted into the wee hours of the morning. Initially using anatomy charts tacked to the back wall near the butcher block, he patiently carved the halves into salable cuts. To begin, I watched Daddy sharpen his butchering knife by moving the blade rapidly across his hand-held, twenty-inch blade sharpener. Sometimes, when the knife's surface was extremely dull, I turned a manually operated sharpening-stone wheel temporarily clamped to the work-counter while he slid the blade back and forth against its surface, occasionally creating sparks that fascinated me.

Daddy then adorned a full chest-to-knee white apron, knotting the waist string neatly in front. I have kept two of those aprons, which I occasionally use for cooking. Even after years of laundering, they still have remnant blood stains that remind me of his laborious, highly skilled butchering that provided fresh meat for his customers and our family.

With the cow- or pig-half laying across the butcher block, Daddy proceeded to carve out the forequarter, hindquarter, and other major portions while explaining them to me. Skillfully using the handheld meat saw, he cut through thick bones, releasing the lever below the handle to replace the thin blade as needed, asking me for a replacement from the collection hanging from a nail on the back wall.

Next, he trimmed away fat and unwanted lean strips, and sliced off a few cuts of pork chops, ribs, and beef steaks. I watched him proudly display those cuts in the meat refrigerator, arranging them on white porcelain platters with artificial green veggies between, sometimes going around front to make sure of the customer appeal.

Daddy attempted to teach me the art of butchering, when I became old enough to be trusted with handling the sharp twelve-inch knife without cutting myself - with knife in hand, serious intent, and his coaching, I had modest success, but never learned well enough to manage the process alone. He never pressured me or appeared disturbed by this shortcoming, and at some point, discreetly discontinued the teaching effort. However, I became quite good at using the knife and saw to carve cuts of pork chops, T-bone steaks, slices of ham and liver for customer orders. And, with the meat cleaver tightly held in hand, I had fun chopping neck bones according to the requested weight.

Daddy used the leftover meat trimmings to make ground beef and pork sausage. Standing on a wooden crate, I helped grind the meat by sending the trimmings through the big, red electric grinding machine that was poised on the counter next to the refrigerator. Daddy cautioned me not to put my hands too far into the machine's funnel to avoid losing part of a finger. He also showed me how to change the chopper plate to obtain desired results.

The pork trimmings were transformed into what we called "pan sausage." After the first grinding, I hand-mixed a special seasoning from a small brown paper bag into the ground pork before pushing the meat through the grinder a second and third time using progressively smaller chopper plates to obtain the right smoothness.

After completing the grinding process, I watched Daddy carefully lump the ground beef and pork sausage into rounded mounds on separate white porcelain-covered metal platters, hands patting softly, and placing them in the display section of the meat refrigerator between artificial veggies. And occasionally, using trimmings from the pig, he made hogshead cheese, a special delight for us and special customers. You can't beat the unique, delectable taste of freshly made hogshead cheese on crackers.

Sometimes during those late working nights Daddy would sip a bottle of beer, which seemed more ceremonial and relaxing for him than for its "great taste." He tilted his head back, took a swig and rested the bottle on the refrigerator. It was quiet in the store after a busy day serving customers. And in the shadowy confines of the market, lit only by two hanging light bulbs, we engrossed ourselves in the much important butchering ritual. Those were special nights and cherished memories for me, staying up late working side-by-side with my proud father in the meat market of his successful business, his dream evolving.

Our conversation was sparse, with knowing silences between Daddy and me, introverts. But there were some important teaching moments, ranging from the details of our work to stories of Daddy's meaningful life experiences, including tales of his western adventures. We also sometimes talked about my store responsibilities, customer relationships, activities with my friends, planned visits with his brothers, and school. The flow of conversation was casual and natural, without probing or pretense.

The night's work ended with a ceremonial wire-brush cleaning of the meat-cutting block's surface to clear away chipped bone and the deposits of salve-like fat, in preparation for the next day. Daddy, with both hands on the wire brush, arms moving powerfully side to side, working top to bottom, made it seem effortless. I swept the concrete floor while he washed the butchering and grinding equipment before pulling the light-string, shrouding the store in darkness, and heading home. This somehow symbolized both the end and the beginning of our valued time together.

Sure enough, the next day customers of all races (until 1954) came to purchase "Mr. Johnnie's pan sausage" which usually sold out within hours after the word got out. My father was famous for his pork sausage. Had he ventured into the wholesale sausage business on a regional or national scale, I think he would have been highly successful, and perhaps very rich. Had I learned the secret of the special seasoning ingredients in that small innocuous looking brown paper bag, perhaps I could have gone into the sausage business myself and become wealthy. Jimmy Dean should be thankful that it never happened.

In the new building, Mr. Johnnies Grocery Store became the second largest general store in Bastrop, an agribusiness and paper mill town of 11,000 residents in northeast Louisiana, just twenty miles south of the Arkansas border. The largest store was white-owned and located a few miles east near the huge, malodorous paper mill. When Daddy's entrepreneurial effort attracted African-American shoppers away from the white store, it would have been expected that the white store owner would have taken drastic counter measures, given the hostile southern racial atmosphere. But my father somehow developed an amicable working relationship with Mr. Parker, the owner, whose store served as a wholesale source of some items for my father's store.

As a preadolescent, Daddy often took me with him to Mr. Parker's store, asking me to wait at the large wood-burning, cast-iron potbellied stove near the center of the store during winter months. They met in the storage room behind the meat market presumably out of sight of white shoppers. I was always happy to see him return, sometimes empty-handed, which leads me to conclude that Mr. Parker was the source of valuable information my father used to manage his own business. This was one of those unusual relationships that was not supposed to exist in the Deep South, a violation of strict southern protocol that prohibited equality in interracial discourse, if permitted at all.

Although Bastrop's racial customs and laws, as existed throughout the South, were designed to keep Black people subservient, poor, and marginalized, my father somehow managed to circumvent that system. Our relative economic independence allowed us to live in a quasi-safety bubble shielded from dire poverty and the worst racial hostilities. Our family was part of a stealthily emerging ultra-small Southern Black middle class rising out of restrictive socioeconomic controls, but where the Ku Klux Klan frequently flexed its muscles to intimidate and enforce the Deep South social order.

According to the Equal Justice Initiative's 2017 report, *Lynching in America*, "Some states and counties were particularly terrifying places for African-Americans and had dramatically higher rates of lynching than other states and counties. Mississippi, Florida, Arkansas, and Louisiana had the highest statewide rates of lynching in the United States."

More than 4,000 people were lynched in the U.S. from 1877-1950, the report said, with 16 of those taking place in Morehouse Parish, Louisiana, our home. The NAACP says that from 1882-1968, 4,743 lynchings occurred, mostly in southern states. Seventy-three percent of lynching victims were Black.

Bastrop's early history is replete with malicious and violent conduct against African-Americans, including lynching. My father described a harrowing story that took place not long after marrying my mother. "We were driving towards town one day, when we suddenly ran into a large crowd of white people walking, heading in the same direction and shouting very loud. They seemed very angry with clenched fists raised, faces all twisted up. And then they started yelling and screaming "Kill! Kill! Kill the nigger! Kill the nigger!" We realized we were in danger; this mob was going to lynch somebody. We had to get out of there fast before they looked too closely at us. So, we took a side street and drove back home as quickly as we could without being noticed."

Having light skin, relatively straight hair, Anglo features, and the fact that they were driving a car, which was unusual for Black people at the time, was probably what made them unnoticed momentarily, allowing them to escape. Back in the safety of his parents' home where they lived at the time, Daddy continued in a painful tone, "We were really scared and so were all Black people in Bastrop. Everybody stayed off the streets, and our house stayed dark all night. That could have been us."

On that day, July 9, 1934, the white vigilante horde broke Andrew McLeod, a Black man, out of jail and lynched him, hanging him from the large tree in front of the Morehouse Parish courthouse in the middle of Bastrop's town square. Sick jokesters later referred to the spot as where Blacks "hang-out" in Bastrop.

As traumatic as that experience was, it did not deter my parents from a lifetime of activism in the pursuit of human justice and dignity for African-Americans. In fact, that personal near-death incident appeared to have galvanized and emboldened them, generating a fierce determination to fight the harsh and violent Jim Crow system that permeated Bastrop and the Old South.

However, their more personal and urgent priority was to protect and nurture the growth and development of their children. They managed to isolate me and my sister Barbara from the most harmful racist atrocities, and Mr. Johnnie's Grocery Store was central to accomplishing that feat. They didn't talk much about their effort. They just did what they felt necessary.

Daddy seemed to have gradually garnered the cautious respect of Bastrop's white elite, successfully managing his small business outside of the white establishment's direct control and sociopolitical agitations, due mostly to cash-only operations. And when he communicated directly with them, he was courteous, respectful, and professional with just the right amount of confidence, always looking them in the face, if not directly in their eyes, something very dangerous for Black men. While home the summer after my first year of college, 1956, I saw this first-hand when an unexpected sheriff's deputy came to the store to collect for a speeding violation I had committed during a return trip from visiting my girlfriend in New Orleans, which I had not yet explained to him.

"Johnnie," the deputy addressed Daddy while sitting down on the studio stool across from him, "I have here a bond that needs paying for, I believe, your son, given the age listed, for speeding through a Parish south of here." The two looked over at me and back at each other. Daddy, avoiding direct eye contact responded, "how much?" The deputy gave the amount and Daddy leaned over the counter and paid him cash. I was totally petrified and ashamed. Daddy did not admonish me for not telling him earlier, probably knowing I had already learned directly an important lesson: Be forthcoming with your father sooner rather than later.

Daddy, quietly, without bravado and fanfare, continued pursuing the American dream while abiding by the existing Jim Crow laws and most Southern customs, avoiding the latter entirely when explicitly racist. But some argue that our family's ability to thrive without experiencing the harshest racist treatments may have been due to our light skin, straight hair, and Caucasian features, attributed to early Jewish ancestors on both sides of our family. I don't entirely dismiss this assessment. But, whatever the reasons, we reaped unusual, though limited, respect and freedom from the most suppressive effects of Jim Crow. But this did not lead to complacency. Given the acute racist environment, I knew to be on guard, always, and to never overstep sensitive racial boundaries. However, Daddy's business did not go entirely unscathed from racial circumstances.

For example, until the 1954 *Brown v. Topeka Board of Education* U.S. Supreme Court school desegregation decision, white people made up almost half of my father's general store customers and generated a substantial amount of its profits. Our store was conveniently located for many of them and provided almost everything they needed. I clearly remember the white families that frequented the store, often making sizable purchases, especially the large, wealthier white families. While shopping, the men sometimes had brief, casual conversations with my father, mostly about the weather or some other safe, impersonal topic.

However, after that historic decision, white customers suddenly stopped coming. Apparently, they took exception to the federal government "requiring" racial interaction; though that was something they had been doing naturally, and voluntarily, for years.

I particularly recall this tall, thin white man who lived only one block west of the store with his young children. Their large house, painted white with a sizable fenced-in vegetable garden in back was on a corner lot directly across from black residents in paint-less shotgun houses, all living in respectful peace and tranquility. This was not unusual for other residential sections in parts of Bastrop.

However, after the *Brown v. Board of Education* decision, this casual geographic proximity and social tolerance changed dramatically. That family moved abruptly, as did most white families who lived nearby. Eventually, white families in Bastrop, living for years near Black residents, relocated to completely segregated sections of town. For poor white residents, the transition was slow with some elderly whites only leaving when they died.

Mr. Johnnie's Grocery Store was part of a small, but vital emerging Bastrop Black business community, similar to ones that were developing in many segregated towns and cities across America with the epitome, Tulsa's Black Wall Street (see *Black Wall Street* by Hannibal and *Built from the Fire* by Victor Luckerson). The West Madison Street businesses included my Uncle Jake's café, the barbershop and dry cleaners mentioned earlier, a bar, pool hall and mortuary, and occasionally a dentist's brief stay. However, Daddy's store was conveniently located within the residential community, a comfortable walking distance for customers. These businesses typically met the unique needs of African Americans, and consequently, were of little concern to whites. But sometimes Black people stopped patronizing white establishments because of objectionable treatment, thereby forging a few duplicate mom-and-pop businesses. Collectively, those modest entrepreneur ventures created wealth for Black families and their communities and helped fuel the desegregation efforts that hastened the death of Jim Crow.

But some whites sought to tap into the somewhat insulated new and growing Black economy to enrich themselves and boost their wealth accumulation. An example was the white man who opened a grocery store in the heart of the Black community, only three blocks west of my father's successful business. In order to gain a competitive edge, he offered Black customers easy credit, but with considerable interest that many could not figure out. His effort initially had a modest negative impact on my father's revenue. But the devastating part was the number of Black individuals who became severely indebted to the owner, not unlike the sharecroppers who were bound to perpetual indebtedness while white landowners lined their pockets with cash from free labor.

With their growing wealth, Daddy and Mama built a large three-bedroom house next to the store, later adding a detached one-car garage and rental duplex. The remainder of the acre lot included a large vegetable garden and a playground with basketball hoop that replaced the orchard. Daddy was the contractor for all construction, hiring carpenters, plumbers, and electricians. Leaving me to manage the store when the duplex was built, I watched him through the store's back windows, learning from his dedicated supervisory skills. He was meticulous for details and punctual work.

Building the house next to the store, turned out to be a strategic convenience for us as an inexhaustible pantry (I did much of the fetching) and an emergency convenience for customers, who only needed to knock for acquiring what they needed from the store.

The white-painted wood structure, on the corner of Pruett and Haynes, was the largest, most contemporary residential dwelling owned by an African American in Bastrop. In fact, only a few elite whites owned comparable houses in size, style, or quality. The pitched shingle-roof design featured high peak lines and sharp angles with a stucco-and-brick chimney that highlighted the front entrance. Contrasting flat roofs covered screened-in porches in back and on the side near the store, which served for occasional summer sleeping adventures for my sister and me. The interior design included three bedrooms connected by an L-shaped hall. There was a full bathroom, gas-appliance kitchen with drop-down ironing board and small breakfast nook, a dining room with two built-in glass corner China cabinets and a living room that included built-in sofa nook and a stucco fireplace with gas heater.

Aided by the later addition of aluminum siding, the house defiantly and beautifully continues to stand today on that prominent corner, after more than eighty years. It's elegant and sophisticated architectural design, though worn, has not diminished, though the neighborhood has been ravaged by the crack cocaine epidemic and the town's diminishing economic capacity caused primarily by the paper mill's gradual decline and closing.

That very impressive and accommodating family dwelling was my parents' joyful pride. They dreamed big, worked hard, and saved aggressively to achieve its reality. But I am certain that at the time it was built it probably attracted considerable attention from Bastrop's white citizens. It was clearly superior in size and quality to most of their homes.

One white-owned house in town had almost the exact design. I suspect that my mother may have appropriated that design and instructed the carpenters to duplicate its features. She wasn't talking, but knowing her strong defiance of white authority, such a bold decision is not surprising. Surely, they must have considered that this Black boldness might invite unwelcomed attention and malice, a risk that could endanger their lives. It was a courageous act. Yet I am not aware of any hostile attempt to deface or destroy our house. From the beginning of their marriage, my parents had dreams to fulfill, and a living standard to achieve.

"The southern racial customs would just have to be tested," they rationalized.

In a broader sense, perhaps their daring feat was meant as a symbolic challenge for the Black community, urging them to also free themselves from restricting their dreams and dare to live beyond the confining limitations imposed by racist intimidation and fear. No law stipulated that a Black family's house could not be equal to or better than a white person's if they could afford it, although southern white supremacy implies that's not a good idea. But such a strategic challenge on behalf of African Americans would not have been unusual for my parents. After all, they were to become founding members of the local NAACP chapter and my mother the first Black woman on Bastrop's City Council. Indeed, not long after their courageous business and residential exploits, other Black businesses and stylish homes followed.

But the best part about the new house was that less than one year after its completion, I was born in the warm comfort of its guest bedroom on September 14, 1938. And with my sister Barbara, two years older, my parents now had their ideal family: two children, one girl and one boy, and later a dog named Troy, for Barbara. Our family was part of the slowly evolving new southern phenomenon – a stable, though small, relatively secure southern Black middle class.

From my first insecure steps, I was a moving fixture in my father's next-door general store, to my eyes, a vast enticing structure and environment. Proudly wearing a cowboy hat that I loved so much I slept in, I moved curiously about, familiarizing myself with the maze-like configuration, surrounded by skyscraper-like shelves and glass enclosed show cases. People coming in, walking the aisles, picking up items, teasing me. Then the cash register rang, and they left, making way for new people. All of that was intriguing, and fascinating.

The skyscrapers were full of colorful items of different shapes and sizes, some metal and others paper-like packages. And then the glass-enclosed cases that were full of assorted goods of all shapes and textures, and big humming white metal containers full of cold objects, apples, oranges and stuff I couldn't get my hands on. So captivating, I gravitated to the strange items, reaching to touch, grasp, pull, and taste, accessible items, but was cautioned at every turn. This was my innocent precocious beginning of many years under my father's watchful, nurturing wings in Mr. Johnnie's Grocery Store.

At four years old, I discovered all the enticing things just lying around within easy reach, begging for my tasting attention, and soon began to sample them with a vengeance. At some point, Daddy started looking the other way, allowing me to eat and drink to my eye's pleasure (and my stomach's capacity) any and everything I could reach.

For several days I feasted happily on Baby Ruth, Butterfinger, Peanut Patties, Mounds, Milky Way and Moon Pies from the candy case, and sugar cookies, potato chips and peanuts, washing everything down with Coca-Cola, Dr. Pepper, RC Cola and Grapette sodas from the bottom of one of the refrigerators, all to my stomach's delight and capacity. That is, until I became urgently sick! My stomach decided to rebel.

I was in the house for several days trying to survive and recoup from my immense overindulgence. After full recovery, my father, the great psychologist, henceforth and forever did not have to worry about his son eating up store profits. My desire for sweet edibles and soft drinks, particularly Grapette was forever altered.

The store was a natural teaching/learning incubator, offering my father many opportunities to instill important and meaningful lessons aided by his subdued, persuasive approach. "Son, it's important how you treat people," my father would often tell me. "They come in the store needing something and we should help them in any way we can so that they will come back. But it's good to be kind to all people wherever they are." Those were words Daddy spoke and paraphrased many times beginning the moment I understood what the store represented to our family and community. Regardless of age, there was always something constructive my father found for me to do, and learn, sometimes in the early years just to keep me out of harm's way and devilment. Profound mentoring and teaching transpired within those hallowed walls and beyond.

Constantly working beside him also allowed me the benefit of absorbing his personal traits and attributes, most profound among them his strong work ethic, self-discipline, compassion for others, and responsible ethical behavior. There was not a time he was not serving customers or working to improve the stores' operation, and I was at his side learning until I was able to work alone. Intense mentoring and teaching occurred while working as cashier, butcher, stock boy, bag boy, customer assistant, delivery boy, sales rep, bank depositor, coal oil pump operator, janitor, etc.

Daddy had enormous patience as he taught me those roles, never exhibiting overt anger, or becoming disturbed by my numerous growing pains and mistakes. "Son, don't forget to turn the can and jar labels forward when you put them on the shelf so they can be seen by our customers, placing the new items in back. And don't forget to feather-dust items regularly with all the dust blowing in from the street," he constantly reminded me. But he was a little more pointed after I took the trash out back to burn and started a grass fire. In deference to my mother, he never administered corporal punishment, though he threatened once when he heard I had boasted to a friend that "My Daddy never whips me!"

His teaching and mentoring extended beyond the store to lawn care and car maintenance. We carved out a small spot behind the store for my own garden that included tomatoes, radishes, and beets. He took me with him when attending special vendor events, such as the opening of Wonder Bread's new facility in Monroe.

My father applied common sense for managing the store, and instinctively knew that success depended on customer satisfaction. He made it a point to know each person that came through the door, determining the greeting and the kind of conversations that produced positive responses, and made a mental note of regularly purchased items. It was all personal, for him and the customer. Daddy had a genuine zeal and dedication to serve and meet their needs.

Special, high-demand products, included Olay and Pond's face creams, Geritol, Hadacol and Black Draught medications, Lucky Strike and Kool cigarettes, Days O Work Chewing Tobacco, and Garrett Dry Snuff. Hadacol was a favorite cure-all, aches-and-pains suppressant, "miracle drug" of the period. No wonder, as it had 12 percent alcohol, labeled as "preservative."

Even with the large, diverse inventory, customers occasionally requested non-stocked items which Daddy acquired quickly and added to his regular inventory. Further, if a customer had an urgent or emergency need for an item during closed hours, they need only knock at the side door of our house next to the store, and we graciously responded. During my teens, I was usually the one to dispatch the item which the customer often paid for later. My father felt access was an important customer service and a unique asset compared to the competition.

Working with and observing my father, I learned generosity and compassion for others, particularly those less fortunate than we were. Practically all of our Black customers were poor, earning little pay doing manual labor on white-owned farms (hoeing, weeding, and picking cotton), at the local paper mill (cutting, loading, hauling, and unloading logs), working for the city and parish (janitorial service, garbage pickup, digging and clearing drainage ditches), and domestic work for white families. Too often those individuals would not have enough money for food, medications and fuel for lighting, heating, and cooking. Some could not even afford simple cold meat cuts and bread for the next day's lunch.

Daddy readily opened credit accounts for many, knowing that some would never be able to fully repay their debt. And he never pressured anyone to do so. I watched him conducting those transactions, how he treated the desperate people in a way that they could maintain their dignity and self-worth. Their debt was something he never spoke about. And often, as a teen, I was the one to record the debt, Daddy's way of teaching me record keeping and compassion. After he retired, I came across the ledger among the store's files that noted many unpaid accounts. His kindness, generosity and sincere compassion for his customers was unparalleled.

Occasionally, at home in the evening while a preadolescent playing quietly in my room, Daddy would yell through the closed bathroom door where he was enjoying a soothing hot bath, for me to come and wash his back. And during the warm sudsy massage my little hands provided, the two of us shared private father/son conversation and the opportunity for bonding. He learned about the wild adventurous imagination that drove my daily play activities. I mostly played alone during the early years. And, I would absorb the quiet soft spoken sincere loving interest in my stories that characterized his humanity. However, another ulterior motive for this scenario, I suspect, was to illustrate the similarity of our male anatomy, the subtle early nudge towards understanding my manliness.

Daddy and mama practiced a strong, determined, and disciplined work ethic that included me and Barbara in every aspect. For that reason, I refer to us in this narrative as "Smith Family, Inc." And on Saturdays, Smith Family, Inc. was its busiest day of the week. It was "all hands-on deck!" for Mr. Johnnie's Grocery Store and clothes washing. While my mother, the family bookkeeper (a skill she learned attending business school in Monroe) managed the checkout counter, my sister helped customers in various departments, including women's stockings and cosmetics, and measuring and cutting fabric. I served as bag boy for large purchases and delivered small orders on my bike to the elderly and disabled. My father and I managed the meat market, assisted customers, and restocked shelves. I also dipped ice cream by the cone and pumped coal-oil.

In the meat market, I became quite adept at filling customer orders for neck bones, pork chops, ham, liver, bacon, ground beef, pork sausage, cold meat, and cheese. We had a manual meat slicer for bacon and cold lunchmeat. Chopping neck bones with a meat cleaver was fun but slicing semi-hard cheddar cheese from a large wheel took all my strength.

Eventually, when I was in my mid-teens, Daddy left me for brief periods to manage the store while he took care of other matters, confident I could respond to customers and handle financial transactions. Though intimidated at first, the awesome sense of responsibility made me feel important and significantly boosted my self-confidence.

"Can I help you? Yes, we have that. I'll get it for you," I responded to customers, just as he had taught me. Only a few had to return initially when I couldn't complete the order or transaction. For him, those were valuable teaching moments.

Some regular customers phoned in their grocery list, or absent a phone, I rode over to pick up the list. Daddy enjoyed taking the phone orders himself as part of his personalized service, knowing exactly how to cheer them up. The larger grocery orders were made on Saturday, and Daddy and I delivered them by car after closing. After learning to drive, I delivered them myself. Some of the lonely but wonderfully engaging elderly customers began to think of me as a son and looked forward to my visits.

The bike was also like a low-tech Brinks money transportation service for the store. With a green money pouch in my open basket, I took weekly cash and check earnings to the bank totally unaware of the risk. Why didn't Daddy enclose the cash in a grocery bag which we had plenty of? One could only guess. Regardless, no one seemed to notice as I sped the three miles powered by adolescence energy.

Clothes washing was sandwiched between store responsibilities and somehow accomplished before dark. During the early years, a wood fire was built under a large, black cast-iron pot in the backyard to heat the water. But with the later installation of a deep double-sink in the store's meat market section to meet sanitation certification, it also served conveniently for washing clothes. The washboard was a perfect fit, and bluing was added for rinsing white items. The clothes were hung to dry on a wire line Daddy stretched across the backyard and were taken down as the sun set. Saturdays were exceedingly long, hardworking days for Smith Family, Inc. But the following day, Sunday, Daddy opened the store only until noon while the rest of us went to church. That afternoon and evening was Daddy's half-day off, spending much of the time in bed listening to the radio.

During the summer months, he closed the store Wednesday mornings for fishing excursions, opening back up midafternoons. Leaving before sunrise, he took us to fishing spots often recommended by customers where we cooked and ate breakfast, fished, and cooked and ate what we caught for lunch. Sometimes joined by other family and friends, it was a cherished enjoyable family time away from the disciplined routine of Smith Family, Inc.

It did not take long for me to discover that working with Daddy did not offer the much-desired pleasure of "idle" time. Whenever I thought there was a break from assigned tasks, he would invariably find me and say, "While you're resting, do..." It's amazing how much work I accomplished while I was resting! And when an unplanned task appeared suddenly, he would quote a blacksmith idiom he probably learned from his father: "You must strike while the iron is hot, son." No thanks, Grandpa.

On New Year's Eve, Smith Family, Inc. conducted the annual merchandise inventory, remaining in the store after closing during the holiday to calculate and report business taxes for the year. The four of us worked in pairs, one counting and the other noting the information. I served as merchandise counter with either parent. However, we stopped briefly near midnight long enough to shoot fireworks and wish each other "Happy New Year!" before completing our task.

We shot the fireworks from the concrete space in front of the store and directed the candlesticks and Coke-bottle rockets toward the vacant field across the street. Strings of firecrackers were lit on the ground next to the store, exploding in rapid succession as we watched at a safe distance. However, before lighting the first fuse, Daddy always instructed Barbara and me in clear, explicit language on safety rules. But that did not prevent me from injuring my hand one year with the too-late release of a "Big Red" firecracker. The pain and throbbing from the blast, confined mostly to my thumb, was excruciating and lasted several days. After that experience, Daddy's cautionary words became a part of my own fireworks safety-speech.

Often during the brisk March winds, Daddy and I flew kites from the front of the store, sometimes using the field across the street as our launching pad. As a preadolescent in short pants, I recall, at his urging, selecting a colorful kite kit from the store's inventory, then kneeling with Daddy on the concrete floor near the entrance to quickly assemble it. Spreading out the kite's fragile paper, two crossed sticks were stretched tightly to the four corner strings. We then attached a stabilizing tail made of tied-together cloth strips. Anxiously anticipating the exciting moment of sending the kite aloft, we stepped outside on the paved area in front of the store hoping the wind was still blowing.

Holding the kite in my raised left hand and the kite string in my right, I ran down the street until it lifted into the air in the swirling wind allowing the string to unwind to the end. Slowly backing up to the front of the store, string in hand, I allowed the powerful wind-swells to carry the kite aloft, zigzagging wildly as it ascended into the waiting vast, blue sky. But I had to be careful of the huge Chinaberry tree across the street, which had a ferocious appetite for innocent little kites.

In 1948, after my tenth birthday, Daddy organized the first Black Boy Scouts troop for Bastrop. That was the earliest age for eligibility to join, and his motivation and target was me. The Scouts provided personal growth and leadership development opportunities through fun and engaging activities beginning at adolescents, something he felt important for me. The closest African-American troop was located in Monroe, twenty-five miles south of Bastrop. Through word of mouth and announcements at school and churches, more than twenty-five boys attended the first meeting. My membership continued through high school, but Daddy's involvement lasted much longer.

During the extent of my father's direct oversight of the troop, he had difficulty finding and retaining Scoutmasters, a persistent problem. He was extremely careful to select men he could trust with the lives of young boys. He looked for individuals he trusted and who demonstrated leadership ability and social skills compatible with our age group and the Scouts mission and values. Unfortunately, there were not many interested men who met those standards.

Occasionally, when we were without a Scoutmaster, or when the Scoutmaster could not attend a meeting or activity, my father would substitute even if it meant temporarily closing the store. However, there were many times when he placed me in the leadership role. As a mid-teen, I oversaw meetings, coordinated projects, and drilled the troop in marching techniques, a skill learned in the school band.

Sometimes Daddy placed me in charge of one-day summer hikes. The gravel-road we often took circled northwest of Bastrop, much of it following Bayou Bartholomew. On those days, Daddy briefly closed the store once or twice, long enough to drive out to check on us. He was confident that I could manage and protect the lives of my cohorts, several my age or older. Me? I didn't give it much thought. I just responded to what was required. However, he counseled us to govern ourselves according to the Scout's motto and rules. Indeed, it was amazing. I don't recall any disruptive internal conflict. But I believe Daddy deliberately seized opportunities to place me in that role to develop my leadership and social skills, especially important for his still shy and socially awkward son. I must say in retrospect, I did perform with unusual authority and confidence in that role, rising to Daddy's aspirations for me.

But there was one remarkable and traumatic summer camping trip that really tested my leadership ability and provided anxious moments for the troop, my father and other parents. It involved an overnight weekend hike to our favorite campsite along an unusually wide, swiftly moving stretch of Bayou Bartholomew, approximately ten miles southwest of Bastrop. The bayou runs more than 350 miles through Arkansas and Louisiana. Unfortunately, when the time came for our scheduled venture, we were without a Scoutmaster. Daddy was unable to find an adult volunteer he trusted for the entire trip, but he did not want us to be disappointed. So, he enlisted the assistance of Rev. Norris, the Minister for Mt. Olive Methodist Church (Presented in a later chapter), the troop's sponsor who could only be with us one day and night.

However, on Sunday morning for the return trip, Daddy pulled me aside: "Son, you'll need to lead the troop back to Bastrop. There's nobody else, so I'll have to depend on you to get everybody back." I stood there attentive, but confident. This is something I'd done before, although for not as many miles. I knew the route well, and my troop mates respected me and responded to my leadership. Their confidence in me always boosted my own. So, at age sixteen, feeling up to the challenge, I was good to go.

However, before Daddy left with the camping gear, he spoke briefly to the troop: "I'm leaving you on your own under John L.'s leadership. I expect you to behave as Scouts and work together so that you will get back safely." He calculated that with a normal walking pace, there was more than ample time to reach Mt. Olive Church well before dark. With water canteens full, first-aid provisions and snacks in our backpacks, our Scout troop was good to go.

But to make sure the trip back was an adventure, I decided without prior discussion with my father that we would follow the bayou rather than use the road. I knew that the bayou intersected with the road near the main highway close to Bastrop's City Limit. I thought it would be much more exciting to walk through the rough, natural terrain and thick, tree-shrouded forest on the edge of the winding waterway rather than trudging in the hot sun on the gravel road. And the experience, I rationalized, certainly would be more relevant to Scouting's nature-related tradition. What I did not contemplate was the bayou's extremely curving, snake-like path.

I took the lead position and began the single-file march, keeping the bayou on my right within eyesight. There were parts of our hike when we were down near the bayou's bank, and at other times high up on a levee well above the water line. I carefully picked my way through the thick forest and underbrush watching out for reptiles and other wild animals. About an hour into our walk, I became aware of the bayou's extreme curvature and the serious impact this was having on our timetable. I considered heading directly north in the general direction of the road but had no sense of how far away it was. Without a landmark such as the bayou, we might get lost trying to find it. But I knew that if we continued to follow the bayou it would eventually take us back to the road at a point close to US Highway 165, the final short leg of our trip. So, we continued our original course following the bayou.

Darkness had begun to set in prematurely because of the tall trees and thick foliage, and the youngest members of our troop started to get scared. We placed them in the middle of the line as I reassured everyone that we were not lost and would soon emerge from threatening circumstances. I forced a courageous facade to encourage them. But I was now concerned about the possibility of being unable to exit the forest before visibility was completely lost. Everything required for overnight camping had been sent back with Daddy, our water canteens were almost depleted and night critters were commencing their threatening sounds. However, at the moment of utter desperation, the gravel road and nearby US Highway 165 appeared. My heart leapt for joy and relief.

But the evening's adventure was not yet over. Since we were late, and it was almost completely dark, I visualized Daddy and other Scout parents getting desperate and organizing a search party. Without communication, we needed to get to the church as soon as possible.

We had about three miles to go along busy Highway 165 with glaring car headlights in our faces. But with only a mile left, to save time I choose a shortcut over large, vacant property that would lead to the back of the Mt. Olive Church building, our destination. I knew nothing about the property I had chosen to march our troop through in the dark. This was another terrible decision I was making.

As we marched, I quickly discovered that the property was vacant for a reason. It was swampland with low-growth foliage, covered by more than an inch of water, deeper in certain sections. By the time I realized the extent of the problem and the need to change or reverse course, I had lost my bearings. I had to quickly recall what scouting had taught me about using the stars to navigate. Fortunately, they were bright. Though inexact, this helped me get our troop back to the highway, then onto Pruett Street, and finally, the church. Once there, my visibly concerned father and gathered parents, happily greeted us. We all breathed a sigh of relief and thankfulness. But as the leader who had made several terrible decisions, I was feeling disheartened.

However, after I explained everything to Daddy, he said he was pleased and proud of the way I had handled the difficult situations that resulted from my misjudgments, realizing it could have been much worse. His encouraging words were: "You did okay. Your decisions were well intended. You got everybody back safely. And that's what's important. Let's get home, your mother's waiting," His positive encouragement was truly meaningful and a sizable boost to my fragile self-esteem and confidence. I really needed that.

Since most of our troop members were from poor families, Daddy paid the annual troop fees and individual membership dues himself. He also purchased our camping equipment, including eight quality two-person tents for camping adventures. However, he and other

Black leaders realized that a long-time established and well- outfitted regional administration and camp site was available for white Scouts, offering them an intense week-long summer camping experience. This racial discrepancy was part of our dinner discussion, and Daddy decided the Black Scouts deserved an equal experience. Over the next year he occasionally disappeared to help establish and build Camp Britton, the new northeast regional camp for African American Scouts. He and a group of Bastrop and Monroe Black men acquired the loan of several acres of beautiful, unspoiled land thickly populated with natural forest southwest of Monroe near US Highway 80. When completed, this became one of five, Louisiana regional camps established for "Negro troops," which were not completely integrated until 1972.

Camp Britton, named for the family that donated the land, was rich with a variety of mature native trees including oak, hickory, cypress and pine, thick sprawling shrubbery, and wild grass on uneven terrain with a small clay bottom pond. Advised by the Scouts regional director, my father and other volunteers laid out the camp's parameters, and cleared living and assembly sites, teaching areas, connecting trails and parking spaces. They cut and configured log seats for the slightly sloping assembly site, and excavated latrines near the troop living areas. A well for drinking water was drilled and linked to outdoor shower stalls, a wash basin, drinking fountain and the newly constructed, partially screened kitchen/dining hall that also served as the administrative hub and camp entrance with American and Scout flags out front. On the inside, picnic tables served for meals and staff meetings.

The natural pond, a short dirt-road hike from base camp, was shallow and just large enough for improvised water games. Though fun, it quickly became muddy from the splashing and horseplay and forced a sunbaked, mud-encrusted hike back to the showers.

The camp's food supplies were acquired inexpensively through the Federal Food Surplus Program, which featured lots of dairy products, dried beans and noodles, fresh vegetables and fruits. Primary meats were ham, poultry, and ground beef, all creatively prepared to please our taste buds and fill our bottomless pits. The cook was phenomenal, but it probably did not take much finesse to please young boys' appetites heightened by the outdoors and vigorous activities. Bowls and platters passed around family style at each table were left empty. Camp directors are keenly aware that the overall experience is judged primarily by the quality and quantity of meals, and Camp Britton passed the test.

Assigned troop camp sites were located north of the kitchen/dining/administration building. Troops were responsible for their tents and sleeping equipment, usually a blanket or quilt, and advised to check underneath for scorpions and snakes each night before retiring. To my knowledge, no one was bitten by either, and I did not see any that summer.

The inaugural opening of Camp Britton was an exciting and historic event for everyone, Scouts, parents, staff, and for Daddy and the building team, particularly. For the first time, all northeast Louisiana Black troops were assembled to share the Boy Scouts most honored tradition: camping. And because of my father's generosity, Bastrop's troop was well represented, prepared, and equipped. The white regional director served as Camp Britton's inaugural summer camp director and brought with him trained staff from the white regional camp to assure a well-coordinated, meaningful and exciting experience. To assure the camp's future, he requested the names of five Black Scouts for staff training. Daddy made sure his son was selected to shadow and learn from the highly experienced, white staff throughout the week's encampment.

My four counterparts-in-training and I arrived at Camp Britton two days before opening. We witnessed the early arrival of the white staff in trucks hauling three large wooden platforms, three Trek canvas cabin-style tents, and six bunk beds, including one for the regional director. With our assistance, they set up their living accommodations in a separate section, which revealed a clear disparity between our camp living accommodations. I later learned that the white T. L. James Louisiana Purchase Council Regional Camp provided enclosed cabins for all Scouts, along with a large swimming pool and other exceptional amenities.

The white staff/trainer I was assigned was very personable; working closely with me didn't appear to bother him in the least. He seemed genuinely interested in teaching me and appeared to really enjoy the inaugural Camp Britton experience. But there was a complete absence of casual conversation, which I suppose was to be expected. I eagerly absorbed everything as I shadowed him throughout the week. At about five foot, eight inches in height, with a muscular physique and medium-length dark hair, he wore shorts, T-shirts, and moccasins. He carried a sheathed hunting knife attached to a wide decorative belt, handy for multiple camp functions. He was confident, knowledgeable, and skilled in Scouting and camp responsibilities.

Under his guidance, I became quite proficient at a number of Scouting shills, including tying knots, identifying trees by foliage, and predicting weather by cloud color and formation. I learned to cook a meal of ground beef, potatoes and vegetables wrapped in foil buried in hot coals and dirt. And one of our daily responsibilities was to lead early-morning five-mile hikes for Scouts earning a hiking merit badge, accruing twenty-five miles toward that goal by the end of camp. After the first day, he allowed me to lead the hikers alone, and that first morning, one of the hikers suffered heat exhaustion. I nervously requested water from a white farmer along the route. After a long suspicious stare while standing just inside the doorway of his house, he directed me to a well on the side. After that experience, we carried canteens for the hike.

Of course, from the outset, no one knew exactly how the camp's white leadership and black/white staff-mix was going to work out. This type of close interracial relationship was new and there were stereotypical suspicions on both sides. However, during the exciting week of intense sunup to sundown activities, racial difference was lost; the presence of the "other" was irrelevant. And as trainees, we were so intimately involved with learning everything we could, from survival skills to leadership roles, that the race of our teachers blurred. It simply didn't matter. The spirit of Scouting took over and made race invisible. Mutual respect, honor and Scouting's motto and laws ruled the day.

On the last night of camp, the staff led an inspiring and emotional closing ceremony inspired by Native-American rituals (now considered controversial) in front of a large, blazing, elevated alter fire. We sat on tiered split-log seats in near darkness, surrounded by tall trees highlighted by flaming lanterns on poles. The trails and side aisles that guided us to the assembly were lighted by candles in open cans. The spellbinding ceremony dramatically culminated our weeklong communion with nature and each other. It was somber and emotional, and an excellent way to end our new regional camping experience.

The next day, families arrived early to pick up their sons, grandsons, and brothers, and many toured the camp before leaving. I saw my father walk proudly through Camp Britton that day with a gigantic smile. He was so proud of what the team of Black men accomplished, and the obvious effect on the young Scouts whose happy faces, along with their families, made it all worthwhile. He was also elated to learn that I had satisfactorily completed the staff training program.

To his credit, my father seized Scouting as an opportunity to encourage and influence my development. But just as meaningful were the benefits I gained from observing him championing and leading the Scouting effort for Black families. I witnessed his quiet, strong, persistent, and dependable leadership while organizing and supporting our troop and building Camp Britton. In those efforts, his subtle compassion, steadfast dedication, and work ethic were unparalleled.

But, also, through his intimate involvement, Daddy absorbed Scouting's profound mission and values. He saw the Boy Scouts of America as not only important for the growth and development of young boys, but its values as worthy of anyone's aspirations, young and old, male, and female. The Boy Scouts Oath encourages individuals "to help other people at all times; and to keep physically strong, mentally awake and morally straight." And the Boy Scout Law describes Scouts as "Trustworthy, Helpful and Kind." Those attributes represented Daddy's life aspirations that I have endeavored to emulate.

Though I discontinued Scouting when I went to college, Daddy diligently supported the local troop several more years, but recruiting volunteer Scoutmasters continued to be a real challenge. However, as it has happened with so many African-American institutions and organizations, desegregation led to the dissolution of the Black troop, and as a result, his direct involvement ceased.

In his early nineties, one of the last requests my father made of me concerned the Scouts. "Son, I sure would like to visit the Boy Scout camp. It's been a long time," rendering a soft tone. "Okay Daddy, we'll drive out to Camp James," I quickly responded. Camp T. L. James, now the integrated regional Boy Scout Camp, was a short drive. He wanted to experience the camp environment once again if only from a distance to remember and reimagine old experiences. We drove the narrow road through the thick, forested acreage getting a distant look at the camp's infrastructure, seeing the central administration building and general assembly area, swimming pool and activity site, along with the living quarters. While riding in the front passenger seat, Daddy strained his eyes to take it all in and seemed delighted with what he saw, registering a slight smile as each area came into view. Scouting was now part of his DNA.

During my early teens, as work for Smith Family, Inc. became routine, I began to wonder how my friends earned their spending money. I wasn't getting an allowance, but when I requested spending change, my parents responded without hesitation, but usually after inquiring "what for?" Often Daddy simply gave me his wallet to take what I thought was appropriate while he wandered off continuing his work. Since I was invested in Smith Family, Inc., that forced me to think carefully about my financial need, which was his point. However, that did not seem to be quite the same as having my own earned "cash in pocket" to spend when and how I wanted, without my parents' knowledge. Those compelling thoughts started to impact my work ethic, dragging a bit in responding to the job, and my parents detected less zeal.

Is John L., Jr. feeling lackadaisical about his responsibilities? they must have asked themselves. Or perhaps they wondered if I'd grown unappreciative of the quality of life achieved as a result of our family's hard work. Maybe they thought I needed to understand and appreciate my unique African-American status.

"Perhaps he needs to experience the other side."

Well, whatever the reason, when the opportunity came for me to explore work outside of Smith Family, Inc, my parents opened the door wide, no questions asked. I suppose they thought that after I tried the grass on the other side of the fence, I would find home obligations more favorable.

So, out of curiosity and with strong enticements from my friend Fred, who lived just down the street, I decided to venture into the world of picking cotton. Besides the peer enticement from him, and seeing schoolmates returning in the evening on the back of an open flatbed truck seemingly happy after a day of picking cotton, it looked like an exciting adventure away from my boring and routine home duties. "That's like fun-time away from home," I thought, "with some spending money at the end of the day."

Convincing my parents was much too easy. They had experienced the grueling reality of manual labor and farm work and figured it was something I needed to discover for myself.

On the day of the big event, I woke much earlier than usual. I was excited! My mother handed me a brown paper bag with a cold bologna sandwich and she and my father waved as I rode off on the back of a truck with my friends into the cool, humid predawn. Close up, no one on the back of that truck appeared happy and joyful as I had anticipated. Perhaps they were still sleepy.

Arriving on the edge of a massive field full of waist-high plants with white fuzzy balls on top as far as you could see Fred helped me select and fit a long, gray cloth bag around my neck. "To earn the most money," he explained "you need to pick and weigh-in early while the cotton's still damp with dew, adding to the weight. You get paid by the pound." So, after a brief picking-technique demonstration, Fred left me to fill the bottomless bag that dragged behind me with the South's white-gold. I later realized that for him this work provided crucial subsistence money. The more he made the better his life would be – not exactly my motivation for being there that day.

The sun's heat quickly became unbearable, drying up the cotton bolls and draining me before I could make my first weigh-in. The hand-pricking burs that begrudgingly held onto the fuzzy white cotton fiber slowed my most diligent and enthusiastic efforts. "Boy, this ain't going too well," my thoughts screamed. "It's not fun." Lunch of my dry bologna sandwich, along with water ladled from a bucket came and went almost without notice. By the end of the long, hot, twelve-hour day, with only two weigh-ins (totaling one full bag and one partial), I had little to show for the exhausting and demoralizing venture. "Boy, that was a big mistake," I agonized, "I should have known better." Arriving home was, without question, the best part of my day, never to be repeated. My parent's sensed the learned lesson immediately, no conversation needed.

However, later that night, I thought more deeply about the arduous endeavor. For everyone on that truck, including Fred, picking cotton was serious business, often the difference between having food to eat and going hungry. But, I wondered, how did anyone, including experienced super-pickers, earn enough money to survive by stuffing the extra-lightweight, difficult-to-extract cotton bolls into a bottomless sack at less than one cent on the pound? It was brutal work for those placed in the position of having to provide cheap strenuous labor or suffer survival consequences. I realized that I was fortunate; I didn't have to do it.

Days later, after taking cotton-picking off my interesting-work list, Fred and H.T., my other close partner, cornered me. "Why don't you go caddying with us at the golf club? We get nice tips." "Well, okay," I agreed thinking that might be closer to my liking. "Yeah," H. T. chimed in, "it's like a walk in the park – carrying someone's golf-club bag and getting some spending change." It sounded like an easy, fun adventure, for a strong, though gangly, young man like myself, and an opportunity to hang out with my buddies away from the daily drudgery of Smith Family, Inc. chores, and getting some discretionary spending cash of my own in the process.

Again, my parents acquiesced quickly to my request to accompany my friends to Bastrop Golf and Country Club to caddy for the club's elite, white membership. Daddy and Mama loosened their protective cocoon enough to allow me the opportunity to discover, once again, what it's like laboring at the bottom of America's capitalist economy, working for someone else.

We walked to the country club early that morning with blue sky, warm sunshine, and a slight breeze, figuring on having a great time. However, when we arrived at the back clubhouse exit to meet the club members, the day quickly turned dark. "Hay nigger, come on over here and get my golf bag," were the first words that greeted me from a white club member exiting, only the beginning of how we were spoken to throughout the day. Having been protected by my parents, I was not prepared for the harsh, demeaning, racist language spewed at us continually until they took their golf bags from us at the end of play and grudgingly placed loose change in our hands. Calling us nigger, cursing us for not keeping up, or for not handing them the requested club, was par for the course, pun intended. I suppose I needed that experience to learn firsthand what my parents were trying to protect me from since birth.

At the end of that excruciating day, I decided that walking behind and carrying a bag of golf clubs for privileged, racist white men, who relegated me to less-than-human status, was definitely to be avoided. It hurt, and I was angry and terrified at the same time. At that moment I rededicated myself with renewed zeal to the demands of Smith Family, Inc., never again seeking to relinquish my membership and responsibilities, no matter how difficult or inconvenient they seemed. Fortunately, thanks to Daddy's vision, business sense and work ethic, I had that choice.

However, understanding this disparity helped spark my sense of humility and compassion for those of limited means, which represented most of the Black people of Bastrop and other places I visited and lived in the South. It's amazing what, and how, attentive and loving parents can teach you.

So, now I knew what I did *not* want to do, but not yet what I wanted to become.

Over the course of my childhood through seventh grade, my parents made enormous and compassionate efforts to cultivate my interest in something meaningful, tangible, and worthwhile that would focus my attention and motivate and nurture my growth and development. They were more than a little concerned about their late-blooming son's unfocused nature and employed aggressive strategies to find a spark that would ignite a life-focus. My life was Smith Family, Inc. and fun and games. School had not yet gained much traction. Daddy even built a roughly constructed lean-to next to our garage as a woodwork shop, and supplied it with basic tools hoping that would center my attention. I spent hours there, even on cold days without heat on damp dirt surface, trying unsuccessfully to figure out a building project. Nothing resulted.

Determining the store and house needed painting, he seized the opportunity to sharpen my focus around a manual skill. After buying the paint and demonstrating the appropriate technique, I took to the task with an abundance of encouragement and minimum oversight from him. Once finished he praised my effort, and then informed me of two neighbors wanting me to paint their houses for pay. With the dollars as incentive, I accepted the jobs readily, but my parents thought the money should be saved for college, a future I had not yet considered. I was hoping for discretionary cash. The two customers were satisfied, I had no interest in continuing to paint, and what I thought would be spending change now had a place of deposit for if and when college day arrived.

However, college for me and my sister was definitely part of our parent's plan weather we recognized it or not, and as preparation influence, newspapers were ever present in the house, including the *Chicago Defender* and the *Pittsburgh Courier*, reputable national Black publications. Those papers were also connections to the Black urban middle class as it rapidly developed in America's major cities. They also made sure Barbara and I were members of the Chicago-based Bud Billiken Club, a unique Black youth education and social organization with members nationwide. Years later, as a member of the Great Lakes Navy Band, I proudly marched in the annual Bud Billiken parade through Chicago's Southside, feeling a real kinship to the organization.

In eighth grade, music and the tuba won my focused attention with plenty parental hoopla. And by twelfth grade, after refining my performance talent, I had earned local, regional, state, and tri-state (Arkansas, Texas, and Louisiana) superior awards in solo contests. Consequently, music scholarships were offered from historically Black universities and colleges in Louisiana, Texas, Arkansas, and Mississippi. But despite those offers, I decided to attend Lincoln University in Missouri, a HBCU nationally recognized for its music program, intending on becoming a school band director.

Unfortunately, Lincoln did not offer music scholarships or other forms of financial aid prior to enrollment. But after thoughtful deliberation, my parents decided to support my choice. So, on their modest income, and money from a small insurance policy, they paid for a total of eight years of college for Barbara and me to attend two of the most prestigious historically Black universities in the country, Fisk for her and Lincoln for me. This included two years when we were enrolled simultaneously. A lot of moola for their kids' education. And a gigantic sacrifice on their part.

This financial sacrifice, similar to other intense situations, never appeared to fluster or intimidate my father, always something he could manage and control, and a trait I have inherited.   On one of our summer fishing excursions, I watched him casually select a green switch from a small tree and calmly chase a rather large snake as though chastising it for occupying our camp site. Me? I would've chosen a much larger tree branch to *kill* it. Outwardly, he appeared as cool as a refrigerated cucumber. But internally, on certain occasions, it must have been very different, particularly given the hostile racist environment in which he lived and worked.

More than a decade before I was born, targeting Black civil rights organizations, the State of Louisiana passed a law that required all registered nonprofit organizations to provide their membership roster to the State Department for review. The 1924 law was never aggressively enforced until 1956, when the white supremacist Citizens Council obtained an injunction prohibiting the NAACP from "doing any business or acting as a corporation in Louisiana" without providing the state with its membership list. This forced the NAACP, which was aggressively seeking social justice for Black citizens, to operate underground while shielding the identity of its membership from possible physical assault and murder by the Ku Klux Klan.

During those threatening years for Black Americans, my parents, charter members of the local NAACP chapter, invited the organization to meet inside the store late at night. The lights were kept off, an outside streetlight shining through the two front picture windows providing ample illumination for the secret gatherings. Somehow, I wound up in one of the meetings, and at the impressionable age of four, it seemed intriguing and mysterious. "Why is everyone standing around in the dark, whispering?" my little mind asked. "Is this a game? Can I play?"

This was a courageous and dangerous act for everyone who attended. If the Citizens Council or the Klan had found out about the meetings, members would have been harassed, physically abused, or perhaps even killed, and the store burned to ashes. But despite the horrendous danger, the local warriors for racial justice participated vigorously in the NAACP's national and state strategy to end legalized racism. It was a matter of dignity and self-respect, for which they were prepared to die. Finally, in 1961, the U.S. Supreme Court ruled the unscrupulous 1924 Louisiana law unconstitutional, freeing the state's NAACP to once again openly pursue its aggressive agenda.

Because of their local leadership role, my parents were familiar with the regional and state NAACP officers, and covertly helped move them and their messages throughout north Louisiana along the U.S.

Highway 80 East/West corridor, from Vicksburg, Mississippi to Shreveport. One of them was Bastrop native, Arnos T. Hall, the brilliant and courageous Tulsa, Oklahoma, lawyer/judge whom my parents and I visited in 1968 when I lived in Oklahoma City.

Though my parents actively pursued racial justice through NAACP membership, Daddy was prepared to take more aggressive action, if necessary, to protect his family, and it's a good thing he did not find the need to do so. He owned two pistols, and during the early years, made sure they were in perfect firing condition. One was a six-shooter revolver like the one Barbara and I saw Gene Autry and Roy Rogers use in the cowboy movies we paid twenty-five cents to watch on Saturdays from the segregated balcony of the Rose Theatre. The other pistol was a small, self-loading 9mm.

One weekend when Barbara and I were teens, he brought both weapons on a visit to our grandparents' farm in Beekman. Away from the house near the edge of the thick pine tree forest where the car was parked, Daddy pulled the pistols from the car's trunk and handed them to us. He pointed out the key components, then proceeded to load the six-shooter and demonstrate how to hold and fire the weapon. Afterwards he assisted us in shooting at a tree not far from where we stood. Wow, did that gun have a kick-back. We did the same with the 9mm.

Daddy conducted his firearms training in a way that clearly communicated to us the seriousness and gravity of using a gun, but I never saw the pistols again. They were hidden away, out of our reach, out of sight, and out of mind.

However, one early fall evening, when my father was in his eighties, an unfamiliar white man knocked at the rear family room entrance of their house and presented himself in a manner Daddy perceived threatening. After the man left, he retrieved the 9mm pistol from the top shelf of his closet where he had kept it hidden all those years. He did this without my mother's knowledge, intending to protect her from the hostile stranger he was sure would return to harm them.

Realizing that the weapon had not been fired in decades, he commenced to quickly clean and oil it while sitting in his favorite chair. In preparation, he took the cartridge clip out, but did not remember to empty the chamber. And just as he began to clean the pistol, BANG! it discharged. Fortunately, it was pointing away from his body, but the bullet severed the first joint of his left index finger. Hearing the loud blast, my mother rushed in to find Daddy in agonizing pain holding his bleeding finger. She quickly placed pressure on the wound and rushed him to the hospital.

My father's reaction to that threatening situation was probably demonstrative of what might have occurred during his younger days given similar circumstances. Though mild mannered, he was fully prepared to defend his family if directly threatened, and courageous enough to take the necessary action to protect our lives. Fortunately, that time never came.

As Mr. Johnnie's Grocery Store profits began to decline in the 1980s, primarily due to competition from new supermarkets that offered substantially lower prices, my mother enrolled at Grambling College (now Grambling State University) to become a certified elementary school teacher to make up for the diminishing income, and in doing so she found her real passion: teaching. After completing her degree, she was employed immediately as a first-grade teacher in the Morehouse Parish School System where she taught for more than thirty years. Her income, medical and retirement benefits proved essential for a secure and comfortable retirement for her and Daddy.

And as the store's customers continued to decline, it morphed into a quick-stop convenience store, and finally a candy and sweets shop for neighborhood children. Daddy somehow managed those changes with classic dignity and a magnanimous spirit as he diligently served the changing clientele.

After my mother started teaching, Daddy assumed more cooking responsibilities, including noon meals in the back of the store for Barbara and me where he used the two-burner gas range. Each day I eagerly walked home from school to enjoy his scrumptious lunch rather than eat the school cafeteria unknowns. Occasionally his menu included hot tamales wrapped in corn husks purchased from a Mexican national pushing a two-wheeled cart. Also, on weekdays, he prepared the meat entrée for our evening meal, which my mother finished after arriving home.

Daddy's earlier Midwest and Western travel was responsible for some of the tasty food he prepared, often while I observed. His recipes featured his interpretation of various ethnic and culturally influenced cuisine including Italian, Spanish, Creole, and Cajun. The spaghetti meat sauce and Cajun-style T-bone steaks were family favorites. I attempted the steak, but never got it right. Daddy said: "You have to hold your mouth just right while you're cooking," ending with a sly grin. "Your mother keeps raving about the steaks, but I think she's just trying to keep me in the kitchen, cooking."

My father's love of family was enormous and infectious, and eating meals together was an essential part of his nurturing routine. Squeezed into the kitchen's booth with a small window framing tree and shrubs for breakfast, dinner and supper were where meaningful conversations about daily experiences, school activities and life took place. And it was here I learned my first blessing: "He who made the little bird made both you and me, so let us thank Him, for great and good is He." Amazing, I still remember it. My sister, Barbara, usually stole the show with her keen, active mind, natural intellect, and school subject interests. And she was active in school clubs and extracurricular activities. Lots to talk about. At preadolescence, I was highly energized, but not yet too interested in school demands, or much else except imaginative play. Nevertheless, the engaging dialogue at the table over time provided life lessons that had lasting effects.

A small radio sitting on the meat refrigerator in the store was tuned to sports games featuring our Black heroes when broadcast: Joe Louis boxing matches and Brooklyn Dodgers baseball games featuring Jackie Robinson, Don Newcombe and Roy Campanella, the first black National Baseball League players. And with one of the few radios in the Black community, customers often lingered to hear the broadcasts. Of course, we were joyous and gratified by the triumphs of the Brown Bomber and winning efforts of the Dodgers, though defeating the New York Yankees in World Series play was regularly ended with: "Wait 'til next year!" In a subtle way, our sports heroes, of whom we took special pride, exemplified an early form of national "Black power" represented by strong, heroic African-American men.

When Barbara and I began playing musical instruments in ninth and seventh grades respectively, at our prompting, Daddy awakened us at 5:30 a.m. when he got up. That was our practice time. Me on the trombone and she on the bell lyre, next to the drums, a parent's worst nightmare. It's unimaginable how they tolerated the rough beginner sounds of unsuspected musical careers at that time of morning. (Barbara majored in music in college and taught music in public school.) But they encouraged our efforts, never complaining. And in the long run, it paid off handsomely for everyone.

After complete retirement, Daddy transformed the general store into a comfortable two-bedroom rental apartment. And the detached garage was redesigned into a recreation room with a half-bathroom featuring a professional-standard pool table, both developed with his usual tough oversight and scrutiny. The apartment provided extra income during their retirement, though it gave them close neighbors for the first time. And, the pool table became a source for life-enhancing, mental and physical gymnastics that helped sustain my father well into his ninth decade. On many occasions, I was the victim of his serious and intense eight-ball challenge. He took no prisoners, related or not, which was another example of how everything he attempted in life was done with the intent to persevere and succeed, thankfully, attributes he passed on to me.

Daddy thoroughly enjoyed his young, energetic grandchildren. There were three from Barbara, and two from my first marriage that visited often. A swing suddenly dangled from ropes tied to the backyard cedar tree branch whenever they visited. Fishing trips got arranged and horseback riding planned, depending on which grandchildren were coming. There were old-fashioned field hockey and badminton games, and backyard barbecue and fish fry dinners. In Oklahoma City where I lived for six years, Daddy relished neighborhood walks with his grandson, Michael, and provided him and his sister, Eva, interesting toys during Bastrop summer visits. And as they aged, he challenged them to eight-ball pool as well, but they lost, just like the rest of us. They loved him and have wonderful memories of their grandfather.

Over the years, overt racism in Bastrop begun to abate, and many white residents began openly demonstrating their long-felt respect for my father. Several visited him regularly while homebound in his early nineties. I remember one gentleman who visited him while I was there was a retired wholesaler who serviced his store for over thirty years. And another who owned a small auto repair shop where my father took his cars, which I later did for him.

Indeed, there were several white individuals who attended my father's funeral at Mt. Olive, four months before his ninety-seventh birthday. In Daddy's quiet, calm, and confident persona, he managed to endear himself to many people, white and Black. Everyone responded to his kind and gentle character, resolute courage, business acumen and the positive contributions he made to the community over sixty years.

Among those extraordinary traits was a subtle spirituality. His exterior façade had always exhibited a calmness demonstrative of Buddhism, Yoga, and other meditative practices. I recall when sometimes summoned by him to the master bedroom, seeing him there after twelve-hour workdays, alone, sitting in his favorite rocker, knees pulled up to his chest with both feet in the seat silently rocking in small motions.

While talking softly, I witnessed him massaging Vaseline into the palm of his left hand to smooth the dry, crusty skin probably caused by some of his early labor exploits. We knew not to disturb him during those personal moments unless called. But I often wonder what he was thinking about in that relaxed and serene state, which was never included in our conversations. Was he in touch with a spiritual source? Was he thinking about the business, or the next fishing trip, or the church in which he was newly involved? Or was he thinking about how to maintain racial harmony to sustain the peace and security for his family? Was he mentally reviewing past episodes of his life, evaluating accomplishments? Or maybe they were just random thoughts about the present and the hereafter. Whatever they were, the quiet, nonverbal man never revealed them to me.

When Daddy fully retired after more than fifty years in the grocery business, he joined Mt. Olive Methodist Church, where my mother, Barbara and I belonged for most of our lives. This was a serious commitment for him. Something he may have thought about for some time, and his powerful intrinsic spirituality made the transition natural, accommodating, and perhaps, reassuring. What seems certain is that he had always believed in a Supreme Being, or some power beyond himself. And in his later years came to realize and affirm that this Supreme Being was God. The organized church, more specifically, Mt. Olive Methodist Episcopal Church, provided him a structural and ceremonial base for confirmation. His life after death was now on solid ground.

Not content to simply attend and sit on a pew, he actively served in meaningful and engaging roles, serving as usher, church treasurer and trustee. When I came home for visits during those years, I attended church with him and mama, and was touched by his religious sincerity and devotion as he worshiped and performed his duties. On his face shone a devout expression I had not seen before.

In conversations with my parents during those years, I found out that reading the *Our Daily Bread* publications and *Bible* references followed by prayer became a daily routine. Daddy was never one to pray aloud in service or otherwise, something else we have in common. This was probably because of his, and consequently my own, private and reserved nature. My prayers are many daily, silent, priest-like supplications of thankfulness, forgiveness and blessings with faith in what God has ordained.

Daddy's life seems to have always exemplified and embodied the true essence of Christian theology: love God, love your family, love your neighbors, love humankind, love yourself, and do unto others what you desire in return. His persistent pursuit of human justice for his Black brothers and sisters, the ethical way he ran his business, the compassionate treatment of his customers, the way he embraced everyone's humanity exemplified God's will. And the devotion and care for his family was all about l-o-v-e, love, on a subtle but grand scale.

Also, after retirement, my father made special efforts to remain relevant around the house. He did not see himself sitting idly while my mother did everything. He insisted on washing the dishes after each meal even when he had also helped with the preparation. He continued for an extensive period writing checks to pay the few monthly bills they had. This he did in the little office-nook just outside their bedroom side-door. One day, he told his wife, "I don't feel like writing checks anymore." And "that was that," my mother said. And for many years he had allowed her to lay out his attire for dress-up occasions avoiding after-the-fact critique. Smart man.

During the summer, he cut the lawn, riding erect and sedate on his mower. That made us all anxious as he cut along the high ridges of the property next to the street, something I experienced during summer visits. He was later convinced to pay someone else to do that job making everyone, me, mama and friends, very relieved.

At times, his mind shifted into youthful-gear as demonstrated when he abruptly climbed the steps and slid down a sliding board at Chemin-A-Haut State Park, north of Bastrop. Mama and I had taken him there for an outing where he could fish in the Bayou Bartholomew. By the time we realized what he was doing, he was at the top of the ladder swinging his legs onto the board, and down he went with the biggest grin on his face you could imagine. We almost had heart attacks, and he got a real kick out of seeing the expressions of horror on our faces. I somehow managed to capture that playful and anxious moment on camera.

Except for the radio, Daddy's exposure to literary culture and the arts was limited. Unfortunately, he was unable to attend any of my college and professional music performances, to witness the results of those early 5:30 a.m. childhood practice sessions, when the sound was more noise than music. But I was never more pleased and overjoyed to witness the dramatic reaction from his first encounter with musical theater.

During one of my parents' last Tampa visits, where I moved in 1972, I introduced him to that musical genre. He was in his early eighties and enjoying late-discovered air travel. He loved the idea of traveling quickly from home to his destination without wasting time on dangerous highways in slow automobiles driven by questionable drivers. Florida and California where Barbara lived were on his regular destination list.

For that visit, I arranged for our attendance at a live musical production of Leonard Bernstein's *West Side Story* produced by the University of South Florida (USF) Theatre Department where I served as College of Fine Arts Dean and music professor. Attending this performance was originally intended to give Daddy a sense of his son's administrative responsibilities, hoping the scope of my authority would impress and make him proud. However, I did not anticipate the aesthetic affect this first-time encounter with live musical theater would have.

We were seated ten-rows back and center of the stage in the auditorium where my father could see and feel the full impact and presence of the performance. Where he could see the expressions of the characters, feel the intensity of the acting and exuberant dances, hear the rhythmic energy and flowing lyricism of Bernstein's music, all encapsulated in exquisite stage, lighting, and costume design. From the orchestra's first downbeat, it was obvious to me that he was captivated by the fast-paced, musical drama unfolding before his eyes.

At first, I was concerned about his ability to keep up with the storyline and tried to help with explanations during intermission. However, at the end, during an enthusiastic standing ovation, Daddy just sat there unwilling to move from his seat with this big, toothy smile; his face and eyes lit with pure joy and delight. Never had I witnessed my father register this level of spontaneous ecstasy and satisfaction. Gone was the usual serious expression. He sat there beaming, wanting more! Waiting for more! This was a new height of personal experience for my father, and I was so pleased to have arranged and witnessed the ecstatic response, one that I will never forget. It was difficult removing him from his seat and the theater.

It was during this same visit that Daddy indicated he would like to plant an evergreen in our yard. I said, "Okay, that's great!" But he wanted to select the plant and place it in the ground himself. "Well, okay" I said, again not sure how much he could really do. We went to the closest nursery and he carefully selected a sago palm. After we returned to the house, Daddy thoughtfully viewed our property, which included a large, unusually shaped backyard with a swimming pool. Because it was primarily a play area for our five children and their friends, it had very few shrubs or trees. But after intense consideration,

Daddy chose a spot in the right corner of the fenced yard, where the plant could be easily viewed from the house.

"Perfect!" he said. "That's where I want to put it."

Once the decision was made, he requested a shovel so that he could get started. "What?", I said. In his eighties and he wants to dig a hole in the hard, sandy earth large enough to plant a tree? "Yes!" he said. And with shovel in hand that's exactly what he began to do. I attempted to help but was waved off. After some struggle, Daddy managed to dig the hole the right size, placed the sago palm in it, replaced and patted the dirt around the trunk, and requested a hose to water it down; all with that typical serious and intense facial expression. With that done, we all stood around looking at it, and him, with amazement. He simply appeared calm and proud of his accomplishment and wondered what we had been concerned about.

Daddy had vigorously completed this important chore much like he had always done in Smith Family, Inc., with pride, humility, and the usual serious concentration. When it was completed, I suddenly realized that my father meant the sago palm to be a living monument to his memory. He wanted me, his son, to never forget his guiding presence during our time together. He seemed very pleased and peaceful having accomplished that task.

Over the succeeding years, I took special care of the plant as a shrine to his wonderful life and what he meant to me. Unfortunately, we later moved to another house leaving the sago palm for others to care for, though its beauty and symbolism is deeply imbedded within my heart and soul.

Daddy's last four years were difficult, as dementia ravaged his mind that controlled a body that was prepared to last much longer. His life played out exactly as he predicted: "Once a man, twice a child." My mother lovingly shouldered the responsibility as full-time caregiver, seldom leaving his side even when Barbara and I and others were there to help.

However, for releasing other burdens on my mother, I was there often to do the things around the house and property that Daddy would have done, things he had patiently taught me, such as repairing or replacing small appliances, making minor plumbing and electrical repairs, cleaning the gutters, trimming shrubs, vines and weeds, edging the front walk, replacing putty around windowpanes, cleaning air conditioner filters and replacing weather stripping and insulation. I secured the now-vacant apartment, took their car to be serviced, and assisted with grocery shopping. I later assumed responsibility for managing Daddy's father's property, the Armstead Smith Estate, where Mr. Johnnie's Grocery Store first started on the front porch of his shotgun house.

I try to push out of my memory the uncharacteristic images of Daddy during those final, tough years. But they come with the package. You don't get to pick and choose.

On the day of my father's funeral, the weather was unusually brutal for Louisiana. It was extremely cold with wind-driven snow and freezing rain causing the burial ceremony to be shortened, forcing us to leave before the casket was lowered into the ground. I will take the liberty to offer my spiritual conjecture that God was celebrating the sad, yet noble, ending of a human life that was lived so close to Christian aspirations and ideals.

I spoke on the family's behalf for Daddy's service, composing my words the night before. There was so much to say, and so little time allowed. How do I pack profound meaning into a brevity of words so that one comprehends the essence of a life? Much of what I said enveloped Daddy's affiliation and love of Scouting, the meaning and purpose of the Boy Scouts. His life was a testament of Scouting's noble standards that inspire human goodness and service to mankind, an endeavor to which we should all aspire.

In writing this story of my father's life and our relationship, it was difficult to express the enormity of his influence on who I am and what I have become, a real struggle of deep-seated memory, interpretation and words. But, for sure, Daddy's life exemplified the complex and complimentary forces of "innate" and "in-person" influences that shape human life, including character and spiritual essence. He provided nature's DNA, and his continual intimate human presence for my growth and development. And the more I define and contemplate his personal attributes, the more I see myself in his image. However, in many instances, I must admit, I fall short.

Daddy set high standards.

As I grow older, my physical features have even taken on those reminiscent of his mature years. And except for moments of extreme anger or disappointment, like my father, an even temperament seems to be the norm for my personal interactions and endeavors. Listen intently, speak softly and smile – the person you are communicating with at the moment is important and matters.

I find myself feeling joy from helping others without expectations of returned gratitude. I work hard tackling whatever the task may be, attempting to complete it with a measure of perfection. I teach my children and grandchildren more by role model than by verbal lessons, though when asked, I will give an oral dissertation, footnotes and all. These are almost my father's exact attributes. However, so many of his lessons were ultra-subtle. I probably missed many.

But there was one overt aspect of Daddy's life that was measurably absorbed by Barbara and me: The independence and self-determination that defined his character and success, and governed virtually every element of his life. As an independent thinker and activist, able to avoid the influence and restrictive intrusions by others, he pursued a life of his own making. Central to that was Mr. Johnnie's Grocery Store, where his customers were his only boss. Even the powerful Southern white supremacist establishment was unable to destroy or steer his course.

That ideal continues to be a powerful and attractive force for me. Having always been employed by others, I sometimes felt the intense desire for independent self-sustaining work. Barbara eventually succumbed to that inherited spirit by becoming the proud owner of a small flower shop in midtown Oakland, California. I was so proud of her, particularly after she described three times weekly 3 a.m. trips to the wholesaler. And though still intensely embedded within my being, I sense it too late for me to follow Daddy's self-reliant model.

But I have been truly marked by the fatherly presence of Mr. John L. Smith, Sr., the incubation of Mr. Johnnie's Grocery Store, and the work ethics of Smith Family, Inc. Who I am, and what I have become, I believe is an extension of my father's life. If this is the case, I assume this life with a badge of honor owed to his seed and profound human presence.

Thanks, Daddy. I love you!

Chapter 2

Roots

"There's Pa-Pa's house! There's Pa-Pa's house!"

Jumping up and down on the back seat floorboard of our family's dark-green 1940s Chevrolet, I was really excited at seeing, over my parents' shoulders, my grandparents' dwellings in the distance. The dark-gray images were perched in the midst of rows of fertile crops and fenced cows, pigs, and chickens. We were bouncing along at the end of a root-veined, two-track dirt road surrounded by dense forest that led to the forty-acre farm where my mother was raised.

"There's Spot! Look! There's Spot!"

My dog, the transplant from home, had barely cleared the wire fence heading to greet us as we neared the gate.

"Wow! Spot can really jump!"

I could hardly wait for the car to stop knowing my hyperactive black-and-white mutt would be waiting with an exuberant tail-wagging, tongue-slobbering welcome. I would quickly spend time with my grandparents and then start my adventure on the farm and in the thick woods beyond with Uncle Jap, my sister Barbara and Spot. The 15-mile drive was just the right distance for my early childhood patience: short enough for a thrilling car ride away from home, and not long enough for "Are we there yet?" boredom.

When the drone of our car broke the quietness, my grandfather appeared on the front porch of the house scrunching his hand-shaded eyes to determine who might be visiting. He would wait next to the door to greet us individually, almost as royalty receiving subjects paying homage. Throughout my life, his distinct stature, conscientious pursuits, and periodic presence, like inhaled magic dust, would lightly but intently bore into the very core of my character and ambitions.

The 40-acre farm property, homesteaded in 1919 in my Grandma Mattie's name (Mattie Evelyn Cotton Scott, 1882-1925) included three gray, log-plank, tar-paper-roofed buildings on tree-trunk pillars connected by short wooden bridges for avoiding dirt and mud, while walking from one to the other. Slatted shutters framed open windows on the side of the square front building, the living quarters, with a porch spanning the entire width. Wide plank steps were near the center. Inside was a hallway with two bedrooms on the left and a great room with a large stone fireplace to the right. The furnishings our grandparents had were simple and minimal.

The kitchen/bath, a smaller structure behind, featured a cast-iron wood-burning stove, cupboard, small table, chairs, and wash tub. Several feet away stood the smokehouse for preserving slaughtered meat. A short path led to the outhouse, a closet-size enclosed toilet with a box-seat over a deep hole in the ground.

In the front yard, a few feet from the house were a shallow well, with a pulley at the top of the weatherworn, twelve-inch square, wooden structure protruding several feet out of the ground for drawing drinking water. During my early visits, I had fun helping Uncle Jap, my grandparents' last child still living at home, pull the rope that lifted the cylindrical draw-bucket up full of cool, delicious water. "Whooweeee Uncle Jap, it's goooood and cold!" I proclaimed, mesmerized each time, seeing water pulled up out of the ground and experiencing its unique, refreshing taste.

The land my grandparents chose to settle on was flat and fertile, excellent for growing assorted plants for survival. Clearing the land of trees and thick shrubs by themselves, they tilled the hard, untouched soil with only a mule and improvised plow that often broke. They added chickens, cows, and pigs to supplement meals, and a horse for transportation. The nearby narrow gravel road (later named Wheeler Road), connecting with Stevenson Road, Highway 142 and Bastrop to the South, made the farm accessible. The bumpy car lane we arrived on that led to my grandparents' property was first a horse path and then a two-track wagon trail indicating their progress and giving them easier access to Wheeler Road.

Those original dwellings, captured permanently in my memory, were finally replaced by our grandparents in the early 1950s with a rectangle shingle-roof, wood slatted house, painted white, with screened double-hung windows featuring two bedrooms, a living room with a fireplace, dining room and kitchen with an ice box. The front porch, where I often sat with my short legs dangling over the side, spanned only half the width of the house with one stone step to the ground.

Visits to my grandparents' farm are much-cherished memories. My early boyhood trips exposed me to their difficult struggles, living in the roughhewn dwellings without electricity and indoor plumbing, so different from how my sister and I lived. Our new Bastrop house, built in 1937, was spacious with all the modern indoor kitchen and bathroom conveniences. Yet, for Barbara and me the difference didn't matter, as we loved Sunday afternoon visits to the farm. With Uncle Jap as our guide, we raced out to explore the planted fields and animals, and the vast wild forest beyond.

However, in retrospect, my grandparents' long hard struggles are to me both infuriating and inspiring. As Black Americans they had so little control over where they lived, how they supported themselves and security from violent acts. Their race left them at the mercy of whites who cared little for their existence, except for exploiting them. Though, as property-owning, rugged and persistent individuals, much like most early Americans, they managed year after year to acquire seeds for crops, plant and cultivate them to provide food for their growing family, secure farm animals for work and consumption, build shelters for living and protection from the elements, and create amicable relationships with Beekman's white population preventing potential harm. I never once heard them convey despair, seemingly accepting things they could not change. But I was also transformed and am still moved by their contentment and perseverance. They not only survived with dignity, but through two marriages my grandfather raised seven remarkable children including three firsts in family college graduates.

"Pa-Pa" is the affectionate name my sister Barbara and I gave our maternal grandfather, Jasper Scott Sr. (1881-1964). He and his brothers Samuel and Julius were born in Bastrop and completed elementary education in a one-room, community-run church-school; the only school available to Black children. Encouraged by their father, a successful blacksmith, Pa-Pa and Julius left for New Orleans in their twenties to attend Gilbert Academy, a Black college-prep secondary school, later incorporated as Straight (University) College and then New Orleans University (now Dillard University). They worked on the bustling shipping docks in the Port of New Orleans and were hired to do yard work and house cleaning for white residents to pay for school and living expenses. After graduation, Pa-Pa returned to Bastrop while Julius stayed to attend the college program.

Once back home, Pa-Pa began dating Mattie Cotton who lived near Beekman. They were married in the early 1900s and occupied and farmed 40 acres of land near where she lived, until it could be officially homesteaded in 1919. Their first child, Julius, was born June 18, 1911, followed by my mother, Julia Mae, on September 3, 1913, and later, three additional children. The family and farm continued to progress steadily with everyone's sunup-to-sundown hard work and persistence. But Pa-Pa's Gilbert Academy experience had exposed him to formal education and the joy of learning, which aroused a passion for teaching he could not ignore. It was not long before he began teaching children sporadically, including his own, at a nearby church.

Tragically, Grandma Mattie suffered from a chronic heart condition and died at the age of only 43, leaving five young children without a mother. She passed away before I was born, so I didn't get to know her. However, my mother often talked about her with love, devotion and pride. "My mama loved us," she proclaimed proudly but sadly. "She took good care of us, fed us three meals a day, sewed clothes for us and prayed for us. Made sure we were as clean as possible." She went on. "She took real good care of Pa-Pa and made sure his shirts were ironed properly when he went to teach. And, taught us lessons too when Pa-Pa was away teaching other children. Then she started to get sick. That's when she started showing me how to cook, iron, sew and take care of the house. She knew she didn't have long to live and told me if she were not there, as her oldest daughter, I was to take care of the family, but she would always be with me."

Over the years she repeated that story, and sometimes after overcoming a difficult situation, or achieving a positive goal she'd say,

"Mama helped me. She's always with me." On the night her mother died, mama described total devastation: "I screamed the moment I was told, and my sisters and brothers all cried way into the night. They let us in for a moment to see her and we couldn't stop crying." My mother never mentioned a funeral or burial service, so there is a blink period. "From then on I had to take care of my father, sisters and brothers, just like my mother told me to do, and I did the best I could," she asserts, "but sometimes I didn't iron Pa-Pa's shirts just right and he chastised me harshly."

A slightly faded photograph of Grandma Mattie surfaced years after her death, and when found, was copied and shared with her children and grandchildren. It reveals an attractive woman with light-brown skin, pronounced cheekbones, full lips, fashionable medium-length afro hairstyle, and kind, soft eyes that peer directly at the camera with the confidence of royalty. Dressed in a neck scarf and loose-fitting coat, she sits on a covered high-back, throne-like chair with a foliage backdrop. I am completely enthralled by this beautiful and powerful maternal ancestor and wish to have experienced her warm grandmother presence.

After her death, my grandfather later married Lucie Nimmer (1901-1967) on March 14, 1926. She was 25 years younger than he was. I only heard my mother mention once the friction this caused in the house, which explains her rather distant relationship with her step mother. My sister and I referred to her as "Maw-Maw." Two more children, both boys, resulted from their union, and were living on the farm when I was born. The youngest, my Uncle Jasper "Jap" Scott Jr., my farm companion, became an important and influential figure in my life (more in a separate chapter).

Pa-Pa was five foot, eight inches tall, of portly stature, with a round face, close-cropped hair, and cream-chocolate skin, which he protected by wearing long-sleeve cotton shirts and overalls when toiling on his farm in the intense sun. He walked in smooth even strides, the knees only slightly bending – as if on a victory march. Business attire, when worn, complimented his portly physique, and with head held high, eyes intense, lips tight, he appeared serious and distant.

My time spent with him was at the farm, or during his visits to Daddy's store, at our house for Christmas and on occasional family fishing trips. During my adolescence, beyond salutations and comments about my growth since the last time he saw me, everything else was in passing: "Can we play in the woods, Pa-Pa?" "Yes, that's okay." "Can I have a glass of water, Pa-Pa?" "Help yourself." "Are the fish biting today, Pa-Pa?" "No. They don't seem to be too hungry."

Not prone to smiles or laughter, he spoke quietly without passionate inflections, clearly enunciating words with few gestures, as if talking to someone not there. In my personal conversations with him over time, he was open and responsive, but did not cater to small talk, or hug and embrace to show affection, sounds a bit like me. Private and proud, Pa-Pa exuded a sense of relaxed confidence.

As a teenager, I heard stories from my mother, aunts and uncles that made me more aware of Pa-Pa's extraordinary farming and teaching exploits, which opened my eyes wider to his astonishing personal history, and consequently, the need to be more reverent toward him. But my shyness and his distance prevented me from knowing him directly and deeply.

Beekman, the closest town to my grandparents' farm, had the only grocery and gasoline outlets in the region, a place where they most often interacted with local whites. It was next to a north-south Arkansas & Louisiana Missouri Railway track that transported pulpwood between Bastrop and Crossett, Arkansas. Each time we approached the track, "Where's the train? I want to see the train!" I blurted out as my early boyhood wish, hoping it would momentarily block our travel so I could get a good look, but was disappointed each trip.

A closer and more convenient store, also with a gasoline pump, later opened at the intersection of Stevenson Road and Highway 142. However, Pa-Pa underestimated the distance one day when I happened to be visiting, and walked to buy groceries. Ordinarily he traveled on horseback. Sometime later Jap and I heard a distant voice crying out from the forest: "Help! Help! I need some help with these things. I can't go any further! Jap?!" The box he carried on his shoulder was too heavy for the return trip. "Hold on we're coming," Jap yelled as we rushed to assist him, quickly locating him completely exhausted. After that experience he never strayed from traveling to the store on horseback with a saddle bag.

Not far from that store was Shiloh Missionary Baptist Church, one of the early churches where Pa-Pa taught classes. The church still exists today, a historical testament to the Black community of farmers' vitality, although all except Pa-Pa's forty acres were bought by white investors. I visited that church with my grandparents and other relatives several times in the 1950s and 60s for special occasions. Most current members, many with direct lineage to original church families, live in Bastrop and commute for Sunday service. Several miles east near Beekman on Highway 142, behind a recycling plant, is the well-maintained Shiloh Cemetery where my grandparents and other Black farm families are buried; families that relied extensively on each other to survive. They traded and, before telephones, communicated across their spacious properties with special vocal signals; I heard Pa-Pa and Jap use as they moved about busily tending crops and animals, signals that communicated greetings, that they were alive and well, and tending their farm.

In the 1920s and 30s, Pa-Pa taught school at area churches regularly, sometimes riding horseback seven miles to Vaughn and beyond. For him, farming was a labor of necessity to provide sustenance for his family. But teaching was a passion, a noble calling that demanded serious intent, preparation, and tenacity. He farmed to live, and lived to teach, and together the two vocations formed a life-mission and passion. He wanted to transform children's lives through the power of knowledge, as his life had been changed through schooling in New Orleans. So, with the loving support of Grandma Mattie and the all-hands-on-deck farm work of their five children, he pursued his true passion, if only part-time.

On days he taught, Pa-Pa happily transformed his identity from farmer to educator. Well-ironed, long-sleeve white dress shirt, suspendered, pressed suit trousers, dark tie, and polished dress shoes or boots replaced coveralls and thick cotton shirts. Hat and coat were added when he mounted his frisky brown stallion, bound for a distant church-school. During the galloping horseback ride, his mind swiftly transitioned to lesson plans that were refined as he reached his destination.

My mother told me later that the children Pa-Pa taught, including her and her siblings, were eager learners, readily absorbing the lessons typical of African Americans little more than 50 years after the 13th Amendment ended slavery. They were hungry for knowledge and the ability to improve their living status. Parents paid what they could, usually farm products, or nothing at all. But this did not matter to

Pa-Pa, for he was a man intending to lift Black children out of ignorance and despair, providing hope and preparation for a better future. It was his joy.

Teaching reading, writing and math by rote and repetition (books were not available); he drilled the students on each subject. But he sought to inspire and motivate their imagination in history and geography lessons, telling vivid stories with picturesque descriptions, knowledge he gained in New Orleans.

Decades later, when my mother was in her mid-seventies, she booked a cruise to Alaska and witnessed the natural beauty of the enormous ice shelves and serene bays that her father had described so vividly many years before, as though he had been there himself.

"It was as awesome, beautiful and inspiring as Pa-Pa had described. It's hard to understand how he did that so well having never been there," she said, herself, now a retired first-grade teacher.

Pa-Pa thought it important to portray himself as a professional educator to obtain his objectives. Ministers and educators were the most respected members of the Black community and he was intent on reflecting that assessment in attire and comportment. He believed that those qualities also influenced parent's trust and student respect.

"They should feel fortunate for the opportunity to learn and be taught by me, and see me as someone to emulate," he rationalized. "They will be motivated to move up in life."

Much later, when public education was finally extended to Black children in Morehouse Parish, he briefly served as an elementary school principal before retiring.

From toddler to age 10, I had so much fun on my grandparents' farm that my parents arranged a weeklong stay one summer.

"Whoopee! Wow!" I shouted when told, thinking about being pampered around the clock, eating Maw-Maw's super-delicious food and playing all day in the woods. Maw-Maw's biscuits, cakes and pies were the best! Perhaps better than my mother's, a comparison I never confessed aloud to anyone, for obvious reasons.

The first night there, with Uncle Jap's help I climbed onto a mattress stuffed with feathers that quickly absorbed me into its deepest recesses. It shifted so much with my every move that it was hard to sleep. And we had to decide whether to open or close the unscreened window-shutter, choosing between stifling heat and hungry mosquitoes. The heat won.

However, in spite of the scrumptious food and personal attention, I didn't have as much fun as I had anticipated. One reason was, there was no one my age to play with. I missed my Bastrop neighborhood and church pals, especially Fred and H. T. Uncle Jap was tied up much of the day with chores, though for some I tagged along. And he assisted me with personal needs. I am not at all sure that Pa-Pa was enamored with my long stay either, though in his own way he made a gallant effort to be a responsive grandfather.

One day, to keep me busy, or interest me in the joys of farming, or both, Pa-Pa placed me behind a mule-pulled plow to till the soil between long rows of three-foot high corn. "Come here John L., we're going to do a little work," he said. "Now grab the reins and plow handle and I'll guide you." I was intimidated and excited. Walking behind me with his hands over mine and the guiding reins, gently coaxing me and the mule along the narrow path with rows of corn on each side, I suddenly felt his hands lift, allowing me and the mule to proceed on our way without him. Panic immediately overwhelmed me as I stumbled along trying to keep up. Gradually, the mule steered the plow over into the raised rows of corn, causing them to collapse one after the other like dominos. Helplessly following the mule while stepping over fallen corn stalks, I was at a loss for changing our path. And the mule, hearing no commands from me, simply charged ahead without slowing. The directional commands "gee" and "woo," I had heard Pa-Pa use, never came to mind. When Pa-Pa caught up and stopped our destructive track I knew he had had enough, and I was upset for disappointing him.

"John L., go check on your grandmother in the house. See what she's doing," I heard him say with forced patience as he waved his hand in that direction.

Banished to the house — never to do farm work with my grandfather again, I should have considered it a blessing given the sun's intense heat. However, it appeared the mule received an immediate reprieve, since he continued to work the fields in return for food, water, and a place to sleep. But I sensed that Pa-Pa was not a patient man for mistakes. That summer turned out to be my first and last extended visit on the farm, an apparent agreement between parents and grandparents.

On a later preteen visit, I traveled on an unusual train that for a short time that transported passengers, mail and freight through Bastrop into south Arkansas passing near Pa-Pa's farm. Nicknamed the "Doodlebug," the two-car train, operated by the Missouri Pacific Railroad, featured an early motorized version of the diesel engine. When told about the trip I got very excited about traveling on the unique train, but also a little anxious about taking the trip alone.

The slow-moving train, without the traditional smoke billowing from the engine, produced a loud clattering sound and attracted the curiosity of everyone who saw or heard it. I had a seat to myself in the front-colored section of the trailer car and stood staring out the open windows on both sides enjoying the passing view of farmland and forest and the rush of the ride. "Wow, this is great!" I yelled since no one was close by.

At a point in the middle of thick forest, I saw Uncle Jap standing close to the track, flagging the train to a halt so that I could get off. Lingering, I was not ready to leave; the trip was much too short, ending a unique thrill. But I nevertheless stepped off onto the ballast gravel, looked back as the train pulled off, felt a little more grownup and followed Uncle Jap through the woods, anticipating seeing Pa-Pa and eating Maw-Maw's cooking once we reached the farm.

When Uncle Jap learned to drive, Pa-Pa purchased a used car so they could travel to Bastrop to shop and manage their personal affairs. Sometimes they shopped at my father's store. Pa-Pa always sat up front on the studio stool, while Maw-Maw gathered items from throughout the store, placing them on the checkout counter. This sometimes provided an opportunity for me to approach him, standing at a respectful distance.

"Hey Pa-Pa.," I greeted hesitantly.

"How are you doing in school?" he would ask.

"Okay."

"Are you learning anything?"

"Yes."

"Good."

As I grew older, because of his reserved character, the abbreviated conversation never changed much, except my responses were a little more descriptive.

During the December holidays, my parents traditionally hosted Pa-Pa and Maw-Maw for Christmas dinner at our house in Bastrop, a formal occasion, with men in shirt and tie and women in their holiday finery. My mother enjoyed hosting those types of dinners, and used the occasions to show off her latest dish and cookware. However, she may have also wanted to show her father how Black middle-class, college educated city-elites lived and entertained, a far cry from the impoverished life she had lived, working on his farm and tending to his needs.

My mother had thoroughly researched and perfected Emily Post formalities that governed formal dinners for various occasions, from table settings to food service. The cuisine was traditional holiday fare, including oven-baked stuffed turkey, corn-bread dressing, cranberry sauce, green peas or "snap" beans, baked yams, lettuce and tomato salad, and homemade rolls. Eggnog ladled from a bowl with ice cream, and pound cake with dark coffee were special post-dinner treats. Everything was perfectly choreographed, from seating to dessert.

On the day after Christmas, Maw-Maw and Pa-Pa traditionally hosted the family for dinner at their farm. For me, this was more exciting for its setting, informality, delicious country cooking, and outdoor fun with my Uncle Jap and Spot.

Maw-Maw, not to be outdone, would stock the cupboard with her freshly baked cakes, pies, corn bread and rolls, which attracted my considerable attention the moment I walked into the house. For dinner, there was plenty of home-cured baked ham and fried chicken, recently harvested candied yams, and fresh ham-hock seasoned green beans or mustard greens. The food was served family-style from bowls and platters passed around the table.

Pa-Pa, beaming with pride as he blessed the dinner from the head of the modestly set table in a tight-fitting dining room, seemed to relish the family gathering at his house: the symbolic site from which we all flowed, the genetic and geographic genesis of our lives. He seemed to communicate "I'm still the head of the family, don't forget." I believe it gave him a needed sense of patriarchal empowerment each year, since all of his children had left the farm, and were all doing well elsewhere, except Uncle Jap, who would not be there much longer. The low-key conversations for both dinners were limited, mostly about family, church, and community. Modest gossip was permitted as long as it was positive.

After dinner, while the adults huddled to chat in front of a warm, crackling fire radiating from the living-room fireplace, Barbara, Uncle Jap, dog-in-residence Spot and I escaped to the beckoning thick woods to walk, kid around and play until dark. However, except for the evergreens, the trees were now bare of foliage presenting a more foreboding appearance. And with the frigid weather, playing in the forest was less inviting, forcing us back to the house where we entertained ourselves shooting fireworks. Spot was not happy about the loud firecrackers, jumping up and down, barking louder than usual in protest.

"Spot! Stop, it's okay!" I yelled, only to be ignored. I think it was a playful protest.

My grandparents occasionally joined us on our summer Wednesday family fishing expeditions, sometimes meeting us at familiar locations. And like my father, Pa-Pa sought fishing spots distant from everyone, but quietly chatted with any adult that happened to be nearby. His soft, almost inaudible voice might be heard saying: "The fish don't seem to be biting today. I think I'll plant some potatoes when I get back if the weather holds up. How're your children doing?" For him, the quiet setting and being around family was wonderful, but not essential.

The last weeks of Pa-Pa's life were spent in my parents' master bedroom in Bastrop due to his severe illness. Attending physicians and a regional hospital were nearby and more easily accessible. While at our home, he passed away on August 20, 1964, at the age of 83. I was in the Navy, stationed at the Great Lakes Naval Base north of Chicago, and was unable to attend the funeral. Sadness overwhelmed me after my mother's phone call. Since 1955 when I left for college, spending long hours on the tuba, followed by a year of work and military service, I had limited visits to the farm, and consequently, the time spent with Pa-Pa had declined significantly. But his passing provoked an assessment of his influence in my life.

Over the years, my mother occasionally confessed anger at her father for remarrying so soon to such a young "girl," and not facilitating her desire to relocate to Bastrop to continue her education. "Papa, why can't you help me?" she pleaded, revealing her story to me. "I want to finish high school. Please talk to Aunt Malley, see if they will let me stay with them." Her desire was for continuing her education, but she also desperately needed to escape the tense relationship with her stepmother and the required household duties. "I cried a lot during the night, and never forgave him," she angrily confessed. Then, her spirit brightened, "I finally convinced Grandpa George, and later Aunt Malley to let me live with them in exchange for doing household chores. And I finished high school with honors!" An irony that her success was partially the result of her father's early teaching.

I find it difficult to explain Pa-Pa's actions. As a dedicated teacher and education advocate, why would he not support his daughter's education aspirations? Was he a male chauvinist and believed that a woman's place was only in the home? Or did he simply enjoy the dedicated family-care and housework she provided, even though a new wife was present. Without thoroughly understanding this father-daughter conflict, I try to look past it in assessing Pa-Pa's influence on my own life.

Pa-Pa simply did not cultivate intimate relationships with his grandchildren that directly influenced our development. That was his character. There were only occasional one-on-one conversations and personal time spent with him. Instead, ours was a relationship nurtured and influenced mainly through ancestry respect, observation and biographical knowledge of his survival, hard-won status and achieved goals. Over many years, that was enough to deeply embed memories of him and pick up subtle traits – echoes of his hard-working, stoic and somewhat distant personality.

My grandfather's serious, confident, and professional deportment, and his passionate self-sacrificial dedication to teaching, made indelible imprints on me. Student centered teaching was a serious endeavor for me right from the start, and I try to portray the appropriate professional qualities for my music and education careers. And my natural inclination is to avoid cultivating close personal relationships, although I have learned to moderate that instinct. For sure, Pa-Pa's influence is a significant piece of my identity, which I graciously acknowledge and wholeheartedly embrace.

Chapter 3

Iconic Image

Summer 1949. I was eleven years old and staring up at this huge white building.

"We're going to visit my Uncle Julius in Marshall. He's now the president of Wiley College. We'll stay overnight at his house," my mother announced a few days earlier. She's walking next to me as we approach the entrance. The two-story structure appears gigantic to my small-town, naive eyes, a massive stately Colonial-style building similar to ones I had seen only on television or In movies. Seeing it real, right in front of me, was fascinating but also a little intimidating.

Tall pillars and spacious veranda enveloped its double doors, overwhelming my sense of space, captivating me as we were greeted by Aunt Bertha, President Scott's wife, apologizing for his absence. Once inside, my eyes lit on the high-ceilinged foyer with a sparkling chandelier that led inside to a grand staircase with Southern opulence and grandeur, another feature of the same movies I had seen. However, on later inspection when I was older, the structural and decorative features matched the historically Black college's financial constraints, along with the sparsely landscaped campus. But, no matter, at the time of my first visit, I felt I had entered a palace, my wide eyes taking it all in and trying to cope with its massive splendor.

Noticing my fascination as we walked inside, my mother quickly admonished, "Don't touch anything, John L." But my gaze could not be distracted from the large, finely furnished rooms while being led into the kitchen, provided a stool at the breakfast table and fed sweet goodies by Aunt Bertha. This was mesmerizing for me, sitting there a young excited boy in short pants, and I was being pampered too.

That night, after I was tucked into bed in an upstairs bedroom, music started roaring-up from the grand piano I had seen in the living room, classical music that completely captivated me even at that early age. It was powerful and expressive, keeping sleep from imposing its will.

Shortly after the music stopped and the incredible joy, I felt subsided, I heard footsteps ascending the grand staircase as though each leg was too exhausted to lift, weighted down by unwanted troubles. Then they stopped at the door to my room. The door eased open as I heard a voice whispering words I could not understand. Not knowing what to expect, I closed my eyes and pretended to be asleep as my heart beat increased. I sensed someone tiptoeing over to the bed, briefly bending down to peer at me, then abruptly turning around leaving the room, silently closing the door. The labored footsteps heard earlier continued down the hallway, gradually fading away to silence. With my fear slowly leaving, I could breathe normally again, but wondered: "What was that all about?"

When I arose the next morning and went downstairs for breakfast, Aunt Bertha informed everyone that Lamar, their son, was home for the weekend from Southern University in Baton Rouge, Louisiana, where he taught piano as a professionally trained classical pianist. But he had already left the house before I could meet him, my only classical music loving and trained relative. Was I sleeping in his bedroom, and in his bed? Was he angry? Or did he just want to see what his little cousin looked like? Questions I never knew the answer to because of his early death.

His piano performance that night completely enchanted me and continues as an indelible memory. As a professional musician and university professor, a unique family legacy and unsuspected early role model, Lamar encouraged me to follow my own evolving classical music instinct, and inspired me later to give my first son the name Michael Lamar.

Aunt Bertha also explained that morning that Dr. Scott had been called away abruptly on university business, and I would not get to meet him until much later. As Wiley's president from 1948 to 1958, he served during portions of my elementary through college years, an impressionable period for me during which I learned from his intellect, character and demeanor at family dinners and other intimate occasions.

One of nine children born in Bastrop to George and Betty Scott, Dr. Julius S. Scott, Sr. (1885-1976), went to New Orleans with his brother Jasper (Pa-Pa), where they completed secondary education at Gilbert Academy. However, he continued at New Orleans University (now Dillard University) earning the Bachelor of Arts degree in 1917 at age 32. In 1920, he was ordained a Methodist Episcopal Church minister after earning the Bachelor of Divinity degree from Atlanta's Gammon Theological Seminary. He later received Honorary Doctor of Divinity degrees from both Wiley and Gammon in recognition of professional success and contributions to their institution's Mission. Those credentials placed him in a small, elite class of college-educated, African-Americans during the first half of the 20th century.

Like his brother Jasper, my Great-Uncle Julius possessed a portly physique on a five-foot six-inch frame, brushed-back, short-cropped dark hair, but with a cream-colored complexion, and similar serious business-like persona, which when combined with his rich baritone voice, garnered one's attention. He was very articulate, enunciating words with grammatical perfection. His manner was formal and at the same time relaxed, demanding respect, yet welcoming access. He was a distinguished and impressive man.

Wiley College, where I spent that one captivated night in the president's house, was founded in 1873 as a liberal arts institution in Marshall, Texas, population 24,000. Its mission was preparing Black students for a productive personal and professional life, and to challenge America's racial injustices. Students were from Texas, Louisiana and Arkansas initially, but later as its reputation grew, it included other Southern and Midwestern states. A Methodist church-supported institution, its graduates excel as educators and professionals.

During my great-uncle's presidency, enrollment grew, a gymnasium and music building were built, and the institution was noted for its academic excellence and cultivating spiritual values. I recall Wiley being touted as one of the best Black colleges in the South, my great-uncle Scott working incessantly for that recognition, traveling as required, to increase alumni giving, acquire greater financial support from the Methodist church and attract grants from private foundations. In 2003, a chapel was built in Dr. Scott's honor in recognition of his success as Wiley's ninth president.

Wiley College is also known as the home of the Great Debaters, the Black student debate team that in the 1930s debated and defeated, though unofficially, the all-white University of Southern California

National Champions. A 2007 movie of the same name starring Denzel Washington and Forest Whitaker loosely depicts this historical event with Harvard replacing USC, making the feat more dramatic.

My mother and two uncles attended Wiley, drawn by their uncle's presidency. She attended a summer session, and uncles George and Jasper, Jr. completed Bachelor degrees. Had the college been located closer to Bastrop, my mother probably would have earned her undergraduate degree there as well. Dr. Scott's position inspired many in the family, including me, to consider education a worthy aspiration and valuable asset, something my mother was intent on passing on to my sister and me.

After graduation, my uncle George, a World War II veteran, remained in Marshall working as public-school teacher, truant officer and community activist. He also served on Wiley's Board of Trustees, where he successfully led the annual alumni fundraising campaign. So, between her uncle and brothers, my mother had incentives to travel to Marshall, most times taking me with her; later serving as her teen-driver.

Though the distance between Bastrop and Marshall is only 160 miles, it took more than four hours on busy two-lane US East/West coast connecting Highway 80, due to many hills and sharp curves, making passing slow trucks a dangerous challenge. "Dead Man's Curve," named for its many fatal accidents, was encountered just before reaching Shreveport, where the city's multiple traffic signals slowed the trip further. Approaching the intimidating curve as my mother's teenage driver, my reaction was, "Uh Uhhhhh, that curve's coming up. Better slow down," not exactly a teen's natural instinct. Gripping the wheel tight with both hands, applying more brake than accelerator, hoping no oncoming car strays into my lane, I was always glad to get past it, live through it.

The highway was also used regularly by my great-uncle, President Scott, when traveling to Atlanta and other eastern destinations to attend professional meetings, conferences and to raise desperately needed funds for Wiley. As an African-American on the road, our house was often his *Green Book* stop for refuge and food, but in our case, also to visit relatives. The *Green Book* was an annually published guide for Black travelers used during Jim Crow laws to locate lodging and eateries that catered to Blacks; they were also safe havens from white hostilities. It was during those visits that his compelling influence more directly made an indelible impression on my life. However, because of Dr. Scott's eminent status and achievements as University president and professor, and an ordained minister, my mother placed him on a pedestal just below God, making his visits both extraordinary *and* fraught with anxiety.

"President Scott is visiting us", my mother would loudly announce several days prior to a planned overnight stay, signaling intense preparation for which I was a full Smith Family, Inc. participant. House cleaning, cooking, dinner preparation, lawn care and appropriate attire were priorities, with a formal Emily Post-prescribed dinner as the main event.

For the planned elegant dinner, Barbara and I prepared the six-seat, classic mahogany dining room table as we were taught and previously rehearsed for Sunday and holiday dinners, setting the table with a specially designed cream-color protective pad, a starched, ironed, white tablecloth and similarly starched and ironed white cloth napkins. Our mother's prized silverware, crystal water glasses and fine China, retrieved from corner glass-enclosed cabinets completed the table settings.

Two days before my great-uncle's arrival, my mother carefully chose the menu and commenced meticulous preparations, which sent me to our garden to pick the selected vegetables. The dishes included salad, three or four entrées served family style, and homemade rolls or corn bread, capped off with rich, brewed coffee and homemade cake or pie. Everything had to be immaculate and smoothly run. And, of course, my sister and I were appropriately attired in casual wear, on our best behavior and exhibiting proper manners.

With all the hoopla and special preparations, my impression was that great uncle Dr. Scott was an exceptional person deserving special honors, someone to be respected and admired. This made everything that he said and did worthy of our utmost attention.

After all, Mama gave the impression that he was just one step below God!

Chauffeured for long trips in a confining, un-air-conditioned car without access to public accommodations, Dr. Scott somehow always arrived looking refreshed and dapper. Barbara and I watched anxiously from the side window of the house as the passenger door opened and he stepped out carefully one leg at a time, dressed in dark three-piece suit, white shirt and a dark tie that was surely loosened during the long exhausting ride. He stretched, looked around the premises and headed for the front door of our house, walking with stiff marching-like motions, similar to his brother Jasper. Entering, he greeted my parents with confident handshakes (No hugs, also like his brother), while acknowledging me and Barbara from a distance.

For dinner, Dr. Scott was awarded the honor of sitting at the head of the table, temporarily relegating my father to the opposite end, a gesture he graciously accepted. Where else would the man who was just below God sit? The four of us took our seats only after he had slowly lowered himself into the only armed chair at the table. When other adult relatives were invited, my sister and I were provided corner spaces near Daddy, where we squeezed in next to him on stools. Once everyone was seated, Uncle Julius blessed the food in elegant, but under the circumstances, brief fashion. Immediately afterward, while eating lettuce and tomato salads, the flow of interesting and invigorating conversation commenced, to which my sister and I were active listeners only.

On the surface, the discussion appeared democratic, though it was obvious that everyone deferred to Dr. Scott. Surely, he knew the solution to all the issues, and given a chance he would enlighten everyone. But he seemed more interested in listening to the ideas that flowed from other voices around the table, the liberal arts tradition. This made the discourse extremely enriching and exhilarating for everyone. The passionate back-and-forth of the debate and the rise-and-fall of the voices kept my attention, my head moving back and forth, even though, until teen age, I did not grasp the meaning of everything said throughout the evening's dinner.

After everyone had served themselves the main entrée, passed around in bowls and platters, Dr. Scott would gaze around the table, causing all conversation to abruptly come to a halt.

"You all will have to excuse me now," he would say. "It's time to indulge in the serious endeavor of eating this delicious meal, Julia Mae has prepared." We all joined him in almost complete silence while devouring the scrumptious home-cooked Southern dishes.

The conversation picked up again during dessert and coffee with even more vigor and enthusiasm, though with a slight variance of tempo due to overly stuffed stomachs. Once I was old enough to understand the discourse this was my favorite part of the dinner.

After brief family updates from everyone, talk focused on education, church, social status and politics, topics seldom discussed by African Americans beyond the few elite family gatherings and NAACP meetings. They were informed debates motivated by strongly held positions and perspectives.

However, the broad discussions quickly narrowed to debating the critical issues currently facing Black Americans and exploring self-help ideas and group strategies to attack pervasive racism and inequality, painful thorns in every Black person's side that sometimes led to dangerous and life-ending consequences. Younger voices at the table, including my mother's, were already promoting direct confrontational tactics years before sit-ins, freedom rides and Dr. Martin Luther King Jr.'s nonviolent protests. "We need to get out and protest against what they are doing to us," my mother's voice rang out, whose assertive advocacy was later felt for sixteen years as the first Black woman, and second Black person on Bastrop's City Council.

This aggressive discourse was unique, given the Deep South Jim Crow sociopolitical circumstances of the 1940s and 50s. Black groupthink and tactical talk in the heart of Dixie that motivated self-empowerment, strategic thinking, and aggressive action to loosen the smothering chain of racial oppression rarely occurred because of the threat of white retaliation. But the unmistakable tone of progressive thought and dialogue motivated everyone around the table to espouse political and social activism, though they knew the time was not yet right. For sure, my great-uncle's and my parents' passionate NAACP involvement greatly influenced the focus and dynamics of the intense discussion – and unknowingly also me. Like a sponge, I was absorbing and storing these urgent messages for future assertiveness and involvement.

However, the point emphasized most by my great-uncle Julius Scott was the power of education to transform lives; its self-empowerment, that prepares African Americans for the incisive leadership required to improve our status. "Education is our greatest weapon," he simply stated more than once. "And more of us need to arm ourselves to achieve our collective goals." As a University president, this persuasive argument was expected, but few could express it as he did, cutting through other shortsighted, though valuable, solutions. And for me and Barbara, hearing that message certainly corroborated and validated what our parents had been stressing since our birth. His endorsement certainly helped coerce my belated decision to attend college.

Soon, between the woozy effect of the delectable meal and the intense, energetic discussion, the discourse began to taper off, until Uncle Scott abruptly pushed back his chair from the table, stood up and stretched his stiff legs. "Please excuse me. We have to get an early start in the morning and I must get some sleep. Thanks, Julia Mae for the delicious dinner." He slowly retreated to our guest-bedroom for the night.

Though preparation for those special dinners was demanding for Smith Family, Inc., Dr. Scott's visits were always cherished and inspiring experiences, thoroughly enjoyed by everyone. At first, I was just glad to have the occasion over with, but through my teen years, the thoughts, assessments and aggressive ideas sparked feelings of important urgency, the mounting pressures for social change and equal justice continues to drive my activism.

One summer not long after my night in the president's residence, my mother enrolled in a short academic session at Wiley College and took me and Barbara with her, so Daddy would not be left overburdened with us while managing the store. Barbara stayed in the president's house with cousins, and I lived with my Uncle George and his wife, Aunt Willie, in their house on the southern edge of campus, spending my time playing with cousins George Jr. and Bari. All was well as long as we ate all the food that Aunt Willie cooked. Those were austere times, just following World War II, and food was not to be wasted. For breakfast, she made sure of that by emptying the pot of grits in our plates.

"No food left on your plates!" she admonished, as we rushed through breakfast so we could play. I loved grits, still do today. So, cleaning my plate of grits was not a problem. However, I can't speak for my cousins.

My mother performed in a student theater production that summer, which I was required to attend, wanting to or not. She possessed overwhelming self-confidence and felt that she could accomplish whatever interested her—and acting fell in that category. The small, darkened, sparsely filled theater the night of her performance left me trying to make senses of what was happening on stage. The costume and set designs were convincing, the lighting not so much, and my mother appeared to hold her own with the rest of the cast.

The murder mystery unfolded clearly enough for me to follow… that is until the very end when the knife, the missing murder weapon, surprisingly ended up stuck in the ceiling. "What! How did that get there? And who did it?" was my curious response. I asked my mother, but she never explained. I'm still speculating.

As an ordained Methodist Episcopal Church minister, the denomination of most of our family members, my great-uncle occasionally preached at Mt. Olive, our Bastrop church home. As a teenager, I remember his very articulate sermons challenging the congregants to think intently about the application of biblical principles to contemporary human conditions and our lives, and to question the strength and validity of our own spiritual fervor.

But he always ended with powerful orations that were typical of the Black Protestant tradition. His voice got louder, the pitch higher and the words faster as he spoke. He repeated short key phrases emphasizing action verbs, arms gesturing wildly, his hand occasionally lightly slamming the podium.

"God wants you! God needs you! God wants you to testify about His saving grace!" his voice exploded one Sunday as some responded, "Amen!" His deep, powerful baritone voice enabled him to rouse the congregation with relative ease. But my mother, and consequently me, was never overtly demonstrative behind the emotional preaching style as were some congregants. Now a Baptist, I could be viewed as a bit reserved in my response during highly spirited worship services.

When I was a nineteen-year-old college sophomore, my mother asked Uncle Julius to serve as co-officiating minister with our church pastor for Barbara's summer wedding. Our mother wanted a "family-member minister to participate," she said. But as Wiley College President, Dr. Scott also brought prestige to the occasion, something I suspect was part of her "Black elite" agenda. And for sure, his participation made the wedding a grand, Black community event in Bastrop, a social sensation.

After much parental anxiety, I finally settled on attending college during my high school senior year and studying music, influenced by Mr. Strickland, my band director (more on him later). I selected Lincoln University in Missouri, considered having one of the best HBCU music programs, along with Howard and Fisk Universities. I was aware of Wiley's music program and new building, but didn't give it much thought. I'm sure that my great-uncle Dr. Scott was disappointed, still president at the time. I've wondered that if I had attended Wiley would his close presence and direct nurturing have been more influential, and my life different? But for sure, his education advocacy and iconic profile helped to galvanize the idea that college was an important and necessary commitment.

After retiring from Wiley, Dr. Scott moved to Houston, Texas, where he founded a new church and continued to serve his faith diligently and inspire people of multiple generations. However, he passed away in San Antonio, Texas, the home of his daughter, August 3, 1976, at the age of 91; four years after I accepted a music professor position at the University of South Florida in Tampa. Later as Fisk University President (commencing 1999), I connected the proverbial dots between his Wiley College presidency, the college presidency of his son Julius Scott, Jr. (Paine College), and my university presidential appointment to Fisk, with the proposition that the former influenced the latter, exemplifying the powerful role model and mentoring impact of my great-uncle, Dr. Julius S. Scott, Sr. I viewed my Fisk appointment as continuing the mission of educating the young, gifted and Black, preparing them for productive lives while challenging racial inequality, a mission born of his influence.

Chapter 4

Brother's Keeper

I am a little brother, which means, of course, that I have a big brother, or big sister, or both. However, it's singular, a big sister, Barbara, as you already know from prior stories. Having a big sister, though challenging at times when we were growing up, worked out very well. She's my champion and sibling role model.

I don't recall ever wishing I had a big brother. But one member of my family, an uncle only six years older, came to fill that role for me in exciting and meaningful ways, and therefore, made it unnecessary to wish for a big brother. He lived with me for only a brief period, so he did not hassle me every day as some big brothers might. But his intermittent and unpretentious presence over many years made a huge difference in my life.

My first memories of my uncle Jasper Scott, Jr. (1932-2003), whom Barbara and I affectionately called "Jap," were during those early childhood visits to our grandparents' farm near Beekman, only 15 miles north of (our home) in Bastrop. As the last child of my grandfather and his second wife, Lucy, he was still living with them after his brother and five step-siblings left for other Louisiana and Texas destinations. They were happy to be away from the meager living conditions and grueling farm work.

But Barbara and I at an early age enjoyed the farm, particularly with Uncle Jap looking after us. Sitting on the edge of the front porch of our grandparent's house with our legs dangling over the side, he often entertained us with his lively telling of stories about Br'er Rabbit, Br'er Fox, Br'er Bear, and Tar Baby, African-American folktales. Moving and gesturing wildly, imitating their animated actions, causing us to giggle and laugh with delight, occupying us while our parents and grandparents were in the house talking grown folks talk.

Pulling a yo-yo from his pocket, uncle Jap dazzled us with its spinning dances, back and forth, up and down and sometimes riding on its own string. And while swiftly weaving his fingers through a string held in both hands, he amused us with magic tricks that left us with blank stares and mouths wide open in disbelief. With his help I tried the yo-yo, but limited dexterity at that age prevented any measurable success. However, I mastered the string trick that gave the illusion of the string cutting through my finger, later testing it successfully on my pals, Fred and H. T. It left their eyes with blank stares, too.

One afternoon, Uncle Jap caught a wasp to show us its stinger, which reinforced why we should keep our distance. And late one evening, with me and Barbara standing in our bedroom window with the shutters completely open, he corralled a few fireflies in his hands and brought them to the window so we could examine the nature of their dazzling light show. We watched the beautiful pulsating glow, but he did not explain the how or why, extending our curiosity. During late afternoons, we eagerly followed him around the farm while he fed the cows, pigs, chickens, and horse, familiarizing us with their purpose on the farm: food, work and transportation.

Although all the farm animals were fascinating at first, the aggressive eating habits and loud grunts of the hogs were disgusting and frightening to me, so I kept my distance. No love lost there. But one day Uncle Jap said, "You know that the bacon and ham you love so much for breakfast comes from hogs, don't you?" I stood silent staring at them, unable to put the two together in my young mind. I didn't alter my eating habits, but gave the hogs a little more respect.

On hot and humid afternoons during our visits, our sweet tooth exploded knowing Uncle Jap's specialty. "Please. Please, Uncle Jap," we shouted, jumping up and down. "Please make us some ice cream!" Consenting, he quickly made vanilla custard, poured it into a coffee can, and then we anxiously watched him rotate the can resting in a pan of chopped ice and salt, rotating it back and forth, with one hand, and then the other, our taste buds begging for resolve.

"Okay! Okay! Hold on, it's almost ready," he pleaded as he tried to speed up the process.

The ice cream never froze completely solid, but it didn't really matter. Sitting on the edge of the porch swinging our legs as the sun set behind the house, with a slight breeze moving through the distant trees expanding over the nearby corn field, the homemade ice cream was perfect and the setting looked like paradise. Smacking my lips, I quickly ate my bowlful and pleaded, "Can I have some more Uncle Jap?" licking my spoon clean after finishing each delectable helping.

During my weeklong summer visit to the farm, I was added to Uncle Jap's long list of chores, and I was perfectly happy with that arrangement—my big brother looking after me. He helped me get dressed and washed up each morning, allowing me to tag along during chores.

Each evening after dinner, the small kitchen turned into the bathing room. Not moving from the dinner table, I sat fidgeting in the shadows of the kerosene lamp watching Uncle Jap prepare my bath. After adding wood to the cast-iron stove to heat water in a large kettle, he poured the water into the galvanized washtub resting on the rough-hewn, hardwood floor. After he checked the water temperature to make sure it was safe, I took off my clothes and stood in the tub while he pulled the lamp close to search for and remove hungry tics stuck to various parts of my anatomy, acquired during my day's adventures. I watched him kill each one by crushing it between his thumbnails or burning it from the heat streaming from the lamp's globe.

I soaped and scrubbed myself as best I could, and Uncle Jap washed my hair and back. All of this he did while talking to me softly about the day's adventures and misadventures, and occasionally singing or humming a traditional spiritual, he loved, *Go down Moses* being one of my favorites. Then, I was off to bed to battle with the unforgiving feather mattress. Lucky for me, Uncle Jap showed great patience with his little brother.

He also took care of my dog, Spot, the mixed-breed, hyperactive transplant from home. However, Spot sometimes attempted to follow my parents' car the full 18 miles back to his first home in Bastrop. We discovered this on one return trip while stopped for gas in Beekman. "Mama, Daddy, there goes Spot!" I yelled as he galloped passed on the road running full speed. "Where is he going?" I worried. "Is he going to make it home?" I was always happy to learn that he found his way back to the farm to greet me on my next visit.

Spot accompanied us when we wandered throughout the vast forest surrounding the farm, following nature's trails, or making our own. Uncle Jap pointed out the different trees and plants we encountered, treating us to wild blackberries, dewberries, persimmons, plums, and pecans when in season. Spot sometimes jogged ahead out of sight only to circle around and run up behind us sounding like some wild animal, scaring us. He got a kick out of that, sometimes repeating it and getting the same reaction.

We often played hide-and-seek in the forest with me doing most of the hiding. Once I climbed a tree, only to look down through the branches a short time later to see Spot proudly wagging his tail, barking, and everyone pointing up at me laughing, yelling "We see you! We see you!" Some "best friend" my dog turned out to be.

I loved tagging along with Uncle Jap; it was always exciting and fun. Cheerful and even-tempered, he made no rules nor set restrictive parameters like parents would. We went wherever the urge or curiosity dictated. He was patient, easygoing and relaxed, appearing not to have a care in the world. Although, in hindsight, being confined to the farm miles away from schoolmates and age-cohorts, I'm sure he must have struggled with loneliness and typical teenage issues.

Only six years older than me, it seemed natural for him to become my surrogate big brother, an unintimidating, fun, older person I comfortably and joyfully interacted with. Also, I believe he thought of me as the little brother he never had. So, it turned out to be a welcomed *quid pro quo*, need-based convenient relationship.

Five foot, eight inches tall with proportional physique, Uncle Jap walked with a casual long-legged stride, more a stroll, never hurried. He did not wear the traditional coveralls of most farming families, but preferred shirt and trousers appropriate for the season. His head, slightly round like his father's, was topped with closely cropped dark-brown hair. His skin was cream-chocolate, a feature of half of our family with the other half, including me, much lighter, depending on the varying strengths of our African and Jewish ancestral genes. Uncle Jap seemed very comfortable with himself, who he was, and his current circumstances. I was comforted and reassured by his self-confidence.

But circumstances changed abruptly when he turned eighteen and was conscripted into the Army, causing him to temporarily disappear from my life. I was twelve, just moving into puberty, and could use his close counsel during that life-changing period. Finding myself uncomfortable in typical boy talk and not particularly interested in girls and sports, I really struggled trying to define myself amongst peer pressure.

For two years during the Korean War, Uncle Jap served as a cook at training and support bases in the US, providing meals for thousands of personnel preparing for war. He found himself in a world far removed from the simple, rural life he knew; confronted day and night with extremely different social and cultural norms that tested his character and personal perspective. The strict military discipline and intense interactions with men of different personalities and backgrounds —all strongly motivated to prove their masculinity—provoked personal change within him as he sought acceptance.

Taking liberty from his military duties in urban bars and nightclubs forced him to adapt quickly to a fast-paced, aggressive, and impersonal culture, where he was bombarded with profanity, cigarette smoking, alcohol consumption, uncontrolled men and risqué women, challenging his conservative roots. In the end, his traumatic and transformative military service had a deep and lasting effect. Uncle Jap returned home to Beekman a different person.

Honorably discharged and intending to pick up where he left off, assisting his parents on the farm while completing high school, Uncle Jap struggled to readjust to the isolated rural life and farm duties.

He despised the 18-mile daily school bus ride to the segregated high school in Bastrop. Fortunately, while he was away, his parents reduced the farm's productive crop acreage and livestock holdings, making his presence less crucial. Eventually, unfocused and restless, Uncle Jap relocated to Bastrop for school and work, a move that more readily reconnected little brother to big brother.

His personality had changed, and his interests were focused well beyond us, seeking out the goodtime social life. Staying at our house temporarily while he looked for lodging and a job, it quickly became more obvious to me and Barbara that this was not the Uncle Jap we remembered. One night, our parents left him as chaperone, which we felt was unnecessary, while they attended an NAACP meeting. The stories he told us that night were too mature for our early teenage ears, containing sexual innuendos and modest violence. Then, he left us temporarily to meet a girl, a secret he suggested we keep from our parents.

At a loss as to how to react to Uncle Jap's changed personality, I was still dealing with my own early-teen issues. There was much concern all around me, including parents, about my quiet, shy, loner traits and the lack of passion for a particular interest, forcing Uncle Jap and me into a new and evolving relationship.

Hearing conversations between my parents, aunts and other uncles, I later learned that following military service, Jap struggled to readjust to civilian life in Bastrop. After the temporary stay with my parents, which I recall, he rented a room in a boardinghouse and began overindulging in alcohol and spending late nights with fun-loving women in juke joints. A fight one night resulted in a severe knife wound that almost cost him his life, requiring time to heal and reflect. Concerned about his life, I recall a meeting at our house of the immediate family, including Uncle George from Marshall, Texas. When I found out the details, my first reaction was worry, but later I was angry, questioning why Uncle Jap would do those things and get himself stabbed. I was so conflicted that I didn't visit or see him during that time.

The family responded with love and support, though my mother harshly chastised him for his behavior. However, the life-threatening trauma, our family's tough love and his reassessing his life, caused Uncle Jap to change direction and pursue a different and more honorable path. He stopped drinking, abandoned his wild social life, and began concentrating on his education.

Uncle Jap and I eventually ended up in high school together with him two years ahead of me. I started calling him "Jap" like everyone else, dropping the "uncle." He called me John L., the same as others, except my sister who called me "Bay," short for Baby Brother. We bumped into each other frequently at the small school but made no special efforts to seek each other out. Nor did he attempt to keep a watchful eye on me, or control anything I did or who I hung out with. This was okay with me, since his new personal traits were not conducive for reestablishing our past close kinship. We were at different places in our lives by then. But through brief chitchat about school and family whenever we were together, we nurtured a new brotherly kinship.

When I was in the ninth grade, Mr. Montgomery, our Agriculture teacher, recruited both of us to sing in the New Farmers of America (NFA) male quartet where I sang second tenor with a changing voice, and Jap sang bass. The NFA was the Black counterpart of the Future Farmers of America (FFA), the whites' only organization before desegregation. Mr. Montgomery taught us the music, but left it to us to develop the style, mostly from hearing traveling professional gospel quartets in concert or on the radio. Our early favorites were *Down By the Riverside* and *Joshua Fit the Battle of Jericho*. Rehearsing and performing together was fun and another opportunity for me and Jap to adjust to our new more mature relationship.

Each year the quartet traveled 194 miles to Southern University and A&M College, the HBCU in Baton Rouge for the All-State NFA competitions where we earned superior ratings, consistently. Because of his age and possession of a driver's license, Jap was hired by our high school principal to drive the school's activity bus – but only after passing the chauffeur test. Our first trip to Southern introduced me to a whole new social and cultural dynamic and I was glad that Jap was there.

For the two-night stay, we lived on Southern's campus in one of the men's dormitories, built in the style of a military barracks. It comprised two floors of completely open space, except for the toilet and shower room. Wall-to-wall single beds were separated only by clusters of six-foot-tall gray metal lockers. We were assigned the second floor, which we shared with hundreds of other NFA students from throughout the state. This was something Jap, the army veteran, was used to. But the rest of his young underlings were not. We took one look and were ready to head home to the secure privacy of our bedrooms. Uncle Jap tried to assure us of our safety, but by the next morning our small-town, innocent world had flipped.

That evening I went to the restroom to use the toilet, entered the stall, shut the door, and sat down. I lifted my head and found myself staring at scribbling on the back of the door. As I focused to make sense of what I saw, shock raced through my body as I read the crude graffiti and gazed at the images. The texts described explicit sexual conduct and the graphics were rough depictions of sex organs and sexual acts. Never confronted by this before, I sat staring, paralyzed, unable to react, knowing I was reading and seeing forbidden material. Then I turned my head and found similar depictions on the other walls.

"Why is this here and who put it here?" I thought, horrified. "Is this what college is all about?" My mind was spinning as I finished my business and hastily exited, hoping to regain a sense of normalcy. I sat on my bed looking around for any reaction from my schoolmates, not knowing how to even begin to talk about what I had just seen. Uncle Jap didn't mention the shocking display, probably because he was accustomed to similar graffiti while in the Army. So, I had to deal with it the best way I could, although that was only the beginning of an unsettling night.

After the lights were turned off, I nervously stretched out among a sea of wall-to-wall beds holding energized teenage boys from different parts of the state, with those from New Orleans, the largest urban city, considered the most fearsome. This was an uncomfortable setting that made sleep difficult. But then suddenly, out of the darkness a loud voice yelled something I did not understand, frightening me. Seconds later another voice rang out even louder, uttering more unrecognizable words, but then a voice close to me yelled, "Yo' mama's so stupid it takes her one hour to cook minute rice!" And another voice followed with "Yo' mama's so skinny, she turned sideways and disappeared!" The cacophony continued of call-and-response shouts of negative prose about someone's "mama," many laced with profanity.

I froze, laying there stiff as a board afraid of the fight that I was sure to come. But as the back-and-forth voices continued from the dark recesses of the barracks, there was giggling, then laughter and then hilarious laughter! The more negative the prose the more vociferous the laughter. I rolled over in my bed relaxing a little, but didn't get it.

"What happened to the fights? It's serious business when you denigrate someone's mother, isn't it?" This continued into the wee hours of the morning, only slowing as the participants yielded to the overwhelming force of sleep.

"Welcome to The Dozens!" Uncle Jap said the next morning without further explanation, looking at our sleepless eyes. I guess this was nothing new for him. But this tradition was entirely new and shocking to his little band of small-town, country-boy protégés; something our parents would probably prefer we had not experienced.

"The Dozens," I later discovered, was humorous wordplay with a uniquely African-American origin, for years ignored by literary scholars for obvious reasons. It is a game of verbal sparring and one-upmanship building on the worst that can be said about someone, in this instance their mother, hypothetically of course. There is much speculation about why this game was called "The Dozens," including one unproven theory referencing unfit slaves auctioned off by the dozens. I never understood the humor of it, nor its acceptance as valued Black folklore. But it was a powerful learning curve for my developing manhood.

Jap, the oldest and most socially experienced in our group, used the NFA trips to enlighten us about the "manly" things he thought we should know, if we didn't already. I believe his main target was me, the quiet, nonassertive person, the loner nonparticipant in young Black male group banter. Only a few years older, he broached the subject of girls and sex with teen humor, which provided needed context and explanation for my emerging feelings. "Now, that's what's going on." However, these subjects only came up in group talks, but never in private conversations. I'm not sure why, and I was not about to bring the subject up myself.

But even with my uncle trying to school me in the manly ways of the world, in many other ways I was also inexperienced, which can be dangerous. During our attendance at a NFA regional convention in Atlanta, Jap and Mr. Montgomery lost track of me when, without telling them, I escorted an attractive young lady to her transit bus stop after a late-afternoon social event at the YMCA where we were staying. We had concluded a short chat, and she was heading out the door. I thought I would try the assertive approach, and as a "gentleman", I suggested to accompany her to her destination, a bus stop, while also thinking, "This will make my big brother proud." However, as a small-town boy, I was not aware of the expansiveness of big cities, and how wide, diagonal, and circular streets could easily confuse a young man accustomed only to the narrow, perpendicular roads of my hometown, where I usually navigated by familiar landmarks and well-worn paths. Adding to the confusion, as I escorted my new young-lady friend, there was a well-attended nighttime parade rolling right up the street where her bus was to arrive.

As I proudly turned to leave her safely waiting at the bus stop, she asked if I knew the way back to the YMCA? "Of course!" I said, with my new-found male bravado. "Yes-yes! Sure! No problem! I know how to get back."

I turned around and promptly headed off into the darkness.

It didn't take me long to realize that I had absolutely no clue where I was, or how to get back to the Y. I went up one street and down another looking for something familiar and found nothing. Lucky for me, a policeman appeared just as fear was consuming my psyche. With the directions he and a few others gave along the way, I arrived at the YMCA where Jap and Mr. Montgomery were waiting, anxiously and angrily, on the front steps for their AWOL protégé. "John L.; where have you been? We have been looking all over for you! You can't just wander off in unfamiliar places like that," Jap admonished. Understanding that I deserved their anger, I was greatly relieved and happy to be back in secure circumstances. Unfortunately, the experience only exacerbated my unwillingness to risk cultivating relationships with the opposite sex— no matter how attractive and socially engaging they might be.

After completing high school, Jap enrolled at Wiley College, where our uncle, Dr. Julius Scott, Sr. was president. Traveling to visit his parents in Beekman, Jap often stopped to invite me to go fishing when I was home for summers from Lincoln University. He loved freshwater fishing passionately and was very good at it, a real pro. His knowledge of the many species and the techniques for catching them was extraordinary. His favorite venue was nearby Bayou Bartholomew, a regular Smith Family Inc. fishing destination.

Fishing was a valued family tradition, but for me it was more an occasion to get away from routine Smith Family, Inc. responsibilities, to cook outdoors, relax and enjoy the open-air countryside and waterways, something Scouting enhanced. Unlike Uncle Jap, I never took fishing, seriously. For a long time, Daddy and Uncle Jap fixed my cane pole with a line, cork, weight, and hook, and said, "Go fish!" I managed to pull the earthworm over the hook to make it look alive before throwing the line into the water. Then my mind drifted off to other places while watching the cork float and bob on the water's surface.

So, when Uncle Jap invited me to go fishing, I eagerly accepted just to be with him and enjoy the quiet, yet exhilarating, outdoors. We fished along the bayou's banks, or while floating in a borrowed twelve-foot, two-seat wooden boat he leisurely, but skillfully, maneuvered. Jap caught the fish, usually trout, bass, perch or catfish, whichever species he was angling for, while I enjoyed the casual conversation, the surrounding moss-laden trees, wide-leaf plants, and dense, knee-high foliage crowding the banks. The sounds of insects, birds and frogs and the wind pushing through the thick tree branches added to the serenity.

Convincingly, I watched the cork bobbing on the water. And if Jap said, "throw your line over there towards the bank near that log, John L.," that's exactly what I did, with no great expectations. Of course, I knew that if the cork disappeared underwater, I should quickly yank the pole with the hope that a fish would be dangling from the end, and sometimes that happened.

"Jap, I caught something. Looks like a catfish," I said on one occasion while raising my line.

"Well, hold on. If it is, I'll need to help you get it off the hook without getting finned," he warned. "But we'll throw it back in the water, they're too hard to clean." He held it down under his foot while extracting the hook, tossed it back in the bayou, and I re-baited my hook to continue my fishing charade.

But those fishing trips were actually surreptitious nurturing opportunities where my uncle/big brother, Jap, continued to influence my growth and development.

"You know, I got into a lot of stuff when I was in the Army, hanging out with some rough characters," he once admitted. "But I wasn't thinking. It's always best to think through things before you do them, and to do the right thing," Continuing, he admitted, "The guys were good to be around, to talk about man stuff, joke and jive, and that's good too, but follow your own path when there's a decision to make." Following a brief silence while altering the position of his fishing line, he went on, "I didn't see girls the right way back then. But later at Wiley, I've learned to appreciate really talking with them, hearing their perspective and how they make you see them and other things in a different light."

Silence from me. Then feeling a bit uncomfortable with the subject, I swung my pole to a new position dropping the hook into the water with a slight splash.

"Well, you know, Jap, at Lincoln," I finally responded, trying to excuse my antisocial self, "all of my time is taken up with music and studying, trying to keep up and not flunk out. There are a few music classmates I talk with often, mostly about music, but hardly anybody else.   Maybe there will be more time later to meet some other students."

More silence before he tried again to provoke a more in-depth reaction from me, trying to help me to become more socially assertive. "So, why is it you can't just open up and talk about things, anything; likes, dislikes, whatever, beyond music with schoolmates?" he challenged, directly. "It could be fun getting to know someone else." I had no answer for that. Uncle Jap was trying to help me confront my social shortcoming, and as usual I was hedging. However, usually his approach was more subtle, planting insightful thoughts and perspectives that may influence my still developing character. Unfortunately for me, during our fishing excursions, much of those lessons may have been lost in the serenity of the moment: I was laid-back, relaxed, and enjoying myself in my own world.

While matriculating at Wiley, the Methodist-supported institution, Uncle Jap experienced a calling to the religious ministry. "*My strength is made perfect in weakness (2 Cor. 12:9)*" could easily be the Biblical reference to explain his dramatic transformation and powerful new urge to preach the Holy Gospel. But there were also earthly factors that influenced his decision.

Wiley's curriculum, programs and events featured many faith-based elements. President Scott, an ordained Methodist minister, spoke and preached often at campus assemblies. Jap's cousin, Dr. Julius Scott, Jr., the president's son, was also an ordained Methodist minister who served at the national office. Uncle Jap's parents and several siblings, including my mother, were devout Methodist church members and lay leaders. And, for virtually all of his life he was surrounded by religious family members, most of them active Methodists.

Those influences also motivated Jap to choose the Methodist denomination for his ministry career, which elicited joy and support from the family. I was certainly pleased and impressed with the direction his life was taking; our connections continuing when he visited Bastrop and Beekman. "Jap is finally getting his life together and pursuing a religious calling as a Methodist minister," the family, including me, extolled. However, he soon discovered that a Seminary degree was required to be ordained as a Methodist minister, mandating an additional two years of study after college.

Already significantly behind his age cohort due to military service and the slow pace at Wiley College due to financial constraints, Uncle Jap figured this would put him further behind, delaying his career and starting a family. Desperate to move on with his life, he concluded that pursuing the Methodist ministry was not realistic.

However, after exploring other options, the Baptist ministry appeared to be the perfect solution. Baptists shared the same protestant theology as Methodists, but did not require seminary credentials for ordination. Further, he could begin preaching immediately at Baptist churches, which he did, starting that year in 1960. Two years later, he completed the Bachelor of Arts degree in Religious Studies at Wiley and obtained his first pastoral position in Longview, Texas, where he married Myrtle Shaw and commenced to raising three children.

During his ministry career, Uncle Jap served as pastor of several churches in East Texas, and preached at churches in Louisiana, Oklahoma, Illinois, Michigan and in other Texas communities. He later confessed during one of my visits to his home, "I really don't like the politics and administrative responsibilities that come with being a pastor. I just want to preach and not worry about the church business." His deepest passion was simply to communicate the powerful Holy Gospel whenever, wherever and to whomever.

I heard my uncle/big brother, the Reverend Jasper W. Scott, Jr., preach only once, and it was evident that he had indeed found his true calling. He stood, composed and saintly, in the pulpit wearing a black robe and slowly moving left and right, dramatizing a Bible story that illustrated the sermon's theme, the same way he entertained me and Barbara with fictional tales on the farm during our early childhood. When he reached the story's climax that symbolized Christ sacrificing his life for the sins of humanity, he looked up to the celestial heavens and extended his arms out from his body as though on the cross. This powerfully illustrated the emotional ethos of the Christian faith. The sermon was captivating and compelling, demonstrated by the shouts of "Amen!" and "Hallelujah!" from the standing congregation. It was evident that Jap's devout spiritual passion matched well with his innate and acquired qualities, enabling him to touch hearts and souls. He was impressive, and feeling the spiritual passion; I was pleased.

Uncle Jap happened to be in Bastrop in June 1961, when I started the drive to Aspen, Colorado, for my first professional job as principal tuba player with the Aspen Music Festival Orchestra. He traveled by bus to Beekman to check on his parents. "Hey," he said. "We're going the same direction, so I'll take the wheel to Marshall, and give you a break on your driving." Well, what can you say, except be thankful? Of course, this meant more time for nurturing his little brother. It turned out to be more beneficial than I thought initially, since I was unable to stop overnight in Amarillo, Texas as planned due to segregated hotels, forcing me to continue to Denver without sleep. Even the managers of "reputable" chain hotels stopped me before I reached the office door to tell me, "No vacancies. Try the Black part of town," even though the lighted sign in front clearly indicated "Vacancy." That was painful and insulting, and it took a lot to compress my anger, and protesting alone in an unfamiliar southern town was not practical or safe.

During my six-year stay in Oklahoma City (1966-72) as a member of the Oklahoma City Symphony Orchestra and teaching at Langston University (more on this in later chapters), I usually stopped at Jap's home in Longview, Texas, to visit the family when traveling back to Bastrop to see my parents. Walking into their modest home for lunch and conversation was always comforting and reassuring; my big brother and family welcoming me and my wife and two young children. The powerful unspoken bond we shared was so affirming and genuine. Once when I drove up, he and a friend had their heads under his car's hood, hands covered with oil. He promptly ended their work, cleaned up and welcomed me for food and brotherly conversation.

With the ministry now his first priority, Uncle Jap fished mostly at night. When I was invited to go fishing with him, I declined, in spite of the wonderful memories of past fishing trips. Out there in the dark with all kinds of dangerous creatures lurking around? No thanks. He had protection from "On High." I was not completely sure I did. However, Uncle Jap's nurturing of his little brother continued unabated. He never gave up on getting me more socially engaged, assertive and wise in the ways of humankind. Pushing the conversations during my visits to reveal the status of my maturity and social development, he never hesitated to offer hints for improvement.

"So, you tell me your neighbor performs in rodeos. Bulldogging, did you say? That's interesting. For a Black man, that's rare. Why don't you know more about him and his family and background?" he asked during one visit. I was embarrassed, but knew what I had to do once I returned home. We also reminisced about wonderful times spent together on the farm, in high school, and during the many Bayou fishing trips, which sometimes revealed missed cues that were intended to assist my personal growth.

During most of his adult life, Uncle Jap worked part-time at various manual labor jobs, at first to pay for college, and later to support his family. Myrtle taught school full-time providing constant income. One job required that Jap carry heavy bags on his shoulder, causing a back injury that worsened with age. The last time I saw him alive was when he drove twenty-five miles from Longview to Marshall, in pain, to see me during a visit with Uncle George, his ninety-year-old half-brother. I was really happy to see him, and we had a wonderful, although brief, reunion. But I felt deeply for him as he grimaced while sliding behind the steering wheel for the trip home, a visual memory I still carry.

My uncle/big brother Jap's intrusive role in my life was symbolic of his greater humanity, a compelling desire to help everyone encountering life's complexities. His ministry, sermons, counsel and friendship offered people hope, inspiration and encouragement for confronting personal issues and obstacles in their lives. It was through helping others that he validated his life, giving it profound meaning.

From my early boyhood years on the farm through adulthood, his loving care and personal attention taught, counseled, and nurtured me until he passed away on December 8, 2003. Lingering in his house with the Scott-Smith families before the caravan left for his funeral, I found myself reminiscing about our precious and loving time together.

In a short emotional, hand-written letter, Uncle Jap wrote to me only weeks before his death, he alluded to his early concerns about my growth and development as a boy and man. But he went on to say that he was more than pleased with the sociable and confident person I had become; I'm so thankful that he took the "uncle" kinship seriously and devoted part of his life to being my beloved big brother, dear friend, and influential mentor.

Chapter 5

Moral Compass

"There they go!" I whispered to Fred, my early childhood buddy, while looking up. "The bats! They're back in our church!"

"Whoooweee, they sure can fly, but they're ugly!" added H.T., my other buddy.

"Lookathere," Fred responded back, "one's gonna land on somebody and bit'em."

With threatening rat-like heads, four of them, webbed wings flapping, circled and swooped back and forth above our heads during Sunday morning service, demonstrating dynamic acrobatic skills. The building's high-pitched ceiling gave them ample space to show off, and they did.

Watching from the pews, we were highly amused, waiting for one of the bats to land on the minister's bald head, so we could giggle and laugh, in spite of the punishment from our parents that would surely follow.

My uncle Robert, head Church trustee, attempting to rid the building of the bats, had fumigated its interior all day Saturday with some awful smelling witches' brew, spewing smoke from a large black bucket. But, as far as I was concerned, the stench that was still there on Sunday morning was worse than the sight and threat of the surviving bats, which we found much more entertaining than anything else going on in church.

Bats or no bats, church was a requirement, an important and intrinsic part of my childhood, an experience enforced by my mother. Every Sunday, look for me at Mount Olive Methodist Church Sunday School at 9 a.m., General Worship Service at 11 a.m., Methodist Youth Fellowship at 4 p.m., and occasionally evening service at 7 p.m. On Saturdays, I could be found singing away in children's choir rehearsal. And when the church women sold fresh-baked pies, fried fish and chicken dinners at the church on some Saturdays to raise money for church programs, I delivered them on my bike, and by car when I learned to drive.

Like most Black children in Bastrop, me, Fred, H. T., and our families had close ties to church, partially as a way of escaping temporarily from Deep South racism. Church was a sanctuary from white people who determined much of our daily life. And, if the church had a progressive education program, along with public school education it increased the potential for attending college and escaping north or west.

The overall spiritual and program success of our church depended greatly on robust leadership from the pastor, the person who each Sunday stood before me and my partners, high in the pulpit (so it seemed) as a moral authority figure, preaching the Holy Gospel. In early childhood, I looked up to that person as a symbol of virtue—incapable of sin and wrongdoing, the perfect role model, my parents wished for me to emulate.

But during a Methodist Youth Assembly retreat I attended as an early teen, that ideal model was shattered. I was standing near my bunk in a residential hut as a scuffle broke out between two boys that escalated quickly. The minister assigned as resident counsel for our hut tried to intervene but without much success, until he pulled a knife from his pocket and, while shouting expletives, threatened the young teenagers for being, well, teenagers.

I watched in horror, paralyzed in disbelief at what I saw and heard. I thought, "How can a minister, a man of God, do and say those things?" For days afterward, I was devastated and confused, as that scene played repeatedly in my mind, until later coming to the realization that ministers were human too, and prone to curtained extreme reactions like the rest of us. They were not God. But despite my momentary personal confusion, organized religion was central to Smith Family, Inc. and since I was baptized as a baby (I had no choice in the matter), I was an active part of it, like it or not.

Mount Olive Methodist Episcopal (ME) Church, where I was a member since baptism, had a small congregation with a high percentage of college educated members, mostly public- school teachers. Organizationally, it fell under the Central Jurisdiction; the national ME Church's segregated African-American Division, which was dissolved in 1968, and Black congregants integrated into the newly constituted United Methodist Church.

Founded in 1874 by my fraternal and maternal great-grandfathers Armstead Smith and George Scott respectively; the inaugural Mt. Olive Church congregation met alternately in their blacksmith shops, one west of town, and the other east. The first church building was constructed in 1911 on the corner of Pruett and Welch, three blocks south of where the house I grew up in was built decades later. The white-painted wooden structure, where the bats enjoyed themselves, was designed in the shape of a cross with a high-pitched roof, ample double-hung windows for the best ventilation, and a steeple/bell tower that covered a small vestibule at the entrance.

Beyond its religious mission, Mt. Olive served as a hub for the Black community, offering educational, cultural, and social programs and events for the general public, which included theater productions, poetry readings, music concerts and outdoor festivals, sometimes featuring out of town artists. During the early years, the church also operated as an elementary school.

I recall as a small, barely walking toddler at one of the outdoor festivals, someone prodding me into a fishing game by handing me a short pole with an attached line, prompting me to dangle it over a hanging sheet and telling me to pull it back over when I felt a tug. "Wow! I caught something!" Much to my amazement, it was a candy-filled plastic fish dangling from the end of my line. Jumping up and down at the sight of the "catch-of-the-day," I promptly ate the candy and excitedly demanded, "More fish, more fish!"

In 1950, one year before I started high school, a new modern red-brick building designed in an L shape was constructed. The side wing, was used for educational and social purposes, included a kitchen and modern restrooms, but could be opened up to expand the sanctuary. A wooden steeple, without bell, rose above the entrance and foyer with small Sunday school classrooms on each side. The original plan was to use the bell from the old building, but the new structure would not support the weight. I don't know what happened to the bell. Sadly, it and its historic significance vanished. Later, central heating and air-conditioning were added, completing the building as it stands today.

Like many Black churches, Mt. Olive was central to the Civil Rights battles of the 1960s and '70s, allowing the NAACP and other groups to use its facilities, supporting progressive education, socioeconomic and political community organizations. As sponsor of the Black Boy Scout troop, of which I was a member, the church supported its occasional use.

The college-educated members served as church trustees, lay leaders, program directors, Sunday school superintendents and teachers. My mother was superintendent during the years I attended and beyond, constantly pursuing a current and progressive agenda including Summer Bible School. I recall everything seemingly running smoothly and part of the greater community.

Between home, school and church, children were under the constant, watchful eye and influence of caring adults who communicated among themselves about our deeds and misdeeds, often intervening with tough love and positive reinforcement. Of course, we kids didn't always see it that way; we saw them as busybodies, much too intrusive. However, the overall effectiveness of Mt. Olive in that seamless child welfare system greatly depended on the interest and leadership of the pastor.

Ordained Methodist Episcopal ministers were required to be college and seminary graduates, well-educated and exceptionally versed in Christian theology and Methodist doctrine, placing them among the Black community's emerging middle-class leadership. The entry level assignment for new seminary graduates was typically a small town or rural church, like Mt. Olive, from which they might advance incrementally to larger and more complex urban congregations for future reassignments.

It seems Mt. Olive was held in high regard as an entry-level church by the Central Jurisdiction and Louisiana Conference leaders.

The church's unusually high percentage of college graduate members, the number of active programs, its financial stability and promptness with required reports provided an above-average profile, making it a high priority for exceptional seminary graduates. And for me, the pastor that stood out above all others was Rev. William S. P. Norris, who served during the first half of the 1950s, when I was an impressionable and vulnerable, young teen.

A veteran of World War II, William Norris graduated from Southern University and A&M College and Gammon Theological Seminary, and married Margaret Ester Taylor, prior to his Mount Olive assignment. Born in Bogalusa, Louisiana, the son of Rev. Timothy P. Norris, a Methodist minister, he was not a stranger to the church and its practices. With little fanfare, he plunged energetically into the affairs and programs of Mt. Olive, showing an immediate interest in the young men, particularly after Fred, H.T. and I got his attention one Sunday in morning service.

We were having a fun, good time, talking and giggling in our pew during the service that Sunday while Rev. Norris was preaching. His eyes were addressing the congregation as much as his notes while delivering his sacred message. Then he stopped abruptly mid-sentence, looked directly at us, and pointed his finger.

"Fred, H.T. and Junior (the name he chose for me out of deference to my father John Sr.), be quiet and stop horsing around!" he said, still pointing that accusing finger at us. "I don't want to hear any more out of you. Behave!"

"What? He called us out in the middle of service," I thought in sheer panic as we sat like statues, except for our accelerated heartbeats. There was complete silence. I could feel the eyes of everyone in the church "village" upon me, particularly the eyes of my mother who would surely follow up with more severe punishment. But, somehow, I sensed that Rev. Norris was not yet done with our behavior modification.

Sure enough, not long after that incident—recognizing we were at that peculiar mid-teen age where boys enter into a unique twilight zone of acting weird, making bad decisions, and doing and saying crazy things without considering the consequences—we became his special project. Only in his late 20s, his youthfulness gave him insight about what we were experiencing during that critical phase, and how he might help.

A few weeks later, he announced from the pulpit that he was starting a special young men's program. And the following Saturday, Fred, H.T. and I were among a small group of boys on the south lawn of the church listening to Rev. Norris explain why we were there.

"I just want to get to know you a little bit," he said, stretching his arms and legs. "See what kind of things you're interested in, and what's on your mind. We'll only get together for about an hour each Saturday for a while. See how things go."

We relaxed a little after that revelation, which sounded a lot less threatening than what we had anticipated.

"Who's the fastest on their feet?" he then asked, surprising us. "Why don't we run some short-distance sprints to find out?"

Wow! We got excited about that and began lining up. This was way better than the dreaded religious lessons we were expecting.

"Man, this is going to be fun," I whispered to Fred. "We can show him our stuff."

For several contests, we gave it our best, with each of us sharing the winner's circle.

"You boys are pretty fast," Rev. Norris finally commented while doing a few more leg stretches. "I think I'll see if I can keep up." And he fell in line with us for another sprint.

We looked at each other as if to say, "What? You've got to be kidding!"

We were vaguely aware that he was a lineman on Southern University's football team, but we didn't know if it was offensive or defensive, guard or tackle. Certainly, older and a bit heavier since those days, he still appeared athletic and physically fit, prepared for gridiron war.

At approximately five feet, eight inches tall, with a large rectangular shaped head, barrel chest, large thighs and muscular legs, his features were ideal for a lineman. And there was a noticeable scar below his left eye that seemed indicative of a wound acquired in gridiron combat.

But he was just a lineman, not a running back, I reasoned. And many years had passed since his college football days. Surely, with his current age and newly acquired heft, he didn't stand a chance against our fox-lean bodies, greyhound-speed and rabbit-like agility. Without question, we would win the race easily, I assured myself. No contest.

He asked for a volunteer to countdown, as we prepared to run. "Three, two, one," and we were off! Out of the corner of my eye I saw Rev. Norris spring forward before my foot left the ground. His legs were moving, it seemed, like the high-speed rotating limbs of the Coyote in the famous *Road Runner* cartoon. I saw the back of his head as the distance between us widened, and he finished at least twelve feet ahead. Hardly able to catch my breath, I bent over and put my hands on my knees, unable to believe what had just happened. My buddies and I stood there awestruck, eyeballing each other, not really knowing how to respond to losing to our much older pastor.

But, for sure, that Saturday Rev. Norris got our attention.

During succeeding Saturdays, he continued to dazzle us with unexpected feats, along with teaching and counseling us about moral and ethical living. We sensed his authentic and genuine interest, eagerly becoming his subjects. Starting with the Ten Commandments, where he dwelled on the Commandment, *Honor your father and your mother.* And later, to encourage humility, he covered the Beatitudes with a particular focus on *Blessed are those who are persecuted because of righteousness, for theirs is the kingdom of heaven.*

The Bible lessons were accompanied by practical illustrations to drive the message home. We were also pulled into discussions that championed perseverance, discipline, and hard work for overcoming life's obstacles and succeeding, with the Reverend often repeating, "One must keep on keeping on," challenging us to grow and develop as responsible young men.

"You should always question negative criticism directed at you," he urged one Saturday as he segued into Black identity, "particularly from a white person. It's often meant to diminish who you are and who you have the right to be." He offered shields for protecting ourselves against racist efforts to make us feel inferior, while boosting our confidence. "Be proud of your Blackness," he went on. "You are smart and can do anything. Don't let anyone tell you different." He also challenged us to exceed self-defeating ideas about our Black manhood, intellect, and ability.

The energy and caring spirit, mixed with fun, opened a wide channel of communication that allowed Rev. Norris' message to resonate with us, granting a path for building character and self-confidence. However, in retrospect, I believe his intense involvement with us may have been due partially to he and Mrs. Norris not having children, and we were surrogates.

Rev. and Mrs. Norris shopped regularly at my father's grocery store, phoning-in a short list that I delivered on my bike. When I arrived at the parsonage behind the church and knocked, Mrs. Norris usually answered the door.

"Hi Junior, come on in."

Bags-in-hand, I followed her into the kitchen at the back of the small, neatly arranged modestly furnished house where I placed them on the breakfast table.

"Sit down Junior, while I put them away. The Reverend will be in shortly," she would say, as she placed the items in the refrigerator and cabinets. Shortly, Rev. Norris joined us, standing in the doorway.

"Great seeing you Junior, how's Mr. Johnnie?" referring to my father.

"He's fine. Told me to make sure your order is right," I responded.

"You're such a great help to your father. Now what have you been up to?"

The brief conversations usually explored my work in the store, progress in school, school extracurricular activities and if I had any idea of what I might want to become. "Well Junior, if you continue to work and study hard, you'll be a success in life for sure," Rev. Norris often commented as I headed towards the front door, and climbed on my bike heading back to the store. I enjoyed delivering groceries to them for the genuine love, inspiration and encouragement. I think that they saw me as a flower bud with strong potential to blossom into an honorable, productive, perhaps less shy, human being if properly cultivated. And they intended to provide small servings of vital nutrients.

Each summer, Mt. Olive youth were offered the opportunity to attend a weeklong assembly at Gulfside, a Black Methodist retreat on Mississippi's Gulf Coast. Established by the Central Jurisdiction in 1923 to serve as a refuge, camp, and conference center, it was located several miles west of Waveland on 300 acres of pristine oak and southern pine property, separated from the Gulf of Mexico by South Beach Boulevard and a two-foot-high sea wall. A private pier extended into the Gulf with covered deck and lower platform for swimmers. A cattle grate with low-slung wire fence on both sides marked the entrance, while an S-shaped gravel-and-sand road curved north, white buildings and trees with white-washed trunks, along both sides.

When I attended in the 1950s, the campus included a two-story, box-shaped administration/classroom building with center steeple and four-square pillars framing the entrance. There was a quaint, rectangular white-stucco chapel with high double-hung windows, double doors at the front entrance topped by a short almost apologetic steeple, and interior with maroon aisle carpeting and matching pew cushions. Next to the chapel was a two-story women's and staff residential facility with a dining hall wing. The remaining buildings included a large multipurpose building for assemblies and social activities, and several small half-screened living cottages.

However, since then, Gulfside has sustained various levels of damage from hurricanes, with Katrina rendering the final death blow (no pun intended) in 2005, completely destroying all of the retreat's structures remaining from previous hurricanes. The once purpose-driven destination for Black congregants and others is now recognized by the United Methodist Church and the State of Mississippi as an historical site with efforts to memorialize its Black heritage.

The Summer Methodist Youth Assembly at Gulfside began in the 1940s as a five-day retreat providing religious education, spiritual renewal, and social interaction. My mother was a staff member starting when Barbara and I were in our early childhood. I remember vividly her driving us on the harrowing three-hundred-mile, full-day trip, leaving Bastrop and traveling through what seemed like the entire State of Mississippi. "Are we there yet?" was not a permitted question under the circumstances. For Black Americans, this trip represented a real and present danger that required extraordinary courage, careful planning and shrewd survival tactics. Restroom and gas stops were unpredictable with no identifiable safe places to stop. Racist white men particularly were a very real threat for a Black woman driving alone with two small children. But my mother was not to be deterred, and somehow, with intuitive strategy and many prayers, our annual trips were accomplished without one life-threatening incident, though there were anxious moments.

The minute we left home, I felt the weight of my mother's heightening tension: "Barbara, John L., you must do what I tell you without question on this trip, do you understand?" She admonished with sharp eyes. "Yes," we responded to her serious demand, which put us on notice; this was not to be a fun drive like usual. While driving, I could see my mother on high alert to everything around us, making me a little fearful and Barbara and I much quieter and less active than usual, mostly looking out the window, sometimes playing a game of counting types of cows. But, of course, nature must have its way.

"Mama, I need to go to the bathroom," I hesitantly announced, only when it was absolutely urgent.

"Hurry up," she'd plead, after stopping on the highway shoulder near a wooded area for me to scamper behind a tree. At first it felt like a game, but on later trips, realizing her apprehension, I tried harder to hold it in.

When she desperately needed to go herself, mama waited until it was near time to get gas. When stopping at a gas station, Barbara and I were instructed, "stay absolutely quiet and don't move," as she immediately headed for the restroom. If told she wasn't allowed to use the facilities, she wouldn't purchase gas there but drive on to a station that had a "colored only" toilet in back that was usually filthy and barely functional, purchasing gas only afterwards.

But the reward that made the fraught trip absolutely worthwhile for me and Barbara occurred near the end, as we drove over a slight incline south of Waveland and came suddenly face-to-face with the sparkling green, restless waters of the Gulf of Mexico, stretching endlessly in front of us. The sun's brilliant reflections across the restive waves spanned the entire horizon. Inhaling the sweet, salty Gulf fragrance further enhanced the captivating sight, increasing my excitement, and accelerating my heartbeat as I danced uncontrollably on the backseat floorboard.

"Mama. I want to get in the water! Please! Please!" I cried out each of those first years.

Having survived the scariest part of the trip, she was now more relaxed, smiled and calmly said, "Soon, we are almost there. We'll get in the water soon."

Turning right onto South Beach Boulevard, we followed the Gulf Coast west, my eyes never leaving the incessantly agitated, glittering water. Wanting desperately to get in, I continued begging as we reached our destination, my mother turning right and driving over the cattle grate into the peaceful, scenic and safe Gulfside, finally.

My early childhood years there were the most exciting, since I swam twice daily, early morning and afternoon, ate three healthy meals, and with no other obligations, played in my room. Trembling each morning as I inched off the pier's platform, down the steps into the cold water during high tide, I struggled to keep my head above the lazy waves. Not knowing how to swim, my first efforts were underwater, arms and legs flailing as I propelled myself between the steps and human bodies. Mama described those efforts as like "a desperate frog underwater."

During my teen years, Rev. Norris was Gulfside's Summer Methodist Youth Assembly's resident minister. He preached for daily worship services, taught Bible classes, and served as youth counselor and discipline director. Part of his task was to make sure a boy's escalating hormones did not overpower his best judgments. For example, during early evenings, all of the youths sat along the seawall to observe and meditate during the sunset's beautiful, multicolor reflections on the clouds and Gulf. However, this also offered an opportunity for nurturing romantic liaisons that may have developed quickly, or those that existed from previous summers. I had my eye on an attractive, rather mature-looking young lady from New Orleans I had shyly spoken to the previous year, and made sure I sat next to her for the devotional sun gazing, and wanted to put my arm around her waist. "Oh man, there he is again, across the street behind us," I thought with anguish. "I can't do nothing!" Rev. Norris and one or two other staff members had as usual positioned themselves behind us, across South Beach Boulevard during the evening's meditation to scrutinize our behavior, keeping romantic notions in check. Later, folk dancing and polite skits led by my mother each evening was our only organized social life, boys and girls together. I heard about arranged late night liaisons, and had one offer from a mature young lady, but my shyness, inexperience and Rev. Norris' camp-presence inspired a blank stare.

Rev. Norris was known for his ferocious appetite, and fast foods were some of his favorites. While at Gulfside, he occasionally "sneaked" away from the campus to acquire fried chicken, burgers and fries from the back window of a white-owned café in Waveland and shared those late-night snacks with his adult peers, including my mother. We students were not supposed to know about this external activity, but it was common knowledge and amusement for the Mount Olive Church .

Of course, at some point all of our fun had to come to an end each summer, and we packed up and headed back to Bastrop. During my teen years, several churches in the Bastrop and Monroe region traveled together using a leased school bus, and employing a driver. However, on one memorable Saturday night return trip from Gulfside, the woman driving our bus became lost while taking shortcuts on the back roads of Mississippi. Not a smart idea when driving a bus load of Black people. That decision developed into a treacherous all-night journey through extremely dangerous, racially hostile territory, making it unsafe to stop for any reason.

Once the teenage cargo was aware of the situation, fear began to creep into our minds as darkness engulfed the lonely back roads. For

Rev. Norris, the only adult supervisor for our traumatized group, the midnight maze of back roads heightened his already deep sense of responsibility. Besides calming our anxieties, he helped the driver find her way, rationed what water and snacks we had, and tried to reassure us, sometimes standing at the back of the dark bus watching over us like an intensely concerned parent.

I was sitting with a girl I didn't know three rows from the back, when she bent over unexpectedly to take a nap in my lap. I was petrified, not knowing what Rev. Norris might think. But I could only wait until she decided to sit up. As we kept going, a few sniffles could be heard from a few younger girls having difficulty coping with the dark unknown.

Finally, around 3 a.m. Sunday morning, the bus driver managed to steer us out of uncharted back roads onto a highway that led into Jackson, Mississippi. However, concerned about the driver's lack of sleep and the general wellbeing of everyone, Rev. Norris made an extraordinarily risky, but courageous, decision based purely on his deep-seated Christian beliefs. He steered the driver toward the First Methodist Episcopal Church in downtown Jackson that served white congregants only, a large white building with stately round columns.

Rev. Norris nervously rang the doorbell of the parsonage next to the church not really knowing what to expect. A sleepy-eyed minister hesitantly cracked open the door and Rev. Norris explained to him who we were and our dire situation, asking if the young people in our entourage could possibly have some desperately needed water, use the restroom and sleep a couple of hours in a church space. I imagine he had prayed that the white clergyman would respond with his supposed Christian conviction, rather than hostile southern racial tradition.

However, Rev. Norris soon returned to the bus, face expressionless, and simply uttered to the driver, "Let's go." That minister was obviously one of the white clergy Dr. Martin Luther King Jr. referred to in the 1963 *Letter from Birmingham Jail* where he was incarcerated. This was a perfect example of the overt unapologetic Deep South white religious hypocrisy he referenced in that profound historic document.

Finally, after stopping beside the highway between Jackson and Vicksburg to allow the driver a brief, undisturbed nap on the back seat while we all sat outside to allow her silence, the bus arrived home safely Sunday afternoon, thanks in large part to our calm, courageous and God-connected pastor.

The Mount Olive-sponsored Boy Scout Troop that my father founded served as an extension of Rev. Norris' interest in nurturing young men. As described earlier, he accompanied us on a planned overnight weekend camping trip along Bayou Bartholomew when our Scoutmaster was unavailable, sharing the duties with my father so that we would not be disappointed. He hiked ten miles with us to our campsite that Friday to stay overnight with my father picking him up the next morning for return to Bastrop.

Arriving early afternoon, I recall Rev. Norris exhausted with tired and sore feet, rushing to the Bayou's shore, sitting on a log at the water's edge, pulling off his shoes and socks and slipping his feet into the enticing cool water. Almost immediately, me and several others noticed him raising each leg slowly and carefully out of the water, his face frightfully ashen. Standing nearby, I looked over the edge of the log and was paralyzed.

Much to my horror, I saw the distinctive red, black and yellow banding of a coral snake floating motionless where Rev. Norris' feet had briefly been. Frozen in place, my unblinking eyes followed it as it floated slowly away with the Bayou's current, past the end of the log and out of sight, its body still.

Rev. Norris got up off the log slowly and backed away, making a Herculean attempt at convincing his Scout troop that he was not at all affected by what could have been a mortal bite from the deadly snake. But we could tell as the afternoon progressed that he was as traumatized as we were.

We never knew if the snake was dead or alive. But if alive, it was a miracle that Rev. Norris was not bitten. For sure, many prayers of thanks were uttered by everyone, particularly the Reverend. But somehow, around the campfire that night, he still managed to muster up his enthusiasm, teaching us life-enhancing moral and ethical lessons before we headed to our tents to bed down for the night.

In the Bayou forest, maintaining a campfire during the night is critical to ward off wild predators, particularly bobcats. But that particular night, an owl hung out in a nearby tree, constantly repeating its nerve-racking call, causing everyone many sleepless hours. The next morning, Rev. Norris not only appeared as sleep-deprived as we, but also anxious for my father to come and take him back to Bastrop.

The camping trip and the experience of living with "Mother Nature" was an entirely new and challenging experience for him, who until then had spent all of his life in urban and small-town settings. It could only have been his love for us, the young Mt. Olive Scouts that motivated him to risk the unknown and personal discomfort, for the opportunity to make a difference in our lives. And in return, we loved him for making our camping trip possible, and being with us through part of the experience.

Beyond pastoral duties, Rev. Norris was also involved in community social and political issues. As a Gammon Theological Seminary graduate, he was thoroughly indoctrinated in Bible-based social liberation precepts, and I am certain that had he lived long enough, he would have joined Dr. Martin Luther King Jr.'s national nonviolence Civil Rights Movement.

However, in one 1951 daring aggressive action planned by the local NAACP Chapter, but strategically pushed by the state and national offices; he, my mother, and the Rev. Julius A. Faulk (a Christian Methodist Episcopal minister, and the brother of Orilla Faulk Rodgers, my godmother) attempted to integrate Northeast Louisiana State College in Monroe (now University of Louisiana at Monroe) depicted in a personal photo just before leaving to challenge the "whites-only" institution.

According to my mother, "We walked unannounced into the University's admissions office, after passing many staring whites, presented our credentials to the wide-eyed clerk and announced our applications for admissions to the Master's in Education degree program."

Laughing, she continued, "Everyone in the office stared at us with disbelief with their mouths open! But once they got over the surprise, the reaction was swift and direct."

"What are you doing in here? You can't just walk in here," were the southern drawl responses she described still laughing. "You don't belong here. Get out before I call the police. And, don't you ever come on this campus again!"

"Of course, this was what we expected, so we left walking resolutely to our car having accomplished our task, a test for upcoming

NAACP litigation eventually leading to the Supreme Court school desegregation decision." As my mother described their daring effort to me, I was so proud of my connection to their legacy and the unknown grooming of my own fierce social justice determination.

Another bold and risky collaboration in the early 1950s that Rev. Norris undertook with the white minister of Bastrop's whites-only First Methodist Episcopal Church involved initiating an annual Interracial Sunday Service to improve Black/white relations. On alternate years, congregations of both churches were to host Sunday Morning Worship Service together. I recall only a few white congregants attending the first service at Mt. Olive. However, Rev. Norris was reassigned to a church in Shreveport before the second year of the planned integrated services. And from there, his effective leadership roles led to increasingly larger and more prestigious churches, ending with his final appointment to Grace Methodist Church in New Orleans, the city with Louisiana's largest and most progressive African-American population. He also served as District Superintendent in Shreveport and New Orleans.

My mother kept me informed of his various assignments and church leadership roles and the chronic health issues that began to overwhelm him, eventually leading to his death in 1972, the year I moved to Tampa, Florida for a music professor appointment at the University of South Florida (more of this phase in later chapters). When I learned belatedly about his passing, I was devastated, feeling as though I had lost a deep and profound life source, my moral and ethical roots.

However, during an early 1980s summer drive from Tampa to visit my parents in Bastrop, I had a "nostalgia attack" while passing through southern Mississippi on I-10 that coerced a detour south to Gulfside, remembering all the wonderful times spent there in my youth with Rev Norris, and the simple beauty and serenity of the place. Aware that hurricanes had been devastating to the Gulf Coast region, especially Hurricane Camille in 1969, I didn't know what to expect.

But as I drove over the old cattle-grate entrance, I discovered, much to my delight, that several familiar buildings still stood, defiantly anchored in place. Memories of my past Methodist Youth Assembly experiences sprung forth, including those of Rev. Norris' presence, preaching daily to us from the pulpit. Unfortunately, the beautifully adorned little chapel where he spoke was gone, leaving only memories of his carefully chosen texts and words that challenged and inspired us to seek spiritual guidance as we confronted teenage choices, just upbeat enough to hold our attention.

Driving past where the chapel once stood, I faced the recognizable white two-story women's and staff residence building with adjoining dining hall, standing as if in steadfast defiance of nature's worst nightmare. My thoughts flashed to a story I had heard from my mother about a minister-in-residence riding out a hurricane, probably Camille, on the second floor of that building, watching as the reported twenty-foot waves leaped up to the broken window's ledge, while bracing for the worst that may come. He survived, but vowed to never again ignore hurricane evacuation notices, regardless of a storm's projected force or the strength of his faith.

Overwhelmed, I parked the car and decided to go in to revisit the interior of that building. The screen door to the front porch entrance still gave that familiar soft squeak and slam as I entered. The young lady at the front desk said they were preparing for a Methodist Women's Retreat. But after hearing my nostalgic narrative, she welcomed me back to Gulfside and allowed me to walk through the building. I first strolled slowly down the first-floor hall of the residence section, peering into the rooms and the communal bath that was halfway. The rooms were clean and sparsely furnished with a blanket-covered bunk bed, a dresser/desk and a bedside lamp table with Bible on top.

At the end of the hall, I took the stairs to the second floor and inched my way back down the hall while casually looking through the door of each room. While doing so, I noticed the silhouette of someone at the other end of the hall heading in my direction. Bright sunlight behind the individual prevented a clear image, but it appeared to be a woman walking slowly, stopping in each room.

As we got closer, her appearance began to ring familiarity bells in my mind. And when we finally came face-to-face it occurred to both of us simultaneously who the other was. Irony of all ironies, standing in front of me at that moment was Mrs. Margaret Ester Taylor Norris, the wife of Rev. Norris, my beloved former pastor, spiritual leader and mentor. Wow! What a phenomenal coincidence! Or, was it meant to be?

Was it more than just a nostalgia attack that brought me back to Gulfside?

That bright smile was easily recognizable, though of course she was older (as was I), and slightly heavier with salt-and-pepper hair. We quickly embraced, which was the first time she embraced me as an adult. I addressed her as Mrs. Norris, and she called me Junior, as if time had never passed. It had been almost 30 years since I had seen her, sparking memories from my youth of welcome, love and encouragement from her and Rev. Norris. We began giving updates about our lives since the last time we were together in Bastrop. She spoke briefly about the Reverend's ministry career and accomplishments, and his passing, during which I could see her enduring sadness etched on her face.

Since Rev. Norris' death, she had continued to serve the church in many roles. On this particular day, she was at Gulfside to assist with the Methodist Women's Retreat and was inspecting the living accommodations to make sure they were clean and comfortable for the attendees, placing relevant literature in each room.

I stood there in awe, connecting the "nostalgia attack" I had to Mrs. Norris standing in front of me on the cherished grounds of Gulfside, the place where Rev Norris taught, inspired and nurtured the young, gifted and Black. Memories overwhelmed me. I thought about the Mt. Olive boys Saturday sessions with him, his commitment to our Scout troop, the quiet conversations with him and Mrs. Norris in the kitchen of the church parsonage, his courageous community activism, and his life-guiding sermons that directed and inspired. Those memories confirmed he was a profound source for the ethical foundation that governed my daily behavior, and how I confront critical choices, sometimes going against contrary social and political forces.

For sure, the many lessons he taught as spiritual leader, role model and mentor guided my path, helping me decipher the high and low roads for crucial life issues, and instilled the courage to take the high road on the side of truth and right, regardless. Along with the help of a few others, Rev. Norris made me an honest and fair man, a precious gift for life.

Chapter 6

Aspiring Bridge

"That stadium's public property!" someone shouted.

"Yeah!" shouted another. "If we played there once, why not again! Especially for our regional championship game!?"

"You're right! Let's go down to the school board office and protest. Make them change their mind", prompting the small group of students to huddle secretly on campus to hash-out the details for the demonstration.

The next day in December 1953, fifteen Black high school students, willing to risk the unknown, began their unprecedented walk to demonstrate in front of the Morehouse Parish School Board office, downtown Bastrop, Louisiana. However, Black education in Morehouse Parish leading to that historic pivotal moment had always been a daunting challenge under white racism.

It wasn't until 1916, when the Parish's population included 4,814 white and 13,971 Black residents; with more than three times the number of Black children ages 6-14 than whites, that Black men, including experienced carpenters, began constructing buildings on 29 acres of donated land west of downtown. One four-room building expanded to others, eventually with school board help, to two white-wood-framed rectangle classroom buildings resting above ground on brick pillars by 1929. I attended first through eighth grade in those structures, vaguely aware of the white paint's incessant peeling. However, in 1947, in the midst of Deep South Jim Crow, the unexpected occurred. It was the construction of a modern designed high school building that opened without fanfare with a new principal for the first-through-twelfth grade Morehouse Parish Training School.

"Wow!" I cheered, looking at the striking new structure after watching it over the past year rise almost magically out of the red Louisiana clay on the north side of the sprawling campus. "That's some kind of building."

Me and my close partners, Fred and H.T., gathered near the almost completed construction site and could not believe our eyes, the slick design, and a front entrance walk we could skate on.

"Yeah," Fred finally responded. "Wish we were going to be in it. We'll have to wait until we're in high school."

The structure was unlike any building ever built for colored people in Bastrop, public or private. The new, strikingly modern facility with its flat-roof design, silver metal fascia, red brick walls and white window and door frames were solidly stationed on a reinforced concrete foundation. And although it marked the beginning of a new era in education for Bastrop's segregated Black youth and community, it was really the arrival of the new school principal that would significantly impact me, all students, and everyone in the community.

The day the new principal, Mr. Henry V. Adams, arrived on campus in the fall of 1949 is probably etched in every former student's memory, high school students particularly.

"Hat's off! No talking! Quickly move into your classroom!" was the booming voice they heard on arrival from the tall, physically imposing stranger, arms waving and fingers pointing, barking orders repeatedly, according to my sister, who was in ninth grade at the time.

"I said hats off young man! Get to your classroom!"

There was no school assembly or campus announcement to formally introduce him. He didn't just casually walk through the halls politely shaking hands, introducing himself as the new principal. And he didn't silently hold up in his office sending out flyers about his arrival. Nope, nothing like that.

The initial student reaction was, "What's this? Who's this man with the booming voice shouting at us?" But they quickly got the message and obeyed. And, there he was again during class changes standing in the middle of the hallway shouting: "Move quickly and quietly to the right of the hall to your next class! No talking! Be in your classroom before the second bell!" Those slow to respond were singled out in a verbal reprimand that carried hints of more serious consequences. By the end of the day, it was obvious that this was the new principal that we were expecting, and things were not going to be the same. There was a new sheriff in town—and he, Mr. Adams, meant business.

That day marked the awakening of a new frontier for the education of Black children in the Morehouse Parish. From 1949 through 1965, Principal Adams led an aggressive movement that vastly improved the educational opportunities and outcomes for Black students. In addition to the new high school building, others followed, including an agriculture/industrial arts building, a cafeteria and primary grades classroom facility. Sweeping changes were made to the curriculum, prompting higher academic standards, expectations and aspirations. Extracurricular programs and activities were added, food services improved, cultural programs and special events presented. Competitive athletics were enhanced and expanded.

Henry Adams was the son of Charles Philips Adams, the founding president of what is now Grambling State University, my mother's alma mater. He came to Morehouse with excellent credentials and experience: that included a Bachelor's degree from the historic Tuskegee Institute and Master of Science degree from Texas Southern University. Prior to Morehouse, he was a teacher and principal at other Louisiana public schools, and recently an instructor and assistant football coach at Kentucky State University.

Over six feet tall with an NFL defensive-end physique, Mr. Adams appeared an imposing figure to students. His head, with medium-cropped hair and slightly receding hairline, appeared small atop his broad, muscular shoulders, barrel chest and thigh-sized biceps, intimidating features. The deep, baritone voice—though not always articulate—carried through walls, reaching distant destinations, such as restroom stalls, a favorite student hideout. His presence was sensed throughout the campus—even when he was nowhere around, making for cautious behavior when considering breaking the rules, on, or even *off*, campus. Consequently, student discipline problems at Morehouse quickly took a nosedive.

When Mr. Adams arrived, our first-through-twelfth-grade school was struggling under egregious "separate and unequal" Jim Crow laws. Stymied by inadequate funds, narrowly defined curriculum, insufficient teaching spaces, books and materials, and underpaid teachers; Morehouse was an uninviting and unexciting place. Nevertheless, since its 1916 founding, alumni had greatly appreciated and benefited from the education provided, some continued on to college degrees and successful careers with a few, including my mother, returning to teach at

Morehouse. Other students took their acquired basic skills and migrated to northern and western states for an improved life.

Bastrop's controlling white establishment made sure there were limits to the education of Black children. Morehouse Parish, primarily a cotton agribusiness and paper-mill region, depended greatly on African-Americans for unskilled cheap labor. So, except for schoolteachers, educated Black people were not considered useful or desired.

However, it seems the all-white Morehouse Parish School Board did not anticipate the magnitude of educational improvements that occurred during Mr. Adams tenure. If they had, they probably would not have hired him. His education and background were centered on sports, as were many Black school principals, hired for imposing discipline at their schools rather than improving academic achievement. But it appears that through shrewd tactics described to me by my mother, teachers and community leaders, he was able to convince the board that a small, educated Black middle class was not a threat to the segregated status quo. However, instead, the small more enlightened and economically independent Black populous could actually help maintain race separation, and that modestly improving black education was okay.

Analyzing Mr. Adams administrative record indicates he recruited young, well-prepared, and highly motivated teachers from premier Black colleges such as Fisk, Tuskegee, and Lincoln (Missouri), and partnered them with the experienced, well-seasoned instructors who had dedicated themselves to Morehouse for many years, under dire circumstances, for little pay. Within three years, Principal Adams hired five new high school teachers for mathematics, English, drama, band, and choral music. He also added three physical education instructors, whose duties included coaching varsity women's and men's basketball, and men's baseball and football teams. I experienced the phenomenal presence of all of the new teachers during my Morehouse years.

Together—principal and teachers—implemented an enhanced curriculum, and motivated students to succeed inside and outside the classroom, boosting student confidence and self-esteem significantly. Teachers assisted with student discipline and volunteered as advisors for extracurricular activities. And, to encourage and support teacher development, Mr. Adams established in-house teacher training programs and encouraged them to seek advanced degrees, with many responding to his encouragement. My mother described anxiously attending graduate studies one summer at Ohio State University, driving there with a colleague. She felt intimidated by the large white school and its reputation. But with her usual disciplined study habits she did well.

I took geometry, biology, industrial arts, and physical education, which were courses added by Principal Adams. Geometry, taught by Mr. Alexander, was my favorite academic course, and he was one of my favorite teachers. Unfortunately, due to scarce resources, the biology class had only one frog to dissect, leaving me out of the actual hands-on experience. And, for those who took chemistry, only one simple experiment was possible per class. The industrial arts class provided materials for small wood- work projects only, although my father paid for materials for constructing a large two-seat lawn swing as a class project, transferring it to our yard after completion.

However, it was the extracurricular activities that Mr. Adams established that gave *school* a new and exciting meaning, including organizations promoting student leadership, social development and school spirit. The student council, New Farmers of America's choir and quartet were ones I participated in. Courageously, I joined the drama club. I was cast in a play, forgot my lines on stage, was embarrassed, and never went back.

Groups such as the concert choir, New Homemakers of America, and the 4-H Club were also newly available for students. Honors Day for high academic achievers and junior and senior field trips were added activities for inspiring learning and developing aspirations. Participation in the various activities helped me to grow as a disciplined and organized teen, although perhaps not so much socially, as my shyness and loaner traits still dominating.

Other first-time activities evolved from school and community collaborations, including homecoming festivities and the Morehouse Parish Cotton Festival and Parade featuring the first-ever Black parades through downtown Bastrop, highlighting marching bands, majorettes and specially designed floats. Decorated cars transported the homecoming queen and court. The May Day international celebration featured pole-wrapping with Scottish, Spanish and Caribbean dances in traditional costumes. Of course, most of these types of activities were ongoing for years at the white school and included their community.

The gymnasium with a stage at one end, extended out from the middle of the building, making regular high school physical education classes possible, where I discovered my speed and agility playing volleyball and badminton. And, our modest but enthusiastic competitive basketball effort could move indoors with night games, off the weather-dependent dirt court where I witnessed "Rayville Red" from Rayville's colored high school make some slick maneuvers and awesome baskets, precursor to Earl "The Pearl" Monroe of NBA fame. We could now host visiting teams with pride: playing on a polished tile floor and offering comfortable dressing/shower rooms with hot water. In fact, our new gym was superior to all northeast Louisiana Black schools, including the larger Carroll High in Monroe which is twenty-five miles south, a major competitor.

But compared to Bastrop High, the local white high school, our gym was smaller, without bleachers and designed for other types of events. For basketball games, folding chairs were tightly lined-up three deep on both sides of the court, which made it difficult for fans to see the game and move around. Additionally, when the gym was transformed into an auditorium, folding chairs, lots of them, were placed in long rows on the gym's floor. However, for us, Morehouse students, these were considered minor inconveniences. We were excited about and took great pride in our new high school and gym, appreciating it as measurable progress.

Competitive athletics, a high priority for Mr. Adams, quickly developed as a source for school spirit and identity. Football, baseball and boys' and girls' basketball were the major teams. He hired excellent coaches, provided sufficient equipment, and we were "in it to win it."

In ninth grade, trying to be more macho, while weighing all of 98 pounds and often referred to as "Too-Thin Johnny," I tried out for the three-year-old football team. However, it didn't occur to me that at that weight it was suicide.

After being crushed by a 200-pound linebacker while trying to run the ball, and trampled by a 225-pound fullback named Cash while playing defensive safety, I came down with the Measles and a handy excuse to hang up my cleats—permanently. That experience, and the one junior varsity basketball game I briefly appeared in because of my parent's attendance, ended any future aspirations for competitive sports.

However, thanks to Mr. Adams, an introduction to music set me on a path that would match my size and passion. He appointed Mr. A. V.

Turner (more on him later) as a roving instrumental music teacher to begin building a band program. Later that Spring, challenging us, Mr. Turner bravely scheduled our small group to march in a Monroe parade in a band composed of students from all the schools where he taught. Mr. Adams also arranged for a school bus for the twenty-five-mile trip.

Without uniforms, boys were instructed to wear white shirts, white or light-colored trousers, a dark tie and shoes. Somehow, I didn't get the message and arrived over-dressed in a suit and tie my mother insisted on. While boarding the bus, I found Mr. Adams there encouraging his musical upstarts. The towering giant looked down at me and boomed, "Son, where's your instrument?" Naturally, I was petrified—frozen in place with one foot on the ground and the other on the first step of the bus.

"Huh?" I stammered while looking up at him. "Instrument?"

Fact was, for our first out-of-town public appearance, dressing for the parade was top priority for mother and son, and we forgot my horn. Standing there dumbfounded, I realized I was not getting on the bus without it. So, my mother quickly returned home to retrieve the trombone. I presented it to him as my ticket to board the bus for the much-delayed trip. That was an embarrassing moment, and a rather unremarkable beginning for a future professional musician.

However, funds for those exciting, yet essential, nonacademic programs were not allocated by the school board. So, Mr. Adams had to create other sources of revenue. One effort that garnered considerable student interest was the occasional full-length commercial movies in the auditorium/gym, complete with freshly popped popcorn, furnished by the home economics department. The aroma floating through the building could not be easily resisted, great for marketing and sales.

Students that could afford it, gladly plunked down the modest fee to sit in a darkened room next to their girlfriend or boyfriend. I was there, usually with one of my buddies, and recall problems with the one projector—time-consuming film changes, awkward pauses caused by broken film, and the annoyance of the small screen and poor sound quality. However, that didn't matter, as I went right back the next time.

As Morehouse progressed, higher standards and expectations continued, and when measured at the regional and state levels, Mr. Adams fully expected winners. Losing or poor performance was not an acceptable option. So, as students, we set high standards and expectations for ourselves and had great pride and passion for our school. Quality, stylish uniforms were provided for student organizations, and when we traveled for off-campus activities, whether attending or participating, we were expected to be well-behaved and appropriately attired. This was not always easy for Bastrop's poor families, but we were all expected to look good and perform exceptionally.

It wasn't long before the Black school in small-town Bastrop was recognized state-wide as competitive, particularly in sports and music. With gutsy displays of confidence and pride, our tiny school from a north Louisiana "country town," often stood up to the big "urban" schools, like New Orleans - once almost winning the state basketball championship. I attended athletic games regularly, either playing in the band that annually received superior state awards, or could be found cheering wildly from the sidelines.

Mr. Adams also arranged culture presentations for the students and community to experience. One night during my sophomore year (1952-53), I sat curiously in the darkened auditorium/gym as Huel and Thelma Perkins, a husband-and-wife duo, dressed in formal attire and appeared on stage to perform classical vocal and clarinet solos. He was a Southern University music professor, and she was an exceptionally talented soprano and Bastrop native.

Although still a musical novice, the technical perfection and musical expression of their performance really captivated me. The clarinet solos, particularly, were technically jaw-dropping, exploring the enormous range of the instrument. I was blown away. I had never heard the clarinet played that way. But the most inspiring part of the evening that made the greatest impression on me was witnessing African-American professionals performing Western classical music, affirming an earlier exposure I had, compliments of my cousin, Lamar at Wiley College whom I much later realized, after seeing the printed program, accompanied the Perkins. The commingling of Blacks and classical music reinforced my own attraction to that musical genre.

One year later, thanks to Mr. Adams alerting my mother, that intermingled connection was further affirmed when she took me to Grambling College for a recital by the internationally acclaimed contralto, Marian Anderson. While sitting stage left, halfway back and high on the auditorium/gym bleachers, I was totally mesmerized as she sang German Lied, Italian arias, folk songs, though I didn't understand the text, and Negro spirituals with astounding poise and artistry. Completely overwhelmed, the audience responded with roaring applause after each composition. But the four spirituals she sang last tugged at their hearts and souls, most notably, "He's Got the World in His Hands." Unknowingly, that concert moved the needle even more toward my choosing music as a focus for college study.

Over time, the spirit, excitement, and enthusiasm of Morehouse spilled over into the Black community, motivating staunch support and loyalty. Parents were more involved in their children's education, assuring attendance and supporting teachers, programs, and policies.

Though there was no official parent-teacher association, Mr. Adams enjoyed their cooperation, particularly regarding student discipline. Not sure we students always appreciated that on and off campus collaboration. However, it cut down on some of our "borderline" schemes.

Community members filled the auditorium to capacity for events, applauding presentations exuberantly, even though some were beyond their understanding. Live theater, recitals, band, and choir concerts were new experiences for most, but they nevertheless responded with zeal, because it was "their" children and "their" school. Many Black business owners, including my father, began financial and in-kind support for activities, and demonstrated fierce pride at athletic events. With so much happening at Morehouse, it was considered the community center, the dominant hub for "their" activities.

However, most importantly, Morehouse was transforming young Black lives and preparing them for a better future. Many parents, those bused-in from rural areas particularly, began visualizing a brighter future for their children beyond the dehumanizing, restrictive shackles of the racism and bigotry that stifled dreams and opportunities. They now saw their children graduating from high school prepared for advanced vocations and college, able to achieve goals well beyond their own status.

As Mr. Adams operated effectively beneath the Old South Jim Crow radar, Morehouse was achieving remarkable success in a few years. Bastrop was not an ideal place for a Black man to push aggressively to improve Black education beyond the desires of the white establishment. The Klan's dark shadow made that very risky. However, his shrewd, stealthy efforts were driven by the passionate belief that knowledge, skills, and self-confidence made a transformative and empowering bridge for preparing young African-Americans to "assimilate" into American society and pursue their dreams.

During my senior year, while once again boarding the bus for an out-of-town event, Mr. Adams was standing at the entrance, as usual.

"Son, what's going to be your major in college?" he asked, surprising me.

He encouraged all of his students to aspire to college, and I was no exception. However, having only recently determined that I would indeed be going, I said proudly, "I'm going to major in music!"

He looked at me, disappointed. "I thought you were going to be somebody," he said after a short silence. "A doctor, dentist or lawyer or something like that."

My chest deflated as I found a seat on the bus. His expectations for his students went beyond the current typical southern Black career aspirations of schoolteacher (including music teacher), preacher and small business owner catering to Black needs only.

At the time, the general understanding among many African-Americans was that education should prepare students for "assimilation" into American society regardless of other aspirations. It was to provide a road map toward integration and acceptance into the majority white culture, and presumably, success. To achieve that goal, it was the responsibility of Black educators, like Mr. Adams, to develop schools and colleges, academic curriculum and programs, and teaching methods that mirrored white institutions.

Although that prevailing concept guided Mr. Adams in transforming Morehouse, success depended on acquiring the *financial resources* needed to accomplish that goal. In the Deep South environment, this meant playing the critical divergent roles of strong Black leader for his constituents, and obedient Black servant for whites. And he must have struggled greatly, walking that thin line between providing the requisite strong decisive leadership for Black students, teachers and community, and simultaneously acquiescing to the personally demeaning commands from white school board and city/ parish leaders for acquiring needed resources.

However, Mr. Adams knew that acquiring needed resources that were in the hands of powerful racist white officials would entail personal danger and humiliation. In school board members' minds, Black school funding, unequal as it was, was not considered a requirement, but rather a "gift" from the kindness of their hearts, a mere paternal offering with limited expectations. This placed him in the difficult position of pleading and begging for resources that were supposed to be governed by a per-pupil distribution policy, but was not adhered to for Black students who were considered less worthy. Nevertheless, he did what he had to do, suffered whatever humiliations and indignities necessary, and turned the other cheek whenever required to get whatever resources possible for Morehouse, for his students and teachers.

In those days, some Black people described Mr. Adams as an "Uncle Tom" for cowing, seemingly, to the racist customs and demands of whites without overtly challenging the disrespectful and demeaning treatment he, and Morehouse constituents, experienced. But little did we know, or appreciate, that without assuming a posture and facade of subservience, he would not have been able to obtain the financial support and administrative flexibility he did, and for which we, Black students and families, were the beneficiaries.

I wonder now, looking back, what it was like for him in those school board meetings. How did he respond to the disrespect and atrocious treatment as though he were ignorant and uninformed? What were his feelings while being considered invisible during their discussions? He probably had to stand, not permitted to sit around the table, when attending to make requests. I don't imagine him looking down, shuffling his feet, while carefully choosing his nuanced words to board members. He would not have stooped that low.

But did he get the "yes sirs" and "no sirs" just right, with the appropriate subservient tone? Was his body language in sync with what he needed to project, and not his "real" feelings? When his requests were turned down, did he smile and back away gingerly before turning around, showing as little of his back as possible to the board as he left the room?

And afterward, how did he internalize the indignation and humiliation in order to maintain a sense of personal dignity? What did he do to avoid allowing the harsh racist treatment to affect his psyche and emotions, so he wouldn't take it out on others, such as his wife, teachers and students—or himself? And finally, how did he rationalize placing himself in such a demeaning position for the fragile vision of improving the education of Black students under almost impossible circumstances?

According to Jim Crow tradition, white people of Morehouse Parish expected Principal Adams to control not only his students and teachers, but also the entire Black community. Considered the "top black leader," or HNIC ("Head Nigger in Charge"), he was to manage and control all of the Parish's Black citizens, or else lose his job. And for good behavior, expected to be satisfied and happy with the crumbs they threw his way. Or at least pretend he was.

But, attested to by former colleagues (my mother included) and others who knew him well, Mr. Adams was never satisfied with those crumbs. He kept returning to the table for whatever he could get, ignoring the humiliating pain suffered with each visit. He requested what he thought was reasonable, and in truth, what he knew was owed his constituents, what they truly deserved. He was willing to do whatever was necessary for his students and teachers.

I was party to one of those subtle tactics, and as a 15-year-old I was fully aware of my place in Bastrop's grossly unequal racist society.

Now the tuba player for the Morehouse band, having changed from the trombone several years earlier, I won consistent superior ratings at the state solo competitions and was often the featured soloist for school programs and events, including my own commencement. One day, during my junior year, Mr. Adams summoned me to his office and indicated I would be performing for Bastrop's Chamber of Commerce at their next luncheon meeting. Without much thought, my piano accompanist and I prepared for the event with the assistance of Mr. Strickland, our band director.

On the day of the performance, I remember entering a dimly lit, windowless room and seeing the stiff, unsmiling businessmen sitting at a rectangular table formally set for lunch. While performing, my concentration was on the music entirely, without any feelings or thoughts beyond. When finished, I stood, acknowledged the polite applause and tight smiles, and left the room. However, I was cognizant of the racial code that enveloped my visit, a Black youngster (me), the first to perform before an audience of white men who possessed extraordinary power over Bastrop's Black lives. Consequently, I felt no sense of honor or pride. It was simply what Mr. Adams, my principal, had asked me to do, and I did so with as much perfection as I could muster, for him and for me.

However, in looking back, I now see that performance as a risky strategy by Mr. Adams to cultivate and influence Bastrop's leaders for greater financial support for Black education. My solo performance was to illustrate the results of what their funding could accomplish, but more importantly, it was a delicate attempt to reach their hearts and gain empathy for future funding requests, a strategy savvy leader often uses with governing bodies and prospective donors. This was cultivation for later persuasion, a tactic I have used in my own academic administration career with fruitful results. But for Mr. Adams to use that strategy then, under those racial circumstances, was courageous and bold. He had no idea what the response might be, but it was crucial to try. Now, with greater understanding, I could not be prouder of him, and my own small part in his effort.

The second situation underscores Jim Crow's separate and gravely unequal public-school facilities, and brings to light the unpublicized Black student rebellion it provoked. Bastrop High, the Parish's white high school, possessed a first-class football stadium with perimeter fencing; level, well-cultivated, manicured and marked turf; bleachers on both sides, night lights; and a press booth with an amplified sound system.

In contrast, Morehouse's football field consisted of an open uneven plot of land at the back of the campus with red dirt and wild weeds, marked-off only for games. It was without bleachers, lights or press booth. The games were played on Friday afternoons. Students, staff, family and friends watched, as best they could, standing around the edges of the field. Often, the dirt from the football game blew into their faces. And the half-time band show was viewed from the same vantage-point with spectators unable to see, or fully appreciate, the formations and pageantry.

In the fall of 1953, my junior year, our young football team, the mighty Tigers, under Coach William Washington (later Morehouse principal) had a successful season and was scheduled to host the district championship game—school spirit had never been so high. However, because of its special nature and importance, Mr. Adams requested permission from the school board to play the game Saturday night at the white high school stadium. This would allow the parents and communities of both Black schools to attend and watch the postseason game and halftime band show under prime conditions. The fact that Mr. Adams made that request was itself an act of courage that has never been acknowledged.

Surprisingly, permission was granted, attributed to the carefully cultivated relationship he had established with the board. When it was announced to the students, we were, understandably, extremely excited, along with our parents and the entire Black community. For the first time ever our football game would be played at night under lights in a first-class stadium, and with the potential for winning a district championship! I was excited, particularly about our band's halftime show finally being fully viewed and heard from bleachers.

However, for the Black community to reach the stadium, it was necessary to travel through white neighborhoods, and most, without cars, had to walk. Even though it was unusually cold that night, the stadium was packed full of Black faces overjoyed by the spectacular environment and hopes of the district title.

The band performed the halftime show to perfection, with me as the sole sousaphone player, while everyone stood and cheered, reacting to the fact that everyone could finally see our intricate marching formations, and I certainly enjoyed performing on the flat, well-maintained turf, and my view of the packed bleachers with appreciative spectators. Our football team, perhaps motivated by the momentous occasion, the frenzied crowd and the quality facilities, won the game that night, *and* the opportunity to host the regional championship game the next weekend. That night was one big-time event for Bastrop's Black community, who sensed a hint of racial progress. I was too charged up to sleep that night.

The following Monday, Mr. Adams made another request of the school board to use the stadium, this time for the all-important regional championship game, optimistic they would approve, since they had done so only a week earlier. However, he was gravely disappointed by the board's denial, based on white residents' bitter complaints about Blacks walking through their neighborhoods, "trampling" their lawns, "destroying" flower gardens and "disturbing the peace" as they walked to and from the game. Although exuberant voices still celebrating the game and minor accidental damage to lawns may have occurred, Black presence was enough probable cause for their vehement, negative complaints.

When this information trickled down to us students, we felt an overwhelming collective disappointment, followed quickly by anger.

"That stadium's public property!" someone shouted.

"Yeah!" shouted another. "If we played there once, why not again! Especially for our regional championship game!?"

"You're right! Let's go down to the school board office and protest. Make them change their mind!"

We viewed this as an overt racist act and a slap in the face to our principal. It required a response. A small group of self-designated leaders without my knowledge met in a corner of the campus away from teachers, and after vigorous discussion decided to lead a protest march to the school board office. When the time came, Mr. Alexander, my geometry teacher, casually standing in the classroom door, did not object when I exited through the window near the industrial arts shop, our meeting place.

So, there we were, December 1953, fifteen students willing to risk the unknown—one-year before the U.S. Supreme Court's Brown v. Board of Education of Topeka, Kansas school desegregation decision, and almost ten years before the first student's non-violent civil disobedience sit-ins—leaving the campus and heading downtown to the school board office, with hastily improvised protest signs held high in our hands. I was very angry as I gripped my sign demanding "Stadium Now!" and disappointed at the small turnout.

Mr. Adams was away from the campus at the time, unaware of our impromptu action, but spotted us as he was driving back and pulled over, blocking our path with his car as we neared the West Madison Black Business District. He jumped out and walked around the car to confront his courageous students defiantly holding-up our signs.

He stood composed, face expressionless, eyes unblinking, as he read our signs demanding, "Stadium Now!" and "Equality Now!" and then spoke to us in an unfamiliar voice: soft, calm, monotone and deliberate.

"I understand your disappointment and anger about the board's decision," he began, "and I appreciate your wanting to take action. But this is not the right way. You don't know the danger and personal harm this march can cause. For your safety, you need to turn around."

We stood motionless, silent, not knowing how to explain ourselves to our principal who caught us off guard by the way he spoke. We were accustomed to loud commands rather than rational persuasion.

Breaking the deafening silence, Mr. Adams continued, "You all have not entirely thought through the consequences of your actions, your protest. This could result in your arrest and the horrible things that happen when Black people, especially Black boys, are put in jail." Then again, I heard the empathetic tone, "I completely understand how you feel, the anger and the frustration, but you have chosen the wrong way to respond. You must turn around and go back to the campus. Now."

Just then, a police car approached, stopping in the middle of the highway next to our small gathering, evoking our usual anxious reaction to white policemen. The cruiser sat there without twirling lights or blaring siren. Intimidating, nevertheless. After taking careful note of our hastily scribbled signs, the uniformed officer on the passenger side addressed Mr. Adams.

"You got everything under control here, Adams?" he said. "Or you need a little help?"

"Yes sir, yes sir, everything's fine," Mr. Adams responded, confident but appropriately respectful. "I'll be able to handle the situation okay. Everything's fine."

The police officers stared silently for another long, intense minute before slowly driving off, probably visualizing cracking a few heads if Mr. Adams did not do what he was supposed to do: Control those niggers.

That must have truly been one of those defining moments for Mr. Adams. "How do I maintain a sense of dignity in the presence of my students," he must have thought. "Providing them a role model of strength and courage, and at the same time portray a subservient demeanor toward the white policemen, in order to *protect them*?"

He perhaps realized that the exchange with the police made it very difficult for him not to appear as an "Uncle Tom" to us. It may have also occurred to him that our protest was early evidence of the liberating, self-esteem-focused education he perpetuated at Morehouse, covertly designed to prepare a new generation of Black freedom fighters. Except this demonstration of our progress was a bit premature.

The combination of Mr. Adams' unusually calm, persuasive voice and the presence of the police—the official racism enforcers—convinced our small group of "warriors" to lower our signs and retreat to campus. Unfortunately, our immediate assessment of our principal was, indeed, not very flattering. Yes, we aborted our courageous mission, but to us Mr. Adams appeared as just another weak Black man, too easily acquiescing to white authority, and consequently, to the whole white racist establishment.

I see now that there were two significant factors we failed to understand at the time. First, Mr. Adams may have indeed saved our lives. Black boys and men in Deep South jails, including in Morehouse Parish, regularly disappeared and died without explanation or judicial concern. (Remember the lynching party my parents witnessed.) To have continued our protest march would probably have ended with our incarceration and unthinkable consequences.

Second, we did not understand that Mr. Adams' subservient interactions with whites deeply compromised his *own* humanity, which he willingly did daily, in order to provide the safe, quality education we were now experiencing, a quality education that was above the accepted Deep South norm.

We, of that generation, found it too easy and convenient to label Black leaders "Uncle Toms", when they appeared to readily cower to white people. We simply did not understand the complex role they had to play to protect us, and assist our growth and aspirations. We didn't realize the extent to which they sacrificed their own dignity and self-respect for our welfare. It was not to elevate their living standards or assume positions of power, as many of us thought.

Jim Crow's enforced, unequal racial segregation and injustice all but demanded that assertive Black leaders give the appearance of appeasing white expectations in order to acquire the resources to improve Black lives and prepare next-generation leaders, a subterfuge that empowered future racial justice activists. But as a tradeoff, many, like Principal Adams, suffered humiliation—and should be recognized now as Black social justice heroes for their personal sacrifice.

As the leader for Morehouse, and indirectly the Black community, Henry V. Adams built a bridge that gave hope to hundreds of African-Americans by preparing young minds for new and better life options. Under his assertive leadership, our school was infused with rigorous curriculum and programs that provided invaluable knowledge, and promoted self-esteem and courage. Small wonder that me and fourteen other students took to the streets to peacefully protest a symptom of America's ethnic apartheid almost ten years before widespread sit-ins rocked the soul of our nation. Our liberated and progressive attitude was no accident. It was by design. And small wonder that me and so many Morehouse students graduated with high expectations.

As a proud beneficiary of his unselfish efforts, I now have a more profound and empathetic understanding and appreciation of his shrewd and courageous leadership. Through successfully managing the difficult and delicate balance between self-sacrifice and pursuing educational excellence for his Morehouse students, I and many of my cohorts were able to pursue the careers and professions of our dreams. For me, my positions of university professor and president, and professional musician, result from the strategic influences of Mr. Henry V. Adams.

Chapter 7

Love at First Sight

"Hey, Mama! Mama! I have a note from school," I yelled, walking into the house. "Something 'bout learning to play an instrument."

It was fall 1949, and I was in the seventh grade, and not yet interested in anything particular.

"Seems the school will be starting classes for sixth- and seventh-grade students interested in playing a musical instrument," she said, reading the letter. "What do you think about that?"

Standing there, hungry and anxious to eat dinner, a top priority with boys my age, I whined, "I don't know. I don't know 'bout no instrument."

I looked up into her face, where her trademark stern, intense stare and knitted brow appeared. "Well, you are *going*," she said.

And that was that.

Mr. Adams, our school principal, determined to start a band at Morehouse, hired Mr. A. V. Turner, a roving instrumental music teacher, to provide evening lessons. Desperate to help me discover a passionate interest in something, *almost anything*, my mother decided this was another opportunity, even though I had rebelled earlier against piano lessons. My sister studied piano, so I thought it was for girls.

Determined, my mother dragged me to the first meeting, probably not expecting a different outcome.

That evening, after everyone settled nervously into their seats, Principal Adams introduced the teacher. Mr. Turner, dressed neatly, strode to the front of the room, smiling broadly and displaying perfect white teeth. He was dark brown, short, with slight midriff girth and closely cut dark hair that tapered to a small bald spot at the back. A pronounced red callus appeared on the middle of his upper lip; the telltale sign he had played the trumpet for many years.

His cheerful, empathetic, non-threatening remarks helped soothe the anxiety that was shared by us young, curious, and not so curious, neophytes. Not knowing what to expect, and not being there of my own accord, I was rather ambivalent about the whole thing. And I was not particularly excited about attending yet another class—being in school all day, every day, was enough.

Still waving his hands in the air, Mr. Turner spoke of starting a band at Morehouse, and how our learning to play instruments would make that possible. His exuberance gave me the impression that learning would be fun and easy. After he announced the days and times for lessons and attendance requirements, he pointed to the group of instruments enclosed in hard black cases on the floor next to him.

"Instruments will be provided to you free," he said. "As long as you come to class."

After answering parents' questions, Mr. Turner began introducing those instruments to us by opening each carrying case and assembling and displaying each, turning them around for a full view before returning them still assembled to the opened cases on the floor.

He then invited us to examine the instruments close-up, and select one to take home that night.

I don't remember anything particular about that moment of personal crisis and decision-making as I peered at the available choices. I wasn't very decisive. There were not many instruments to select from, but there were not very many of us either. So, after viewing the small assortment, knowing that my mother expected me to leave with an instrument in-hand, I chose the trombone, possibly because of its unique shape and slide mechanism. I really don't remember for sure why I made that particular choice, but it was a pivotal moment.

After everyone had chosen an instrument, Mr. Turner instructed us individually on how to assemble and hold the instrument for playing, followed by demonstrating the proper technique for producing a sound.

"Put your lips tightly together and blow through them to make a buzz," he told me, and after modest success, he continued. "Now do the same thing in the mouthpiece on the trombone."

I produced more noise than sound, but good enough for starters. After showing me how to put the smelly oil on the slide using a dropper, and correctly placing the instrument in its carrying case, I was on my way home, where things were never the same for Smith Family, Inc.

Or me.

I don't recall measurable progress during those first weeks, but several months into our weekly sessions, Mr. Turner decided to cast us into the midst of a real live music performance, sensing we were losing interest from the monotonous concentration on basic skills and scales without actually playing music. So, to re-energize our efforts, he scheduled us to perform in a parade.

The Black community in Monroe, a larger town 25 miles south, was sponsoring a parade to celebrate a special event. Mr. Turner committed to providing a band, which would include students from all the schools where he taught, representing various levels of musical growth.

I was very excited about this new adventure, if for no other reason than the out-of-town bus trip. And since Mr. Turner lived in Monroe, he met us at the parade's starting site and quickly introduced us to the other band members, while hurriedly placing us in formation. I noticed several students appeared older than the typical school age, and learned they were military veterans returning to finish high school.

Beginners were placed next to advanced players, who served as band formation guides. But some of the veterans bantered throughout the parade, which I thought was rather strange, given the discipline I associated with marching bands. And some of their chatter was about mature subjects with sexual innuendos, which my innocent ears shouldn't have been hearing.

Even though Mr. Turner did his best to teach us by rote the two marches the band would play, I was expected to march in line, hold my instrument properly and pretend I was confidently playing the music. He and the advanced musicians were to carry the performance burden, which they did admirably.

"Wow! This is exciting," I thought. "They're cheering, whistling and clapping their hands for us on both sides of the street. I wish I could really play my trombone." One of the two marches we repeatedly performed was W. C. Handy's jazzy *St. Louis Blues March*, featuring Mr. Turner's big, mellow penetrating tone on trumpet, playing melodic lead, carrying the whole band as he marched along side. After that experience, I doubled down on my practice, and learning to read music.

As student interest in playing musical instruments gradually increased, Mr. Turner brought other instruments to class to meet the demand, offering different types required for a traditional school band.

One evening, as I sat in the back with my trombone in hand prepared for our lesson, he informed us that a school band needed a bass horn for proper balance and for playing all of the music parts. He then held up an enormous, tarnished silver instrument, covered with dents and dark smudges, and rested it on top of the desk in front of him while looking around the room.

"Who wants to play the tuba?" he asked.

My eyes quickly spanned the instrument up and down, seeing an immense bell pointing towards the ceiling ready to catch rain, or whatever else fell from above. Three huge piston values protruded at an angle from the side of the elongated tubing that coiled around itself, seemingly infinitely, ending with a large mouthpiece extending just below the bell, large enough for covering both lips completely, and then some. It looked as though it weighed a ton and hadn't been cleaned or polished in years.

"Who wants to play the tuba?" I heard Mr. Turner ask again, and without any conscious effort, my hand was suddenly waving vigorously in the air signaling my overwhelming desire to play...what was it again... the tuba?!

"I want to play it. I want to play that instrument," I heard my voice involuntarily announce. Having never seen the instrument before, or having any idea about what it sounded like, or what it would take to play it, didn't matter.

It was love at first sight, an impromptu mutual sense of belonging together between the tuba and me despite its huge size and my thin body frame, appearing as a colossal mismatch.

However, it was at that moment in time that the tuba, and music, began dominating my life with extraordinary persistence, and continued for more than forty years. The quiet, shy person that I was, had found his expressive voice and the genesis for a satisfying and productive future.

I did not become principal tuba player with the New York Philharmonic, an early goal, or President of Harvard, mind you, but my many achievements as performer and educator were certainly nothing to sneeze at, given the expectations for me at birth. I eventually served as principal tuba player with the Aspen Music Festival and Oklahoma City Orchestras and president at Fisk University. Quite possibly, absent racism, my achievements as a professional tuba player might have reached a higher level, maybe the principal tuba player with a top-twenty symphony orchestra. Or, maybe not, given the number of orchestral tuba positions that represents, twenty, one per orchestra, and an ultra-slow vacancy rate. Those guys live forever! Oh, excuse me, the first woman tuba player for a major symphony orchestra, Carol Jantsch, was finally appointed, joining the Philadelphia Orchestra in 2006. A big hallelujah for that!

However, conversely, had it not been for something called "Affirmative Action," an aggressive though controversial counteraction (reparations?) to institutional racism (Struck down by the Supreme Court June 2023), my remarkable achievements in higher education may not have been realized. In 1971, the University of South Florida (USF) created a faculty position specifically to hire an African-American, and my race and other qualifications perfectly matched the job description.

Of course, once appointed, like all faculty, tenure and academic advancement was entirely left up to me, and at USF African-Americans were not faring well in those categories.

Unfortunately, in both my music and education careers, race played a determining role, negatively for one and positively for the other. But in a perfect world, race would not have been a factor in either case. Yet, it was my introduction to and passion for music that placed me in careers that not only challenged my capacity to achieve success, but also to effectively negotiate racism. To succeed at one, I had to also succeed at the other.

No one, least of all me, could have known or anticipated the ultimate impact of that single gesture from Mr. Turner, and his significant influence on my destiny of success. He introduced me to one big-old, beat-up, ugly tuba, and by doing so, launched my life's journey into the exciting world of music, with its many gifts and pleasures.

In the spring of 1950, my eighth-grade year, Mr. Turner's small band appeared in an assembly in the new high school auditorium/gym. In a photo taken that day, I'm sitting near the back, in front of the bass drum, head barely visible behind the enormous tuba that I am somehow balancing between my left hand and my skinny right thigh, while concentrating on the music in front of me. It's a hilarious shot, but a reminder that successful life ventures are derived sometimes from unusual and unexpected origins. And it is often a caring individual, like Mr. Turner, who provides the impetus for that amazing journey.

Many years later, in my mid-fifties, I visited Monroe specifically to find and thank Mr. Turner for that tuba encounter—a moment so pivotal in my life I will never forget it, or him. I wanted to tell him about all the joy and professional success I had experienced since, with the hope it would boost his pride in being an inspiring teacher. Anxiously anticipating the moment, when I would see him after so many years, and wondering if he would remember me, I located his home south of downtown, but no one answered my insistent knock. I was so disappointed, wanting desperately to thank him in person.

After all, he was the matchmaker for the lifelong love affair between me and my tuba, setting the stage for my next instrumental music teacher and mentor to nurture that love affair into a fully blossomed passion.

Chapter 8

Just Light and Stoke the Fire

The music was urgent, unpredictable, full of energy; and sounds that were alien to my ear, yet, I listened intently.

Head bobbing back and forth, left to right, slightly slouched with alto saxophone held loosely in both hands, the music maker spewed out intoxicating jazz riffs filling the room's nooks and crannies, reflecting his vacillating mood and temperament. He was obsessed and desperate to find a unique voice to deliver his compelling message.

Facing a window, I watched him through the periphery of my eyes standing in a corner not far away, seemingly digging deeper and deeper within, connecting soul and mind with his dancing fingers, testing the instrument's capacity to respond to his artistic will.

Feet slightly apart, planted firmly on the rough, wood-slatted floor, eyes closed tightly embracing an anxious frown, Mr. Charles Strickland, our new Morehouse Parish Training School band teacher, seemed completely oblivious to me and other students in the band room. It appeared so personal, that I felt as though I was intruding while listening to the new and unfamiliar style.

But in retrospect, that scene highlighted a personal resemblance between Mr. Strickland and the great and popular jazz alto saxophonist, Julian "Cannonball" Adderley (1928-1975), who I met and watched perform years later in the 1960s; it was the same intense musical expressions, gyrating gestures and physical features.

Their heads were almost the same roundness, topped by short-cropped dark brown hair with lengthy sideburns that extended well past their ear lobes. There was a hint of Fu Manchu mustache above and around the corners of their upper lips. A slightly pronounced midsection protruded between arms that appeared too short for their five-foot, eight-inch frames, and arms that connected to fat hands with short fingers, perfect for manipulating saxophone keys. Their physically proportioned legs extended down to small feet enclosed in thick-soled shoes that appeared to anchor their highly animated bodies, keeping them from toppling over. So very similar, Mr. Strickland, my band director, and Cannonball Adderley, the jazz great. But Mr. Strickland's improvisation that day vaguely connected my ears to an earlier childhood experience.

My mother, out for a Friday or Saturday evening drive with me and Barbara in the back seat, sometimes pulled her car off West Madison and parked across the street from the Brown Eagle, Bastrop's Black night club that featured weekend big band blues and jazz. The music's persistent rhythmic energy blasted out through the building's windows, doors, and cracks in the walls into our car as I watched her swaying contently in response, head gently bobbing and fingers softly snapping, and my ears absorbing the genre.

However, what I was now hearing in the band room from Mr. Strickland was a different sound—more direct, more personal, and freely expressed without predictable patterns. He was introducing me to a new dimension of what's considered jazz, the unique musical expression of the African-American experience. Not taught in public schools, yet, we were hearing Mr. Strickland sharing the excitement of jazz with us, his students. He would spend sixteen years at Morehouse Parish Training School, our Black school, until integration closed it in 1969, transforming, nurturing, and inspiring me and many other students through music, including jazz.

If I were to select the one individual who played the most pivotal role in my music career, it would be Mr. Charles R. Strickland or "Strick as he is affectionately known by all who loved him. He provoked that *eureka* moment in me that my parents had long awaited and prayed for, by unleashing and cultivating an intense musical passion that jump-started a career path leading to unimagined heights. He encouraged me in exploring the one thing that I was more than willing to give up food and sleep for: playing my tuba.

In 1952, our School's principal, Mr. Adams hired Charles Strickland, a recent Lincoln University, Missouri, graduate as the school's first permanent band director, charged with building a first-class band and instrumental music program. And since most Black families in the Morehouse Parish were poor, Mr. Adams provided funds for the purchase of all instruments for the band, making it possible for any student to participate—no matter their financial status. Strickland grew up in Minden, Louisiana, only 80 miles west of Bastrop, and based on his college record and passion for teaching, Principal Adams believed he would be perfect for Morehouse. His excellent college music preparation was confirmed several years later by his Lincoln professors when I attended the same school.

From Mr. Strickland's first day at Morehouse, my excitement made me a regular in the band room where he freely availed himself. Walking in each day before classes started and during my lunch and study hall periods, I shouldered my sousaphone, sitting down playing music that was in my band folder. The previous year, I was switched from the tuba to the sousaphone for marching band requirements. Band rehearsals were each day after classes ended in a corner room of one of the old buildings.

On my first day in the band room after his arrival at Morehouse, Mr. Strickland wandered over, pulled up a chair next to me and started offering playing tips: "That note should get two full beats," he observed, beating out the time with his foot, sitting with me and going over the music until I got it right. This was one-on-one, the best way to learn an instrument. And he did this with every student who came to the band room. He eased into the chair next to the student and began calmly providing technical suggestions, and a big dose of encouragement, without any formality whatsoever, as if saying, "I'm your big brother here to help you make sense of your instrument and the music in front of you."

With Mr. Strickland's individualized teaching approach, and his constantly raising the performance bar, we were soon on a fast track for establishing a competitive school concert and marching band. And sensing our progress, we were compelled to work even harder on our own, exactly what Strick intended. *Just light and stoke the fire*, describes how he motivated, managed and expedited our learning.

Playing my instrument daily was a wonderful match for my shy traits, with the many required hours of concentration without conversation. It was me and the sousaphone working together, and I was in charge, manipulating it without discussion, arguments, or protests. The required buzz from my lips into the mouthpiece produced the notes that came out the bell, as I altered the pitch by adjusting my lips and pressing the valves.

But what I was putting in was not always coming out as intended, and oftentimes wasn't improving with practice, causing my frustration. "Why isn't this getting better? I'm practicing all the time," my mind questioned. The next thing I knew, Mr. Strickland eased into the chair next to me, calmly suggesting ways to improve, often with a simple fix like, "pull the corners of your lips a little tighter." Or, "Don't let your cheeks blow out." And, once satisfied with my adjustment, he stands up and leaves to help someone else in need, while I continue perfecting the fix. Quietly encouraging my efforts, he was also nurturing my own voice through the sousaphone, resulting in my playing the instrument more expressively.

Band rehearsals each day after classes caused me to rush through the halls to the band room anxious to play and perfect the music we were rehearsing. With Mr. Strickland up front on the podium confidently waving the baton, I enjoyed playing the music, completely unaware of time. Sitting in the back row of the band gave me a direct eye line to Mr. Strickland, but also a great view of my band mates. When he paused conducting to give instructions or point out mistakes, his hands froze midair ready to start playing at any time. This kept everyone's attention, and minimized potential chaos from thirty-five-plus students holding instruments in-hand and mouths ready to gab. But when student disruptions occurred, he addressed them in a soft-spoken, low-key manner; his personal trait, without threats or extended reprimands, quickly moving on, not dwelling on the interruption, concentrating on learning the music.

The two-hours-plus band rehearsals went by quickly, sending me home at dusk for dinner in high spirits; the enticing aroma reaching me before I reached the door, the results of mama and daddy collaborating in the kitchen.

Our momentum and enthusiasm pushed Mr. Strickland to add morning rehearsals to our schedule, one hour before classes started, and to open the band room Saturday mornings for students to practice individually (with his coaching available, of course), sometimes staying well into the afternoon. But the weekend Smith Family, Inc. responsibilities in the store and at home prevented me from taking advantage of that opportunity.

Football season meant marching band and preparing halftime shows; and the sousaphone's weight on my shoulder seemed heavier with each game. Rehearsing Strick's music and pageantry took place in the band room and on the uneven dust-prone football field, sometimes practicing until it was almost too dark to see who was standing next to you. This encouraged us to chatter, wander out of position and doodle on our instruments, sometimes producing a rare uncharacteristic angry rant from our usually calm and collected leader: "Be quiet? Stop the noise! Get back in line where I placed you and stay!" We would then quickly and silently scamper back into formation, in no hurry to test his patience again anytime soon.

Unaware of any benchmarks for measuring our efforts, and Mr. Strickland not imposing preconceived limits, I later determined we were performing concert music at a level above normal for the short time the band was established. Our first concert included the final movement of Antonin Dvorak's "New World Symphony," a *tour de force* orchestra work transcribed for band. Although classical music was alien to most of our ears, concentrating on learning our parts, one note at a time, provided us incremental steps for understanding the music. And, after productive rehearsals, the composition began making sense, increasing our interest and excitement. However, for me, classical music was already appealing to my natural instincts, and playing Dvorak's music was an absolute delight—the abrupt dynamic changes, forceful accents, and memorable melodies.

Like all college certified band teachers, Mr. Strickland's music education at Lincoln University was focused on Western classical music exclusively. Jazz was forbidden for study and performance. However, as he later told me, "Often, late at night in the music building's practice rooms, I would improvise jazz into the wee hours of the morning from tunes I heard on recordings and the radio. And I wasn't the only one. Sometimes several of us got together for jam sessions, and got paid gigs from the student government to play for dances."

At Morehouse, though jazz was likewise excluded from teaching and performance, Strick sometimes stole moments from his young pupils for jazz improvisation in the band room, spewing out motifs and riffs on his alto saxophone, based on harmonic progressions only he could hear. Although those momentary episodes may in part have been an outlet for managing his stressful teaching responsibilities, I believe he also wanted his students to hear and appreciate jazz as a legitimate musical form, and improvisation as free personal musical expression.

Some of my band mates, trying to improvise like Strick, found it difficult at first, but managed a degree of success after continuing their efforts. I did not develop a strong enough interest in jazz to attempt improvisation on the sousaphone, though later as a professional musician, I regretted not making an effort. Yet, the unique musical style and expression seeped deeply into my soul, for future reference.

During Strick's second year at Morehouse, the band was suited up in stylish uniforms featuring white coats that were an unfortunate catch-all for junk food, spilled soft drinks and mishandled ballpoint pens, requiring frequent cleaning. Regrettably, it was also the cause for one of Strick's most embarrassing and potentially job-ending moments.

The marching band was invited that year to participate in a Saturday out-of-town parade. I enjoyed traveling to perform and show off our new uniforms, happily blasting away as the band's only sousaphone player and playing my favorite march, Getty H. Huffine's *Them Basses.* Unfortunately, it rained on our parade that day, literally drenching us, completely soaking our uniforms as we faithfully finished the parade.

When we returned to Morehouse, we changed out of the wet uniforms, and following Strick's instructions, placed them in the clear plastic bags designed and used for their protection. We hung them neatly on racks in the unventilated uniform storage closet, which was a huge mistake. When he returned to campus Monday morning and checked the storage room, there were all our uniforms, staring at him, our white coats now mostly green with mildew.

For Strick, that must have been a sickening sight, turning his stomach and weakening his knees. Speculating on Mr. Adams' reaction, his life must have flashed brightly before his eyes—ending with unemployment. Given the precarious situation, I feared we would lose our cherished teacher. However, he survived, somehow, and I was happy to see him back in the band room later, although he seemed to struggle internally with guilt for months afterward. The coats benefited from a special chemical cleaning, but were never quite the same bright whiteness I had grown so proud of showing off.

While spending a lot of time in the band room practicing during my junior year, I noticed some of my peers working on solos that Strick had given them. He sometimes plopped the music on their music stands saying, "Here, try this out," usually to a flute, clarinet, trumpet, alto saxophone, or euphonium player. The music sounded more complex, flashy, and musically appealing than the band music I was playing, and appeared more fun. And if the student learned to play the solo well enough, Strick entered them in the annual state solo competitions at Southern University in Baton Rouge.

One day, I asked Mr. Strickland, "Are there any solos for the sousaphone?"

He hesitated for a few seconds, looked away, turned back and said, "I'm not sure. The sousaphone is not really known for solos." Another embarrassing pause, then, "Why don't you check at the music store and see what they may have."

The following Saturday, my mother drove me to the Paul Hewitt Music Store in Monroe to see if they stocked sousaphone or tuba solos. It was the largest music retail business in northeast Louisiana. If sousaphone solos existed, they would probably have them, I rationalized.

The salesman directed me to the instrumental solo sheet music section where my eyes lit up at the sight of "Tuba" on one of several bins. "There are solos!" I shouted while dashing toward the sign. "Let me see what's here." With my heart thumping wildly, I hastily thumbed through the few that were in the file, discovering only two that seemed to have some of the same "flashy" qualities I heard my cohorts perform: lots of notes moving up and down the staff with a nice melody in between.

Noticing a broad smile on my mother's face as she paid for them (titles long since forgotten), I could not wait to play them in the band room on Monday. Admittedly, the sousaphone is large and long, with a big cup mouthpiece and clunky valves, but it didn't occur to me that it should matter. Unbeknownst to me, this was the beginning of my life's mission to play solos on the tuba at a level equal to other instruments, and being appreciated by others. My naive mind had no preconceived prohibitive notions about what could, or could not, be played on my beloved instrument.

I entered the band room that Monday, smiling anxiously, as I hoisted the sousaphone onto my shoulder, placed the music on the stand and sat down to play my first solo. Mr. Strickland was already teaching one of several students in the room, but as I played through the first several notes, everyone's eyes turned toward me surprised at what they heard, the up and down fast-moving tones, though I was fumbling some of them. I stopped, smiled at their reaction, and started over, putting my simple logic to the test: the sousaphone can be flashy, too. Mr. Strickland, unaware of precedence for sousaphone or tuba solos, and observing my persistence, was encouraging as usual, but mostly left me to work out the music's challenges, as if saying, "Let's just see what he's going to do with this."

Weeks later, I was sitting in the band room practicing my solos and I sensed Mr. Strickland, as usual, easing into the chair next to me, but this time he totally interrupted my playing.

"Excuse me John L.," he said, "I notice you're really coming along well on the solos. If you agree, I'll enter you in the state solo competitions this year."

Wow. That was music to my ears. Intimidating, yet my goal from the start. "Yes, yes… I think I would like that," I replied, trying to sound confident. But this was a new game, and a new test, and I asked myself, "What have I gotten into?"

A month later, my nerves were fighting a war with my mind's attempt to remain calm as I stood before three judges in a Southern University classroom playing for the first time in the state solo competitions. I must have appeared as a curious oddity to the judges, not accustomed to sousaphone soloists, but there I was, instrument on my shoulder, ready for the test.

"Please play," one of the university's music professor judges said, and I did. With unwavering concentration, I managed to perform without an obvious mistake, and learned later that day I received a superior rating, the highest possible award.

"Oh boy! This is great! They like my playing," I thought thrilled to no end, and Mr. Strickland was proud of his one-of-a-kind tuba soloist. And when I told my parents, they were pleased and supportive of my newly found passion. But that was just the beginning. With his subtle coaching, I received superior ratings the next year at the state and tri-state competitions. He also entered me into the Grambling State College Omega Men's "Talent Hunt Program" competition, where performing Carl Frangkiser's *Melodie Romanza* earned me a tie for first place with a *vocalist*, a new statement for the sousaphone that I didn't immediately grasp. With the general nurturing, support and confidence of my parents, I managed to take all of this in stride, as though it was meant to be as it was unfolding and I was confidently enjoying the ride.

However, the most critical solo performances that Strick helped me prepare for were Bastrop's all-white Chamber of Commerce concert, arranged by Mr. Adams, and later was for my 1955 Morehouse High School commencement, where I stood on stage in cap and gown playing G. E. Holmes's *Emmett's Lullaby*.

I didn't really know at the time that I was performing above the national norm for sousaphone and tuba players, and would not know until late into my college studies, when performance benchmarks were being established for the instrument. It was then when I realized there were other tuba players pursuing similar goals, playing the instrument in uncharacteristically musical ways. In the meantime, with Strick's coaching and encouragement, I was pushing an envelope that appeared to have no mailing address.

"John L., you think you might want to help me out this year with the band?" Strick inquired at the beginning of my senior year. I didn't know exactly what he had in mind, but an immediate "yes" was the only correct response for my teacher/mentor. "You can help with setting up for rehearsals, handing out music and loading the bus for travel, for starters," he said, as I thought about all of the things that he did as our band director.

Shadowing Strick that year, while performing my assigned tasks, gave me an excellent overview of a band director's job and responsibilities, which was informative, daunting and surprisingly vast, from teaching to community relations. However, I gained intimate insight regarding his personal motivation and passion for the job. He loved music, and thoroughly enjoyed teaching and inspiring students through music, always greatly concerned about their lives, their future.

Helping Strick with the band and continuing to perform on my sousaphone was playing out during my own senior-year crisis, deciding "what next?". I discovered finally that what I really wanted to do with my life was exactly what Strick was doing. I wanted to be a school band director, teach music and enjoy the personal rewards from influencing young lives.

Later that spring, I sensed Mr. Strickland, once again, lowing himself into the chair next to me, stopping my practice. He was smiling as a bearer of good news. "I have been contacted by several colleges with scholarship offers from band directors, wanting you to attend next year and play in the band." We both sat there silently for a moment, relishing with pride what that meant: the rewards for extraordinary teaching and learning. However, if I intend to follow exactly in Mr. Strickland's footsteps, I knew I must attend Lincoln University in Missouri, his alma mater, and study music education while continuing to play the sousaphone, which is what I did, graduating from Lincoln in 1959.

Strick continued teaching at Morehouse while I studied two years at Indiana University, earning the Master's Degree, taught a year at Grambling State University, and spent four years in the US Navy (More on this period in later chapters).

In 1969, ten years after my graduation from Morehouse, a federal court ruled that Morehouse Parish must desegregate its schools (U.S. District Court v. Morehouse Parish School Board, 1969). The ruling was a full *15 years* after the Supreme Court's historic Brown v. Board of Education desegregation decision. Mr. Strickland was still teaching at Morehouse, and I was in my third year as principal tuba player with the Oklahoma City Symphony and music professor at nearby Langston University. The District Court's ruling resulted in the closing of the Morehouse Parish Training School, our historically Black school, ending the incredible 53-year legacy, the source of so many great experiences, wonderful memories and successful lives.

Even though many African-American citizens saw it as the price for racial justice and Black progress, the school's closing was very difficult for me and hundreds of former Morehouse students. Reacting to this historic benchmark, the *Place Aux Dames* Civic and Social Club, an astute group of Bastrop's Black women, published the *Morehouse Memory Book 1976*. The book memorialized our experiences and the school's legacy; it was "a permanent record to pass on to posterity the history of our school, Morehouse 1916-1969."

On the surface, it appeared the court's decree and agreed transition plan was implemented according to the District Court's intent. However, through later conversations with my mother, a teacher during that time, and other Black Bastrop teachers and citizens, it is evident that things were not at all as they appeared. There was a much more tragic and devastating reality that occurred underneath that tranquil façade. Black teachers, parents and students did not benefit as anticipated, partially due to the massive white flight of students from the area's public schools to private schools, which were not compelled legally to desegregate.

According to those sources, when the white Morehouse Parish School Board made teacher assignments under the newly constituted desegregated system, Black teachers that were assessed as "highly qualified" were reassigned to predominantly white schools (my mother being one of them, reluctantly), and the "least effective" white teachers were assigned to Black majority schools. Consequently, many Black students ended up in classes taught by less competent white teachers. Many of those teachers believed African-Americans were intellectually inferior and incapable of learning, not exactly a scenario to improve Black education, which was the original argument for desegregation. And in the reassignments, I understood that none of the white teachers lost their jobs, but a number of Black instructors felt pressured to retire.

Strick's outstanding reputation and accomplishments as Morehouse band director were well known to both Black and white communities. And based on those strong positive assessments, he was selected to become the band director for the newly desegregated Bastrop High School, formerly the Parish's prestigious all-white institution. He was one of very few Black teachers reassigned to that school.

As the Bastrop High School band director, he held one of the most coveted positions in the school system, given its high visibility, and public relations and community ambassador status. I was thrilled and proud to learn that Strick was chosen, a position he absolutely deserved.

He brought everything he knew to the new assignment for continuing the band's acclaimed reputation, including a new unfamiliar marching band and halftime-show style adopted from the world-renowned Florida A&M University (FAMU) Marching 100 Band under the leadership of Dr. William P. Foster, a style he embraced after I graduated. The band's moves featured fast-paced, high-stepping, exaggerated body motions for marching, and full-band dancing to popular R&B and Soul music at halftime shows. I was completely enthralled when seeing the FAMU band's halftime show live for the 1974 Tampa University vs. FAMU game in Tampa Stadium, two years after my relocation to Tampa from Oklahoma. The two teams made history in 1969, as the first football game between Black and white universities, and FAMU won.

With the FAMU band's nationally televised appearances for the National Football League playoff and Super Bowl games, the Afro-influenced style spread like wildfire to other historically Black colleges, public schools and beyond (including a prestigious predominantly white Tampa high school), and Strick, as the Morehouse band director, was no exception.

Bastrop High band's transition from its traditional slow, long-stride marching style, and halftime shows featuring moving patterns and figurative formations performed to show tunes and marches to Strick's new approach represented a difficult challenge. "I mixed features of both styles together initially in half-time shows as a transition to ease the big change," Strick later explained to me about the struggle he faced, "but white anxiety, mostly adults, only grew."

Justifying his decision to institute the new style, he continued, "I really thought this was what desegregation was supposed to be about: learning, experiencing, and appreciating different cultures so students can grow." Silent in thought for a moment, he went on, resolutely, "And anyway, this wasn't anything new, white teenagers nationwide were eagerly consuming and emulating Black-originated popular music and dance."

"Strick, I couldn't agree with you more," I said, trying to ease his anxiety.

Sensing an impending crisis regarding this issue, Strick invited me to Bastrop High in fall 1977 to present a tuba master class for band students and parents, hoping to boost their confidence in his teaching and leadership. By then, a music professor at the University of South Florida, I accepted without hesitation, and prepared to do my best to show the results of Strick's profound foundation that led to my successful performance and academic careers.

"Good afternoon, it's a pleasure to be with you today," I began the presentation, facing a small group of mostly white faces sitting in chairs on the tiered band room floor.

"You know, some years ago I was in Mr. Strickland's band, not unlike youngsters are today, eager to learn music and stylishly march on the football field for half-time shows. And what I got from him was not only the joy of those experiences, but so much more," I said. "Our band was the best, winning top awards for concerts and being highly recognized for our halftime shows, enjoying playing music together and showing off together. However, Mr. Strickland also taught us life lessons regarding humility, honesty, teamwork, discipline and respect... life lessons that have served me and my schoolmates well throughout our lives."

I paused briefly to see if they were attentive, then presented a snapshot of my career, and continued with my personal testimony.

"I am absolutely sure that without Mr. Strickland, my teacher, band director and mentor, life for me would have turned out quite differently. And, I'm certain I would not be here performing for you today."

Another pause; looking, seeking their eyes, and allowing my message to resonate, then I continued.

"Although most of Mr. Strickland's former band students did not follow musical paths as I did, all of us benefited significantly from his generous spirit, knowledge and humanity and are pursuing meaningful and productive lives all over the country, coast to coast. So now, enough said, let me play for you." And I did, dazzling them as best I could with my performance on the tuba.

Leaving Bastrop that day, I wasn't really sure if I had made a difference for Strick, but hoping, maybe, that I had added respectful credibility to the virtues of my teacher/mentor. Unfortunately, a year later, Strick's tenure as Bastrop High School's band director came to an undesirable end, shortened by the polite, covert racist politics that often controlled the destiny of so many Blacks after desegregation, some resulting in defensive litigation (See Pegues v. Morehouse Parish School Board).

The School Board announced Strick's removal as a promotion to *Coordinator of Fine Arts*, a newly created system-wide administrative position, and an action I immediately interpreted as a dishonest racist scam. It was obvious to me that the "promotion" was to avoid legal entanglement and confrontation with the Black community if he was outright fired. The new title sounded important enough, but the position was without any specified authority, responsibility, staff or budget, and no department or personnel direct reports above or below. Presumably, a salary increase was part of the new assignment, although I never confirmed this with Strick.

Although, at first glance, this seemed like an ideal situation, being your own boss, deciding what to do with your time. However, I learned that Strick struggled desperately to define a meaningful role that provided a sense of purpose and self-worth. After all, he loved and enjoyed teaching for more than twenty-five years, and was good at it. So, eventually, adhering to his own values, and living up to the expectations of those, including me, who knew and respected him, he established a string program and taught middle-school violin classes, a void in the Parish's school music program, which he did passionately until his spring 1985 retirement.

"What? Strick's retiring?" I responded to my cousin Bill, when he called with the news. "Last time I talked with him, he seemed content with teaching strings to middle school students in Mer Rouge." Bill was as surprised as I was about Strick's sudden decision.

Still stunned by the information, I thought, surely this milestone will not pass without Strick being appropriately recognized and honored in Bastrop; too many lives were touched and influenced profoundly by him, certainly mine and Bill's, a revered school band director himself. However, after phone conversations with several home town contacts, it didn't appear such plans were being considered, so I put on my thinking cap. "What can I do from Tampa, 800 miles away?"

My first consideration was a typical reception or banquet in Bastrop, featuring personal testaments, but was logistically problematic due to distance. I would be unable to manage the details to assure a quality event. And there were few people there I could depend on for the intense planning and implementation.

However, after several days of brainstorming other possibilities, I arrived at an idea that would appropriately honor Strick and entice his former students and colleagues to participate: a four-day Caribbean cruise, several of which Juel, my wife and I and other family members had enjoyed immensely. Using a travel agent would significantly minimize my involvement in logistics and management, so I immediately requested a travel agent plan for a Nassau, Bahamas itinerary from the Port of Miami. To the best of my knowledge, Strick and his wife Evelyn, also a retired teacher, had seldom ventured far from the state of Louisiana, not to mention off America's shores, and the cruise would make the celebration special, memorable, and something they would enjoy.

On the day of the cruise, August 30, 1985, I waited at the ship's boarding entrance to greet over 50 participants arriving from across the country for the celebration, hoping to recognize those I had not seen for many years. Tables were clustered together for our meals, with the first evening's dinner allowing time for introductions, reconnections, and interactions. In some ways it was a surprise party with almost everyone being surprised to see someone they hadn't seen since high school graduation. Our meals together were also occasions for sharing old memories and amusing stories involving Strick, our beloved Morehouse, and our experiences as students. But between meals, everyone floated (pun intended) independently throughout the ship and on Nassau Island enjoying the sights and sounds.

Besides seeing Strick on an outer deck relaxing in a lounge chair with a colorful drink in hand, I also witnessed him splashing happily like a child in the ship's swimming pool. And during our shore venture on Nassau Island, I watched him dressed in Bermuda shorts and a colorful tropical shirt smiling broadly as he walked among the shops and restaurants carrying a small bag of souvenirs. My mentor was having the time of his life, and I was pleased.

After our last lunch, I arranged for a group photo on the aft deck, and during our final dinner that evening, we toasted Strick with champagne and personal testimonies. Keeping my emotions in check, I managed a tribute.

"Strick, this celebration is for you from all of us," I began. "Your Morehouse students, whose lives you touched by waving your magic baton and sitting next to us, using music to reach and teach us life's many lessons. And from me specifically, thanks for nurturing and exploiting my passion for playing the tuba. You launched my life's mission and made a huge difference in all of our lives, and for that we can't possibly thank you enough."

Once testimonies were completed, Strick, standing in a white three-piece suit, champagne glass extended in hand and smiling. He responded graciously in his usual understated manner, acknowledging our thoughtful tributes, appreciating the sight of so many of his former students and colleagues, and thanking me for making the occasion possible.

"Evelyn and I are truly overwhelmed from this special cruise retirement celebration," he responded. "We love you and thank you so much."

I have experienced many moments of great personal satisfaction in my life, but this celebration of Mr. Strickland for so profoundly influencing the lives of me and so many others, and to witness the gracious, modest and joy of his response, was beyond rewarding.

Over the years, I checked in on the Stricklands several times at their restored two-story home in Bastrop. They always mentioned their joy and appreciation of that retirement celebration cruise. Strick continued teaching music, as a volunteer, to individuals and small groups of children. And former students, including me, continued to rely on his quiet counsel while pursuing our careers. Concerned about the self-esteem and lack of an appropriate social hub for middle class Black men in Bastrop, he established and managed a small private club. During two of my visits, I met him there while he waited for snack and beverage vendors.

My demanding work at the University of South Florida kept me quite busy, but Mr. Strickland was never far from my thoughts. However, on December 1, 1991, I received notice that he had passed, age sixty-three. He was way too young to leave us, and I certainly wasn't ready for that message.

My foundation was shaken. My guru was gone.

I called Mrs. Strickland, offering my condolences and shared grief, unable to find the words for my feelings. Her voice, filled with pain, but also courageous, thanked me for calling, and she then detailed tentative plans for Strick's Celebration of Life, a memorial service on December 3rd. "I would like for you to present expressions during the service if you could make it," she softly almost apologetically requested.

"Of course," I said without thought, "I would be honored."

The service was held in a packed new auditorium, appropriately on the previous Morehouse Parish Training School campus, now a middle school. The afternoon program, inclusive of musical tributes, was well attended by Strick's former students, teaching colleagues and community friends. And as one of several former band students who spoke, I opened my remarks with the following:

> *i have been seeking*
>
> *what i have never found*
>
> *what i don't know what i want*
>
> *but it must be around*
>
> *i been upset*
>
> *since the day before last*
>
> *but that was so long*
>
> *i done forgot when it passed*
>
> *yes almost forgot*
>
> *what I have not found*
>
> *but I know it must be*
>
> *somewhere around*
>
> —Langston Hughes

"According to Langston," I said, "life presents the ever-present challenge of seeking and searching for identity. Mostly, it's a search to define oneself: Who am I? Why am I here? For what purpose do I exist? But for Mr. Charles Strickland, or 'Strick' as we all affectionately knew him, this was not a problem or personal dilemma. He was a proud African-American man, and his life's mission was to serve the needs of young people -as simple as that.

"Once in a lifetime, if you are lucky or blessed, you may be touched and your life altered positively by someone—that rare individual, whose goal in life is service to others rather than self-serving."

I concluded my remarks with, "If we, his former band students are truly faithful to Strick, and all that his life embodied, we will continue his legacy through our own lives of love, generosity and compassion."

Whenever I return home to Bastrop, I visit Strick's burial site at Bastrop Cemetery, the same cemetery where my parents and other ancestors are buried. On North Washington Street, the main north-south highway through the small town, and only three blocks from its center square, the well-maintained cemetery sits quietly across railroad tracks from the sprawling former International Paper Mill (building now demolished). The contrasting noisy infrastructure and towering smokestack that existed to the east, overshadowed and conflicted with the cemetery's peaceful solemn ambiance. Originally established for Blacks only, Strick's gravesite resides in the newly integrated St. Joseph Catholic section on a northern slope—appropriate, as he taught both Black and white students.

During those visits, I stand facing Strick's brightly tinted and stately headstone that symbolizes his unwavering humility. "Band Director" scripted on the stone's surface succinctly defines his passion, but greatly understates his extensive life-enhancing value to me and so many Morehouse students. Standing there, I feel a powerful connection to the profound foundation that ignited an explosion that lifted me off the launch pad toward a rewarding life.

PART II

They Shaped My Purpose

Chapter 9

Inspiring Image

"It's almost time to leave. I've got to catch my train," were my thoughts. "But first I need to see my girlfriend one last time before I go." So, I told my parents I'll be right back, as I got in the car and drove off, much to their amazement. I dashed the 25-miles to Monroe for a quick goodbye, though our relationship had been off and on for several years. Now with that done, I was back in Bastrop ready for the eleven-mile drive to the tiny, rural train station in Collinston, leaving with them later than planned. Approaching the station, I watched with horror as the train's club car disappeared down the track. "I missed my train," I meekly offered since I was the reason for missing its departure. My parents, angry but showing calm resolve knowing I had to be at Lincoln University in Jefferson City, Missouri in two days for freshmen orientation, suggested we go inside the station to ask about the train's route and where it might be stopping.

Speaking to the slow-moving, all-purpose agent at the colored-only window in the back, we learned that the train had several stops on its way to Little Rock, where I would change to a St. Louis bound train. Quickly checking the road map, we discovered that the train track paralleled highways 138 and 165 in Louisiana and southern Arkansas. "We need to see if we can catch that train," I heard my mother command, "John L, you drive!" They took to the back seat as if saying,

"We don't want to see this!" And off we went—my teenage driver instinct for speed about to be unleashed.

Our new Super Rocket 88 Oldsmobile responded to my persistent foot, as darkness fell and the headlights made stark silhouettes of the telephone poles and picket fences running swiftly in the opposite direction. Perspiration gathered from body pores as I kept a lookout for stray cows on the road, Southern police speed traps, and my parents in the rearview mirror, tense, holding hands and praying.

The two-lane back road was near the track at times, and distant sightings of the colorful club car lights told me we were gaining ground, until, there it was, my train stopped at the old brick McGehee, Arkansas station almost 75 miles from where we started. I grabbed my carry-on bag from the trunk, said a quick goodbye to my parents who were prying themselves from the back seat, climbed aboard the train and placed myself in the capable care of Black porters.

Finally, I exhaled as I flopped into my seat, feeling the train leaving the station and my familiar world behind. Then, a different anxiety set in as I thought about my journey, traveling alone and out of state for the first time, and attending college to become a school band director, completely new experiences.

Debarking in the middle of the night in August 1955, to wait for my train to St. Louis, I found my way to the Little Rock station's stale and barely lighted colored waiting room, smelling enticing food that wasn't meant for me.

From Little Rock, it took a while getting accustomed to the newly integrated train to St. Louis, though there was self-selected segregation. Intimidated by the city's frighteningly crowded colossal Union Station, I somehow managed to board the right train. Three hours later, the train slowed to a stop and a sign out the window confirmed my destination: Jefferson City. "Whew! I've arrived," I announced to myself. "Jefferson City and Lincoln University, home for the next four-years," already missing Bastrop, family and friends.

My parents didn't agree to Lincoln as my college choice initially. "How can we overlook the music scholarships from all the other schools?" they asked. "Mr. Strickland went there," I hastily responded, "and he said the music program was one of the top for Black colleges. And Barbara is attending Fisk University in Nashville, a top school without a scholarship," I continued strategically. "So why can't I go to a top school, too?" Yes, I unabashedly played the sibling equity card, and it worked, with my parents not explaining the anticipated financial hardship this would cause.

Leaving the train, I was met by a group of upperclassmen who escorted me and several other new arrivals to campus aboard a van. They were upbeat and cheerful but serious, hoping to ease us out of our travel woes and into college life. Having seen only low rolling slopes while driving in Louisiana, the van's window I was looking through could not capture the high hill behind the Lincoln signage gate as we entered the campus. I was awestruck to see the university built on and around a high hill, one of the tallest in Jefferson City, only four-miles south-southeast of the business district and state capitol building overlooking the Missouri River.

My heart raced as we drove up the curved main road into campus, paralleled by a stair- walk and sparse trees with brick and stone buildings coming into view, denser toward the top. The buildings at the peak faced a flat, treeless grassy quad with crisscrossing concrete walks. Turning right, the van let me out at Foster Hall, the freshmen men's dormitory, situated conveniently across the street from the Blue Tiger, the small café where I would soon happily discover my favorite twenty-five cent hamburgers (pickles only) and ten-cent bowls of chili. This provoked memories of being on the college campuses of Wiley College when my Great Uncle Scott was president, and Grambling College, my mother's alma mater, but they were not on a hill. And this was completely unfamiliar territory where I would be spending a lot of time.

Being the first to arrive at my assigned first floor double dorm room, I chose the bed on the left and the window-facing desk that provided a beautiful, sloping, tree-shrouded valley view. In the frigid winters, that window's ledge would serve as a refrigerator for snacks and the occasional baked-ham care package from Daddy. I later met my roommate Sylvester, a chemistry major, who was as quiet as I was. As anxious, studious freshmen, we passed each other daily in our shared room like kayakers in shark-infested waters. Our pairing as roommates was a great match, providing a quiet dorm room for study and sleep without the incessant need for conversation. The next year I was in a different dorm with a new roommate who, unfortunately, was more gregarious.

Freshman orientation's socializing intent was intimidating, walking all over campus and group activities with strangers. An introvert and loner, it was difficult engaging with other students, the circumstances increasing my uneasiness. But I jumped at the opportunity for self-expression by volunteering to perform a sousaphone solo for the orientation talent show, a confident means of communication. I'm sure it was an unusual musical treat for everyone... a sousaphone solo? The week ended with class registration and a formal notice that all freshmen music students were to perform for a seminar class the first week of classes.

Sitting in Page Auditorium the next week, nervously waiting for the seminar to start, I was aware of the high volume of student chatter, coming from all directions. Suddenly, a distinguished looking man strolled onto the stage, positioning himself midway in front of the baby grand piano. Well dressed and obviously in some official capacity, he stood there holding a sheet of paper in his right hand with the left tucked into his trouser pocket, patiently waiting for quiet, which happened quickly without anyone needing to shush.

"For those who don't know me, I'm Dr. O. Anderson Fuller, Chairman of the Department of Music, here to welcome you to Lincoln University."

"Wow!" I thought. "He not only looks distinguished, he is distinguished."

After he completed his remarks, each freshman was presented to perform a solo, the final certification for becoming a music major.

Born September 20, 1904, in Roanoke, Virginia, Dr. Fuller was this country's first African-American Music PhD recipient. According to a 1982 unpublished dissertation of O. Anderson Fuller by Dr. Steven Houser, he was awarded the PhD in1942 by the University of Iowa after earning the Master's degree there, as well. He received a Bachelor of Arts degree from Bishop College in Marshall, Texas, where his father served as academic dean. He later studied at Boston's New England Conservatory of Music.

Though admitted to Howard University's Medical School in 1924, Dr. Fuller accepted a music faculty position at North Carolina Agricultural and Technical University (instead), beginning an academic career that lasted fifty years. In 1929, he was appointed Chairman of the Music department at Prairie View State Normal & Industrial College (now Prairie View A&M University), continuing there while completing Graduate studies at the University of Iowa. Influenced by a Lincoln University faculty member, who was also a UI doctoral student, Dr. Fuller accepted Lincoln University's Music Chairman offer starting fall 1942.

Not yet a university priority and without a clear institutional identity, the music program was dispersed in different buildings across campus when Dr. Fuller arrived at Lincoln with his wife, Edith and daughter, Patricia. However, quickly acquiring the president's support, he established the Department of Music and achieved National Association of Schools of Music (NASM) accreditation in 1950, only the third HBCU to acquire that status (Howard and Fisk Universities were the others). The process brought new faculty and academic program funding, and eventually a new building that opened in fall 1956, my sophomore year. Attached to the new building was the 1,200-seat Richardson Auditorium, a professionally designed performance space, where I was often on the stage or in the audience for faculty, student and guest-artist recitals and concerts.

New faculty, Dr. Fuller recruitment included Juilliard graduate and Carnegie Hall recitalist, Eugene Haynes (See *To Soar with Eagles: The European Travels - Remembrances of Isak Dinesen*, Xlibris, 2001.). He established new degree programs in music therapy and performance, responding to career opportunities recently opened for African-Americans.

It wasn't long before highly talented students from throughout the Midwest and South started enrolling, some who went on to distinguished careers, notably: Metropolitan Opera and European operatic diva, Felicia Weathers, jazz artists, Oliver Nelson and Julius Hemphill, Fifth Dimension member Ronald Towson, one of the first Black American Airline pilots, James Tilmon, and the first African American

White House Secret Service agent, Abraham Bolden, serving President Kennedy (See *The Echo from Dealey Plaza*, Harmony Books, 2008). Except for Oliver Nelson, they were all at Lincoln at some part of my attendance.

With the new music building opening my sophomore year, all programs and faculty were finally under one roof for classes, rehearsals and individual practice, a closely configured intimate setting for study and social engagement, accessible almost 24/7. Surprisingly, I felt part of a warm, music-loving family of fellow students and dedicated faculty and staff with Dr. Fuller as our "fatherly" figure. We spent enormous hours together in classes and rehearsals, and hanging out in the lobbies and hallways.

It was a really supportive and nurturing environment for me, managing to develop a few close male friends. Living across the hall from each other in our junior/senior dorm, Gerald, Leo, Hopper, and I, developed close connections and attended Second Baptist Church on Sundays together. And, at Gerald's invitation, I spent a wonderful holiday weekend at his home in St. Louis, visiting Leo in his family's apartment while there.

Interestingly, my urban schoolmates seemingly believed that southern Blacks lived on plantations or similar racist imposed impoverished conditions and were fearful of traveling South. They never queried me about my living circumstances, which was Black middle class. Conversely, I was surprised and astounded by the huge, crowded Black slums I saw in St. Louis, the urban North, not an inviting place for my aspirations.

Although I was studying to become a school band director, weekly tuba lessons were required. So, the new building's practice rooms were my regular habitat: four walls, upright piano and no window. (Windowless to help concentration?) Those rooms were sanctuaries for my intense efforts of mastering the instrument, availing myself to sometimes harsh and brutal self-criticism. The discipline I acquired through Smith Family, Inc. at home was effectively brought forth in my practice. Although, the room's solitude also allowed for spiritual resolve that softened my self-analysis, so I didn't beat-up on myself too badly.

The Fine Arts Building was located at the foot of the hill on the North side of campus, most essential buildings clustered around the top and my junior/senior residence hall was near the hill's foot on the South side.   My days and nights entailed trudging the steep incline often, which was a necessary thankless routine. Three meals daily in the cafeteria on top of the hill assured my vigorous hike. My urban schoolmates watched with amusement as the Deep South poster child, me, each morning with a tray full of bacon, sausage, eggs, grits, hash brown potatoes, biscuits, jelly, and milk, head to a table, sit down, and consume everything. I gained a little weight in the wrong places my freshmen year, but inheriting my father's metabolism, the extra weight never lasted.

The size of the music department and curricular format made classes small with familiar faces seen daily. Music theory was a two-year course requirement sequence for all students with Dr. Fuller teaching it the sophomore year, something I was looking forward to. However, it was disappointing to learn that he would no longer teach the class, depriving me of the learning experience that upperclassmen raved about and often demonstrated the knowledge gained from his teaching. Intent on experiencing his teaching, I courageously convinced Dr. Fuller my senior year to allow me to take two independent studies classes with him: counterpoint and composition.

Counterpoint was a slam dunk with its straightforward rules, but composition was another matter entirely. After hearing my two short compositions performed at the semester's end, I knew to continue focusing on becoming a band director/tuba player; the world didn't need yet another bad composer. It also explains Dr. Fuller's lack of critique in class sessions. It was what he wasn't saying that told the truth about my composition efforts. And although the independent studies classes allowed me direct access to his teaching, it was really my four-year participation in the concert choir where his profound presence in my life took hold.

The concert choir, considered the music department's premier ensemble, didn't require an audition, so I don't recall exactly how I became a member my freshman year, particularly as an instrumentalist, not a voice student. Though I had participated in high school and church choral groups, I didn't profess to having a great singing voice, not even in the shower.

But I felt comfortable and confident singing in a group, blending successfully with the excellent voices around me, as I did in my high school NFA quartet. And as an instrumentalist, I could read music better than the average singer, making me an asset to any choral group. However, regardless of how it happened, regular rehearsals and concerts in Dr. Fuller's close-knit concert choir gave me direct access to his wealth of knowledge and musical genius, and for me, his overall mentoring and role-model qualities.

I can't say for sure whether Dr. Fuller's wardrobe gave him the "dress for success" image, or if his handsome features, charismatic personality and professional qualities gave his wardrobe that appearance. He always wore a refined tailored suit, or matching sports jacket and slacks, with long-sleeve shirt, cufflinks and matching tie, along with a Stetson hat with the front brim turned down fashionably and a black cashmere topcoat were added for cold days.

I even saw him outdoors once puffing a cigarette, stylishly extended from a holder and slightly tilted-up like FDR. However, for choir rehearsals, he discarded the coat, loosened his tie and rolled up his shirt sleeves to respond vigorously to the music's demands.

Choir rehearsals were laboratories where I learned great choral music and more, as much about life as about music. It was a powerfully influential setting for Dr. Fuller, positioned in front of us, his talented, eager, and open-minded pupils ready to respond to his slightest gesture or suggestion, and absorb the knowledge he freely conveyed.

For rehearsals, we sat in chairs four deep on a quarter-circle, tiered concrete floor, close to where he stood or sat on a studio stool centered in the curve of a baby grand piano with a music stand in front of him. I was in the back row singing baritone with three other guys, trying to be accurate and blend our efforts.

Dr. Fuller enjoyed and seemed to savor every moment of exploring the intricacies of the music being rehearsed, often tying the importance of detail, discipline, dedication, and perseverance for learning and perfecting the music to confronting and overcoming life's many challenges. His anecdotes seemed to imply that in life, as in our music performances, we should strive to carefully confront issues, design and perfect strategic resolutions, and be prepared to go the distance to achieve success. This approach, reinforced by other teachers/mentors, certainly describes my own method for dealing with complex issues, particularly later as an academic administrator.

As a tuba player, or an instrumentalist in general, the notes on the page were the usual starting point for learning new music. However, when introducing new choral compositions in rehearsal, Dr. Fuller proclaimed, "the angel is in the text," and before launching into the music, spent time discussing the text's meaning and exploring the root source, definition and proper enunciation of English and foreign words. If you had not studied Latin, and I had not, this was an introductory course.

Dr. Fuller also believed that, when possible, classroom knowledge should be applied to the real thing.

"Can anybody tell me what's the overall structure of this composition?" was a question I needed to be prepared for as a junior and senior, recalling what I had learned in music theory and form and analysis classes. "What good is textbook knowledge if you can't apply it to actual music?" he said after a fruitful discussion.

"Now that's why I was required to take those classes," I belatedly thought as I made the connections. But more importantly, the in-depth knowledge we gained in rehearsal prepared us for rendering an artistically convincing performance, presenting the music as the composer had intended.

For concert performances, the choir stood on risers facing the auditorium, with Dr. Fuller in front with his back to the audience. To the audience he was virtually motionless, unlike some conductors whose arms flail energetically. His conducting was discrete, as he mouthed words silently and used slight hand and finger motions, "So as not to distract the audience from the music itself," according to him. But after grueling rehearsals, where he persistently sought and demanded perfection, small movements were all that was needed in concert, since we were well prepared.

Each year during spring break, the concert choir toured the country as Lincoln's ambassador, usually the week before Easter Sunday; something I looked forward to. Sponsored by alumni chapters, we performed regularly in Kansas City and St. Louis, Missouri; Chicago, Illinois; Cleveland, Ohio; Detroit, Michigan; Louisville, Kentucky and Gary and Indianapolis, Indiana, where relative geographic proximity made consecutive evening concerts possible, with grueling all-day bus travel in between. I enjoyed the travel, seeing different landscapes and city skylines, although the diesel fumes sometimes made me nauseous.

Performing in Black churches, or occasionally a small school auditorium, we usually arrived late afternoons, set up the rostrum for the concert, ate dinner provided by the alumni chapter and dressed just before the evening concert. The music performed featured excerpts from operas and cantatas, classical art songs, folk music and traditional Black spirituals, music Dr. Fuller selected carefully for audience appeal and enlightenment. One year, four choir members performed the famous quartet from Giuseppe Verdi's opera *Rigoletto*, with Dr. Fuller as piano accompanist. The audience was astonished, and so was I, sensing the music's difficulty. But the "Negro Spirituals," coming at the end, was the most popular part of the program, including such arrangements as "Live-A-Humble" and "Yonder Come Day."

Standing on collapsible risers used for our tours, I cherished the moments when Dr. Fuller, facing the audience, made introductions before certain selections. He was always so elegant and articulate in those brief and concise presentations, perfect enunciation and diction. Seemingly improvised, the well-chosen words in clear, crisp voice provided relevant historical context or scene settings for enhancing the audience's experience. Setting the scene for *Rigoletto*, for example, was especially important for the listener's experience, and mine. His representation was an impressive model that I've tried to emulate. Although, usually falling short, I keep trying anyway.

After our concerts, we broke up into same-sex pairs, usually the same for the entire tour, and were transported home by alumni hosts for overnight stays. My roommate was Hopper, from the bass section and a year behind me in graduating class. The next morning, our host provided breakfast and made sure we were back at the church on time. But if we arrived early on the day of the concert or left late the next day, our host sometimes planned an interesting activity for us.

Once in Detroit, my host took me to her block association's early-teen girls' fashion show in a nearby apartment. That was a unique experience. Introduced by the host as a college student, I presented myself as a role model for the giggling young fashion models. It was informative to learn about the existence of "block associations" in a large, urban city for nurturing Black youngsters; reminding me of the southern small-town nurturing environment I experienced growing up in Bastrop.

My first year at Lincoln, 1955-56, was one year after the groundbreaking Brown v. Board of Education of Topeka Supreme Court decision mandating public education desegregation. My freshmen class that year included two white, female music students who were studying voice, among the first white students to attend Lincoln. Even though this was historic, Dr. Fuller did not provide any special recognition of their presence for our first performance seminar. They performed as I and all freshmen did, anxiously walking up on the stage and giving their best effort, though it was obviously a milestone for the music department.

However, the two young women quickly became part of the socially cohesive, tightly woven music department family, just another one of the talented, highly competitive artsy music students focused on developing their artistic capabilities and intellect. Due to the intimidating Deep South racial rules where I grew up that prohibited Black and white social mixing, particularly between Black males and white females, which was strictly taboo and unsafe, I kept my distance. But thanks to Dr. Fuller's not calling attention to the racial anomaly, the jovial chatter that characterized the lobby and halls of the music building, and the serious conversations about academics and music, never changed due to the addition of white students.

My freshman year at Lincoln proceeded okay, although I struggled in my English and biology courses. However, there was one important new destination added to our spring concert choir tour schedule that made the year exciting. The concert choir was scheduled to perform on the nationally televised Ted Mack *Original Amateur Hour*, a weekly ABC talent show broadcast live on Sundays from New York City. As special guests, we were scheduled to sing spirituals at the beginning and end of the Easter Sunday show. Dr. Fuller never explained how the invitation came about, but I am certain he had an influential role, for which, although a bit anxious about the new experience, I was really grateful.

My first year of college was now going to include a visit to the big city of New York, who would've thought? In less than a year, going from a small town in the Deep South to the Big Apple. And the choir's television appearance, a major national media coup for the university, would be seen in my parents' home, and many others, back in Bastrop.

Concert choir rehearsals took on an added urgency that year, particularly for the two selected spirituals, increasing the intensity. With Dr. Fuller's usual assertive quest for perfection, our progress was sometimes stalled, frustrating everyone. When that occurred, he abruptly stopped conducting the music, hands in mid-air, panned the choir with his eyes, smiling slightly. Then after a brief silence, with hands dropping slowly, delivered a humorous monologue, a human-nature joke or story that relieved the pressure of the moment. I don't recall any of them, but it always worked.

After our laughter subsided, he would say, "If we don't get some humor out of life, we'll just...die," with the entire choir joining him with the final word "die." Then we energetically leapt back into the music, this time with productive results.

With the mixed-race makeup of the choir that year, Dr. Fuller's planning of the tour's interstate travel required additional preparation, particularly the meals and rest stops between destinations. Howard Johnson's national chain restaurants near interstate expressways, one of the first to accommodate African-American travelers, had become reliable for our Black choir. When he made reservations for this tour, Dr. Fuller advised the restaurants of our racial mix, and they responded by extending their usual welcome.

Reviewing tour rules with us before leaving that year, Dr. Fuller stressed more than usual the need for appropriate behavior and decorum, particularly at rest stops and restaurants. He cautioned us to be vigilant and attentive to the reactions of others around us and avoid giving restaurant managers an excuse to deny or terminate service. We were to walk in, sit together in an orderly fashion, talk softly while seated, be courteous and decisive with waiters and remember to say "thanks!"

Although a sizable group of thirty-eight African-American and two white, female students, plus Dr. and Mrs. (Mama) Fuller, we were to call as little attention to ourselves as possible, which, of course, was no small matter, like asking the restaurant patrons to ignore the Tyrannosaurus Rex walking in, occupying immense space, and then sauntering out.

So, during the tour, I could not help noticing the overt reactions to our group at restaurants. For some white patrons, the sight of the two white female students walking, talking, and sitting next to Black male students was more than they could handle, showing their utter contempt with facial contortions and loud whispers, painfully reminding me of my Deep South upbringing. Thankfully, no one overreacted, and I was always happy to get back on our bus, safely away from the hostile setting.

Since the Ted Mack show's producers had not actually heard the concert choir perform previously, as a precaution, they required us to audition the prepared music Easter Sunday morning only hours before the live telecast, requiring two trips that day between our hotel and the network's mid-Manhattan studio. Presumably, we were expendable if we did not measure up to their expectations. Fortunately, Dr. Fuller had advised us to be prepared for contingencies that may occur. However, none of us, including Dr. Fuller, were prepared for the audition experience, which I later discovered to be fairly typical of New York City showbiz.

When we arrived for the audition, the choir was quickly ushered up several floors via elevator into a poorly, lighted windowless room with black walls, barely adequate for our large ensemble. After positioning ourselves on bleachers, I realized there was a table in front with a man reading a newspaper. All I could see was the back of the newspaper, two hands holding it, and thick cigarette smoke swirling above an invisible head. We stood silently for what seemed like an eternity waiting for him to acknowledge our presence, but instead he yelled "Please start!"

Startled, Dr. Fuller turned around to face us, gestured to calm our anxieties, and led us through the two spirituals.

Although my eyes were focused correctly on him while I was singing, I could also see the cigarette-smoking man seated behind the table never ceased reading the newspaper throughout our performance, flipping from one page to the other while smoke swirled above his head. When we completed the two songs, there was more nerve-racking silence before the voice behind the newspaper commanded, "You may go!" without ever recognizing our presence or giving a courtesy "Thank you."

"Wow!" I thought. "Welcome to New York!"

After Dr. Fuller received confirmation that our performance was still on, we returned to the hotel, ate a late lunch, changed clothes and were back at the studio in robes two hours before the telecast. I was a little nervous, due to the live nature of the show, aware that mistakes would be heard in millions of homes, including those of my Bastrop extended family. When the time came, we were moved quickly into performance position on bleachers facing glaring lights where we quietly waited for our cue. Our anxiety increased the level of adrenaline that pushed to new heights the polished musicianship and strict discipline Dr. Fuller had instilled in us, his premier choral ensemble. So, from his downbeat, we were on autopilot.

From my perspective, our performance was perfect, but then I was not out front or viewing on television, somewhat limiting the value of my assessment. However, during the bus ride back to the hotel, Dr. Fuller, standing up front, spoke glowingly about our singing and expressed his appreciation for our exemplary effort, confirming my critique. For the moment, we were happy in New York, making him and our university proud. But we would sleep really well that night, knowing that Dr. Fuller had scheduled the next day for us to freely explore and enjoy New York City, our exciting reward!

Early Monday morning, we charged into the city with the adventurous spirit of adolescents in Disneyland. I and several others courageously took to the unfamiliar subway for the riding experience, and to reach more landmarks that day. We quickly got lost, ending up somewhere in Brooklyn. But after educating ourselves about the system, we visited the Empire State Building, the Statue of Liberty and Coney Island.

And it was at the Coney Island amusement park where I did something I would never, ever repeat: ride the gigantic, historic, world-famous 85-foot-high wooden Cyclone roller coaster... alone! All my peers declined the adventure, and I was surprised at my own courage, or was it stupidity? My body was tossed uncontrollably into the air at the roller coaster's peaks and slammed solidly back on the seat at the bottom, and gravity in collusion with the curves, zipped me from one side of the seat to the other. Disembarking, I noticed that a certain part of my anatomy was just a trifle sore as a result of my solo venture, a fact I kept secret from my cynical choir mates who had watched my wild ride on the ground while munching on heavily mustard chili dogs.

As the evening progressed, we discovered that people in New York City did not sleep, so we joined them in that idiosyncrasy, walking up and down Broadway, and in and out of stores until they closed. I wound up back at the hotel earlier than most of my cohorts, the shy Southern freshman a bit overwhelmed. The next morning, Dr. and Mama Fuller were pleased to see all of their tired, sleepy charges accounted for on the bus as we left the Big Apple for Jefferson City. They must have enjoyed the momentary quiet bus ride with all of us sound asleep.

Mama Fuller, Mrs. Edith Whitfield Fuller (1902-1986), was our surrogate mother and girls' chaperone for choir tours. Hers was the soft voice that corrected unprofessional behavior, and the raspy whisper in our ear when a personal rule had been violated. Discreetly, the powerful woman behind the man, she was unabashedly deferential to Dr. Fuller, quietly supporting and counseling him through his various responsibilities, demands and decisions.

Mrs. Fuller was an attractive, full-figured, Southern sophisticated lady with light complexion, and though evident that she possessed long straight hair, she always wore it curled around and on top of her head. Her attire was formal, when necessary, but dress-casual when we traveled.

The couple owned a modest bungalow just two blocks from the Fine Arts Building; close enough for Dr. Fuller to walk for lunch. It was said that he insisted on being prompt for 12 o'clock lunch, and seldom returned to his office before 1:05 p.m., due to an obsession with a television soap-opera during that hour. Although the rumor seemed plausible, no one had the courage to confirm its accuracy, certainly not me.

Dr. Fuller's highest priority was his music students, carefully monitoring our progress over four years of undergraduate study. The weekly music performance seminars allowed him a real-time opportunity to observe and measure our musical growth and artistic development. He was particularly sensitive to a student's confidence and self-perception during our solo presentations, especially important for Black students who were also being prepared and groomed for social leadership roles in their communities. So, occasionally, when he believed a valuable lesson could be offered, or confidence fortified, Dr. Fuller interjected himself into seminar performances. He never wasted a teaching moment, and I was to be a beneficiary.

For one seminar, I was performing on my tuba a memorized movement from Bach's *Suite* for an unaccompanied cello, when I experienced a memory loss, getting to a point in the composition and unable to go any further. "Oh no, that's never happened before" I said to myself. Pausing to collect my thoughts, I confidently started over from the beginning. Then, getting to the same place in the music, I was again unable to remember any further. This time I was upset with myself, and embarrassed, sensing faculty and students staring at me and waiting. But I was still convinced the music was in my memory after many memorized rehearsals. "I know the music and must get through the piece to the end," I told myself, and started from the top, only to face the blank wall once more, totally frustrated.

Then I heard Dr. Fuller's calm voice.

"You know, John, this sometimes happens to the best artists. I've seen many who have memory slips here or there," he said. "I have had an occasional memory lapse myself. And it's okay. But why don't you get the music and read it all the way through for us to enjoy."

I quickly grabbed the music and performed the entire movement flawlessly, feeling success, rather than that earlier sense of failure, confidence instead of incompetence. He made a huge difference in my self-perception that day.

My mother visited Lincoln during my junior year to check on me and observe the environment that was spurring her son's remarkable progress. Concerned initially I might find college overwhelming; she was more than pleased with my perseverance and success. After sending Dr. Fuller a letter advising him of her visit, he and Mrs. Fuller graciously hosted my mother for lunch at their home. Daddy, grounded at the grocery store as usual, could not make the trip, but I nevertheless felt his steadfast presence.

The two ladies had several things in common: light complexion, southern sophistication and relatively straight hair swooped up on top of their heads. Both were socially engaging, enjoying each other immensely, my mother told me later. I was so proud of the special invitation from the Fullers and the opportunity for my mother to meet them. She was as impressed with them as I was. And Dr. Fuller's casual comments to me later indicated he was equally enamored with my mother: the articulate educator and energized social activist.

During my senior year, Dr. Fuller graciously responded to my request for a reference letter for graduate admissions to Indiana University's School of Music. And two years later, he was an important reference for my first college teaching appointment to Grambling College in Louisiana (now Grambling State University). Both letters were crucial in achieving those objectives.

In August 1966, financially strapped, I and my wife, Janie were making an urgent, 800-mile drive from Naval Station Great Lakes north of Chicago, where I had been honorably discharged after four years of service. I was headed to my new position as principal tuba player with the Oklahoma City Symphony and trying to arrive for the first rehearsal for the Orchestra's season-opening concert. Responding to my desperate phone call, Dr. Fuller paid for a badly needed overnight hotel stay while passing near Jefferson City, unable to stop in for a visit.

Six years later, in 1972, I joined the faculty at the University of South Florida (USF) in Tampa as a tenure-earning tuba and music theory assistant professor, and enrolled in doctorate-level courses the following summer at the University of Missouri-Kansas City (UMKC), about 155 miles west of Jefferson City. I phoned Dr. Fuller to say hello and accepted an invitation to visit, which I looked forward to since I had not seen him in fourteen years.

The Saturday morning drive for lunch at the Fuller's home was filled with anxiety that intensified with each passing mile. I felt as though I was still a student about to have a personal encounter with the chairman of Lincoln's Department of Music, the musical giant, my role model and mentor. Although it had been fourteen years since graduating from Lincoln, given my shyness and his status my nerves were fraying. I couldn't believe my uncontrollable feelings.

The door opened briskly after a short doorbell rang with Dr. and Mama Fuller greeting me warmly with handshakes, their appearance barely changed. Passing a front window with a view of the Fine Arts Building across the street, they ushered me into an informal dining area, where the table was set for lunch. After placing salad plates, rolls and ice tea glasses on the table, Mama Fuller apologetically disappeared.

Surprisingly, Dr. Fuller insisted that I sit at the head of the small rectangular table as he sat in the chair to my left. I was deeply honored by that gesture. With anxiety still tightly gripping me, our conversation began haltingly, and as I reached for my napkin, I knocked over my glass of tea. "What? Oh no!" my thoughts rang out. "You clumsy dummy!" Although I managed to upright the glass quickly, I looked down to see the spilt tea slowly heading in my direction. Sitting paralyzed with embarrassment, the tea started to drip onto my lap. Then out of my mental fog I heard Dr. Fuller's commanding voice.

"Man, get up so you won't get wet!"

I quickly pushed back my chair and stood staring at my tea-spotted trousers, feeling really dumb, thinking, "This is awful! Right in front of Dr. Fuller, my mentor."

However, somehow, lunch was salvaged after Mama Fuller helped with the cleanup. And I managed to calm my nerves enough for respectful conversation, ever mindful of who I was with and what had taken place, thinking, "I don't believe I did that." Before leaving, I quickly filled in Dr. Fuller on my life since graduation, including career changes, and the reason I was attending UMKC that summer, thankful that my trouser fabric was fast-drying as Mama Fuller joined us at the door.

Dr. Fuller appeared proud of me, as I saw him as an impressive figure to emulate. Over the passing years I have assessed the huge magnitude of his influence on my personal and professional life inspiring my efforts for excellence. But on the drive back, I kept wondering what he must have thought of me sitting there paralyzed watching iced tea dripping onto my lap.

A year later, Dr. Fuller retired, an important decision he failed to mention during my visit. A special retirement event was scheduled by the university on a date I could not attend. So, disappointed, I hastily composed and sent a mailgram that was intended for reading during the program. It read:

"Being as I am, a man of action and few words, it is at this time that I wish the reverse. But how exactly does one find adequate words to express immense gratitude for having been influenced, guided, and inspired by you; provided access to your knowledge, wisdom, human generosity, and the refined black model for us to emulate; and being exposed to your musical genius through teaching and conducting; all

attributes you freely gave as you crossed the paths of hundreds of students like me. Thank you and best wishes for your retirement."

Not long afterward, I learned about the death of Mama Fuller, followed a short time later by his daughter Pat's death in an automobile accident on the way home from visiting him. She was a music senior when I was a freshman, and I recalled her senior piano recital with her signing my program afterwards. Tragically, Dr. Fuller suffered immensely from those closely occurring losses and never completely recovered.

In my last phone conversation with him, he was as articulate, courteous, joyous, and professional as ever, but obviously did not recognize who I was. I kept talking and we had a delightful conversation, but I knew his once impeccable memory had begun to fail.

Dr. Fuller died one year after my appointment as Dean of the USF College of Fine Arts, a position for which he was a profound source of inspiration and preparation.

He was, and continues to be, an exceptional model to emulate.

Chapter 10

Gentle Wind

There we were, March 1, 1959, mentally and physically exhausted.

Standing front and center stage with my tuba in-hand and Fred next to the grand piano, bowing, looking out into the vast mostly empty auditorium. The glaring lights were keeping us from seeing clearly the people who were enthusiastically applauding, trying to sound like more than they really were. We glanced at each other with tentative smiles, happy for this moment.

I had just completed my senior recital, a crucial final test for the Bachelor's degree in music at Lincoln University, and Fred was my piano accompanist. I felt very good about our performance.

The recital also represented the capstone presentation of my arduous four years of tuba study under Professor Marshall M. Penn, also my mentor. I could see him out of the corner of my eye standing stage right, smiling proudly, waiting for us to exit after the applause ended. We would soon be joined by others, congratulating us for our achievement.

Four years earlier, I met Professor Penn for the first time to acquire a sousaphone for my solo performance for the freshmen orientation talent show. "Hello. Welcome," he pleasantly greeted me while sitting at his desk in a white shirt, dark trousers and narrow tie. "I have been expecting to see you," "Oh?" I responded. "Yes," he went on, "I listened to your audition tape. I teach brass and percussion instruments, and I'm director of band and orchestra." Not knowing what to say after that I explained why I was there.

Asking me to follow him to the instrument storage room, I took casual note of his broad proportioned six-foot frame and bald spot at the back of his head. His walk was purposeful, propelled by steady legs and large feet in thick-soled shoes. "Thank you. I'll bring it back right after the program," I said, putting the instrument over my shoulder. He smiled warmly and responded, "I wish you the best for your performance."

Later that evening, when I returned the instrument, Professor Penn advised me: "All instrumental music students are required to be in the band or orchestra each semester. And the marching band starts next week. So, come by the wardrobe room and pick up your uniform as soon as possible." Well, okay, I thought, after orientation's intimidating social agenda at least that's something familiar and exciting to look forward to.

The following day I entered the fortress-like Old Memorial Hall, went to the second-floor uniform storage room, entered, and was immediately struck by the spectacular panoramic view I faced through large windows. I was looking down the tree-shroud, grass covered hill towards the University's main entrance through which I entered just days earlier. I stood for a moment taking it all in before Professor Penn interrupted.

"That's a nice view, isn't it? Welcome again. Come on over, let's see if I can get you fitted," as he pulled out the tape and began measuring my waist.   Except for an old wooden office desk and matching chair, the room was bare.

"I understand you are from Bastrop, Louisiana, where Mr. Strickland, one of our alumni, is the band director. Tell me a little bit about your home," continuing the conversation as he pulled a uniform from the crudely built closets.

"It's a small paper-mill town," was my short response, wondering how he knew that about me.

"What is the population?" he quickly followed up, probably sensing my shyness already.

And that's how the dialogue went that day: questions, short answers. By the time I was suited up, he had gleaned tidbits of information from my reticent responses. However, during the abbreviated conversation I had digested desperately desired things about him: kind eyes, genuine spirit, congenial attitude and warm smile, relieving some lingering anxieties and loneliness.

Turning to academic-related business, he indicated, "You will be having private tuba lessons with me, one hour each week, which I'm looking forward to. Come by my office to arrange a time after your class schedule is set."

"Weekly lessons? With him?" I thought. "Wow, this college business is serious."

And as I was preparing to leave with uniform in hand, Professor Penn's final words were, "Please let me know if I can help you with anything at any time while you're here at Lincoln. Help with anything whatsoever."

Walking down the stairs and out onto the campus quad, his soft voice still with me, a relaxing sensation swept through me that I had not felt since arriving on campus. At that moment, I sensed there was at least one person, an adult authority, a non-intimidating teacher at Lincoln—an angel of mercy—of whom I could avail myself, and trust.

Walking into the gymnasium for class registration the next day, I panicked. Panning the large student-packed facility and hearing their deafening voices, it seemed like total chaos. "What am I supposed to do here?" came my frantic thought. However, above the talking heads, I made out an instructive sign: MUSIC COURSES. Working my way over, I discovered a line of students leading to the sign where Professor Penn stood handing out class-assignment cards. When I joined the line and reached his post, he again welcomed me to Lincoln and gave me my class cards explaining, "These cards provide you information about the time and place for your music classes." Adding softly while smiling, "And don't forget to come by my office on Monday to set a time for your tuba lessons."

"Thank you," I said as I left, excited, and a little anxious, anticipating my first private sousaphone lesson, though he said *tuba*, lesson with him.

Leaving the building, sunlit by large westerly windows, I glanced around observing the hard bleachers on the building's east side where I would eventually sit and cheer for our basketball team, and hear concerts by Dave Brubeck, George Shearing and Duke Ellington—totally in awe of Ellington, the revered Black musical icon, continuing to grow my own jazz lexicon.

Monday morning, I awoke feeling anxious anticipating attending my first college classes. And anxiety was still prevalent when I went to

Professor Penn's office to arrange my sousaphone lessons. His large office served as a traditional classroom and private lesson studio. The idea of one-on-one lessons with him was intriguing, not knowing what to expect and what would be expected of me. I knocked, the door swung open, and he greeted me with that warm smile as if saying, "Welcome to a wonderful and enjoyable world of learning." And then he announced, "I have something here you might be interested in," pointing to a sparkling, brand-new, gold-plated concert tuba displayed in its open case on the floor next to his desk.

I stood there stunned, mouth open.

"Well, what do you think?" he said, breaking the silence. "We needed to give you something better to play. Something that's better than the sousaphone for solo and concert work."

I didn't know what to say but, "Thanks, that really looks great. I can't wait to play it," uttered while I gradually approached the instrument and slowly raised it from the case. The upright bell-front tuba was a recent design for concert bands, and as I later discovered, it was indeed a substantial improvement from the sousaphone I played since tenth grade—easier to produce quality tones, and play in tune.

"Now," I thought, "this private lesson business is getting off to a great start."

Given a key to the instrument storage room where it would be kept, I was ready to start playing it, a meaningful phase for my continuing development, and signaling my teacher's compassion.

Professor Marshall Miller Penn was in the early stage of Doctoral study at the University of Michigan in 1947, when Dr. Fuller appointed him to the Lincoln music department to expand and enhance the instrumental music curriculum and serve as band and orchestra director.

His assignments included teaching instrumental conducting, music education and music history classes, along with providing private studio lessons for all brass and percussion students.

Born April 9, 1921, in Kansas City, Kansas, Penn attended high school in St. Joseph, Michigan. After serving in the U.S. Army during World War II, he returned home and earned his Bachelor's and Master's degrees in music education at the University of Michigan.

College music studio classes are weekly, one-hour, one-on-one lessons for music students, enrolled in each year while pursuing a degree. The three years of studio tuba lessons with Professor Penn (as he was on sabbatical my sophomore year) were the most profound learning and nurturing experiences at Lincoln. They were intimate settings for ongoing dialogue and sharing, including detailed discussions of music and musical expression, methodical approaches for technical development, and counseling regarding personal issues.

In spite of my shy nature, during those lessons, Professor Penn extracted enormous personal details that provided him insight that helped guide my artistic, academic, and personal development. He quickly found out how passionate I was about music and playing the tuba. And, he became aware that I had the self-discipline required for mastering technical performance qualities, which meant he would not have to worry about my motivation for music studies or regular practice. Through subtly peeling back the protective layers of my innermost self over time, he was able to influence many aspects of my education at Lincoln, even serving as surrogate parent during my difficult freshmen year. He was my go-to source for questions and concerns.

The studio lessons allowed us to explore many musical unknowns and choices regarding the tuba, one of the last instruments invented for the Symphony Orchestra in 1835. And unlike the other older instruments, it was without clearly defined and well-known pedagogy, or "how to" technical performance knowledge. William Bell, tuba player with the New York Philharmonic, and Arnold Jacobs with the Chicago Symphony, the country's highest regarded tuba professionals, were teaching select students at the time, but how and what they taught was not generally shared or known. So much of this type of technical information is traditionally passed on over generations through apprenticeships, such as private lessons and master classes. To a great extent, that left Professor Penn and me to chart our own course in my studio lessons. However, thankfully, I was to later study with both Bell and Jacobs (more details later).

Professor Penn brought years of advanced trombone study and musicianship, and I brought my natural instincts and what I learned earlier through trial and error, together defining what worked best. As for interpreting the music, he allowed me much latitude, but offered helpful suggestions. "How do you feel about ending that phrase a little softer," he might ask as I prepared a solo, suggesting I try that approach to see how it sounded and felt.

His low-key teaching method and trust in my judgment challenged me to think and feel the music while considering alternatives that might be closer to the composers' intentions, though with limited musical knowledge at the time, this was intuitive and from general musical listening.

Solos were the primary focus of our tuba lessons, from which I learned the technical necessities and nuances for the musical objective. And similar to Mr. Strickland, my high school music teacher, Professor Penn set no boundaries for what was possible on the tuba, always placing the primary emphasis on playing musically.

"What are you trying to say in this eight-measure phrase? It's not saying much to me," he critiqued my playing, as I was polishing off Leo Sowerby's *Chaconne* for a seminar performance. It was an easy piece technically, but the extended melody implied emotional intent, and I needed to think and feel as a pianist, violinist or cellist would, while playing a very delicate melodic line. This is not easily done on the tuba.

Professor Penn and I soon discovered the lack of credible published solos for advanced tuba players. So, to compensate, he borrowed music from the solo repertoire of other instruments, transcribing them as needed. They included Bach's unaccompanied *Suite* for cello, Stravinsky's *Berceuse* from the *Firebird Suite* for bassoon, Mozart's *Horn Concertos*, and Handel's bass solos (voice) from *The Messiah*. He guided me expertly through mastering each composition before I played them on a performance seminar, where I was a regular.

Years later, I learned that during the same time frame that Professor Penn and I were liberating the tuba from its musical confinement, there were also others doing the same. And in the 1970s, that thrust resulted in a period fondly designated "The Tuba Renaissance," officially launched in 1973 at the first International Tuba Symposium hosted by Indiana University's School of Music. By then, I was the new tuba professor at the University of South Florida, and attended the inaugural event bringing two of my students with me. The "Renaissance" sparked some notable composers' interest in writing solo works for the tuba, and providing challenging new music for my USF students.

Professor Penn also taught music history, a survey course of music from antiquity through modern, required for all music students.

"Mr. Smith, how would you generally describe the music of the early classical period, say, the music of Haydn and early Mozart?" he asked me once in class, addressing students by full name or title and surname.

My response was in the ballpark, but a foul ball in the left field stands.

"Well, that's good." He smiled at me, "But let's see if we can dig a little deeper into that." He didn't embarrass me for my shortcoming, or any of us for incorrect or incomplete responses. Instead, he used the moment to spur deeper thought into the topic.

A serious, no-nonsense taskmaster, not catering to excuses, Professor Penn was intense though outwardly relaxed, demanding but encouraging, always showing sincere empathy for student efforts. Well prepared for all of his diverse assignments, he appeared to know exactly what he wanted to accomplish, constantly challenging us to believe that with hard work anything was possible, a cultural aspect of HBCU institutions.

Sometimes, to enhance our learning, Professor Penn arranged off-campus experiences, including public-school class observations, attending off-campus events and performing with community music ensembles. "I'm going to take you with me to visit Jefferson City High School," he announced one day. "I've arranged for you to observe a band rehearsal." He drove me to the all-white school in his pride-and-joy 1953 Buick Special Coupe, staying with me the whole time. During the drive over he pointed out things I should look for in the rehearsal. And on the return trip, we evaluated the experience to examine the most valuable takeaways, most notable, teaching methods and rehearsal protocol.

But in case he felt he was a little too intense, as I exited the car that day, he said, "Keep up the good work, Mr. Smith. If you continue to work hard, you'll do just fine here at Lincoln. You'll succeed in music, but also in life." That put a smile on my face and provided a motivational kick.

In my band conducting class with music pouring loudly from the portable record player on his desk, we students stood in rows around the room behind waist-high stands holding music scores, while Professor Penn moved energetically between us waving his arms in sync with the music, exclaiming reassuringly "Yes! Yes! Yes! You can do it!" encouraging our tentative efforts.

"Mr. Smith, look ahead. You must cue the oboe for its entrance," he pointed out in one class, sensing I was behind in reading the score. "Ah, you missed it. You must remember to look ahead, to lead, not follow the musicians." Exasperated, I looked ahead, only to lose my place in the score entirely. But I'm always thankful for his critiques, because they clearly defined a benchmark from which I had to improve.

However, I learned most of the finer points of conducting through studying Professor Penn when he was conducting our band and orchestra for rehearsals and concerts. Slightly bent over the music stand, his hands articulated the music's beat, while also gesturing cues for instruments to enter. Softly singing various parts and giving verbal directions, his long, outstretched arms resembled wings attempting to lift his body airborne. Every move and critical observation he made became my own—to recall and use when I'm on the podium.

For Professor Penn's marching band technique and pageantry class, my halftime show was based on the popular 1956 movie, *Giant*, starring Rock Hudson and Elizabeth Taylor, arranging the movie's musical theme for band. "It sure would be nice to see my show actually performed on the football field by a live band after all of this hard work," I thought sadly. But our marching band season had already ended.

Professor Penn was on sabbatical during my sophomore year, replaced by David Baker, a young doctoral student from Indiana University (more on him in the next chapter). And I really missed his encouraging and nurturing presence after a productive and fulfilling freshman year. However, when I walked into my first tuba lesson after he returned for my junior year, he announced gleefully, "I have something for you," followed by a short silence for dramatic effect. "I've obtained a service award for you that waives your out-of-state tuition." "Wow, Mr. Penn. Thank you," standing frozen in place, eyes wide, mouth half open. "That'll really make my parents happy." "I need your assistance with managing the band and orchestra," he explained, "to set up the chairs and stands, pass out music, and serve as student conductor for the two ensembles. Warm-up and tune them for rehearsals. And conduct them in my absence."

That last responsibility, "conduct them in my absence," expanded my chest, but nerves quickly kicked in as I recalled that faculty sometimes joined the ensembles. "Thank you, thank you so much, Mr. Penn" was my joyous response. "I'll do my best."

Later that night, after a bit of devilish ruminating, I decided not to tell my parents about the tuition award. Instead, I pocketed the difference after paying my university fees with the check they had given me. "This is some more pocket change for movies, late-night snacks, and chili and hamburgers (pickles only) at the Blue Tiger," I cheerfully thought. But when Mama and Daddy received the university invoice noting the out-of-state fee waiver, a tense phone conversation ensued, with my mother demanding an explanation. "What do you mean, not telling us about the waiver?" she shouted. "You think money grows on trees around here?" I am sure that at least a few strands of the signature twisted top knot of hair on her head shook loose as she condemned my action, spinning me into embarrassment and dejection.

I don't know why I thought I could get away with that sleight-of-hand scheme anyway, but I guess I thought it was worth the risk. Mama and Daddy simply reduced the monthly discretionary cash they usually sent me in equal proportion to the waiver. So, nothing was gained except a good verbal thrashing.

For the marching band each fall football season, Professor Penn faced a growing dilemma. Most historically Black college bands had over 100 members, including our main football rivals: Langston University in Oklahoma, and Tennessee State in Nashville. And down at Florida A&M University (FAMU), the Marching 100 was the trailblazer for setting the Black "mega band" standard, well over one- hundred. At Lincoln, we were more like the "Strolling 45," if that.

The large HBCU bands achieved their size mostly by awarding scholarships or other financial incentives, while Lincoln did not offer any financial assistance for the band, or other purposes. Our band was made up of music students mostly, including voice and piano majors who had played an instrument in high school, and other university student volunteers. Yet, large or small, a halftime show was expected for our football games and Professor Penn took the responsibility, seriously.

So, his challenge was to somehow present a halftime show that would not call overt attention to the band's small size, tackling the problem as though "small" was "normal," and limited pageantry was an asset; making do with what he had, never showing frustration. It was the willing and enthusiastic students, led by the determined and capable Professor Penn. "Okay, listen up," we often heard him say in rehearsals, hat on, scarf around his neck tucked beneath his black overcoat, walking hastily to and fro with the show's outline in his hand. "Keep the lines straight as you're moving between formations." The show would go on, with Professor Penn attempting the miraculous with humility, grace, and aplomb. For me, that was a great lesson in commitment and adaptability to achieve goals and satisfy expectations.

However, Professor Penn inexplicably took the "challenged" marching band to Nashville for Tennessee State University's homecoming game; like Jonah venturing into the mouth of the whale, or David confronting Goliath. It was so cold during the homecoming parade we could not perform music for fear that our lips may freeze on the metal mouthpieces. But I don't recall being embarrassed for our half-time show because of our size. That 438-mile bus trip, problematic as it was, may have been an incentive or reward for our band's dedicated effort that year.

With me spending so much time with Professor Penn in the music department, including classes, rehearsals and work assignments, my music department cohorts fondly referred to me as "Penn Junior." Of course, that was a badge of honor for me, but I played it down, modestly. Most importantly, I was benefiting greatly from the relationship: absorbing his knowledge and expertise, receiving his advice and counsel, and being motivated by his constant encouragement.

Of course, there were many general education and elective classes I was required to complete for my degree, and several were disasters, although not failures. When not in class and ensemble rehearsals, I was either at the library, in my dorm room studying and listening to classical music on a small portable record player, or in the Fine Arts Building practicing the tuba, piano and other instruments.

Social life, a relatively low priority for me, included attending cultural events, basketball games, movies and a few dances to hear the student combo, not very encouraging quantities for social development. During my freshman year, heavily partying dorm mates left a note under my door castigating me for not joining them. Unfortunately, many of them were academically ineligible by the end of the year. So, my social apathy probably contributed to my academic survival that year.

Music was clearly dominating my university life. And since shyness limited my dating, and social fraternities were not beating down my door with invitations, that left more time for music studies. The few Lincoln co-eds with whom I managed dates, unfortunately, found me boring, distracted, and unversed in the current macho attitude and jargon.

One very attractive freshman from St. Louis and I seemed to make eye-to-eye connections my junior year while leaving a university assembly. When I saw her again, I invited her to a Saturday evening social at the recreation center. Turns out, the sheltered young lady was at Lincoln looking for an assertive and ambitious upperclassman with excellent financial prospects to marry. However, that rather awkward date convinced her I wasn't the one.

So, just as Duke Ellington admitted in the title of his book, *Music is My Mistress*, (Da Capo Press, 1976), if you substituted a girlfriend for a mistress, that summed up my social life. And growing socially, an important part of the college experience, was exactly what my Uncle Jap back home was continually encouraging me to do, but I wasn't helping much.

Oh well, anyway, I went to Lincoln on a serious mission: to become a school band director. And there were people I left in Bastrop, foremost my parents, who were hoping, praying, and paying for my success. I didn't intend on disappointing them. If sacrifices had to be made, including social development, so be it.

Entering my first tuba studio lesson my junior year after Professor Penn's return from sabbatical, I was greeted with that now familiar gregarious smile. "Next week," he joyously announced, "you will be joining me with the Jefferson City Symphony as the tuba player." "Oh? What do you mean?" I responded, only vaguely aware of the orchestra. "I've been a member for a couple of years, but seeing that they didn't have a regular tuba player I recommended you to Maestro Burkel as my student. He gave his approval."

The band was the extent of my large music ensemble experience on the tuba. Lincoln had a small orchestra, but I did not play tuba with it because of its size and limited musical capability. However, I was very familiar with the symphony orchestra sound from classical music recordings dating back to those my sister, Barbara, bought for me when I was in high school. It's a sound I fell in love with immediately. And now I get to play tuba in one. "What's that going to be like?" my anxious mind queried. "You'll be riding with me to transport the tuba," Professor Penn interrupted. "Rehearsals are once a week at night."

My first rehearsal found me distracted initially, sitting in the middle of what I customarily hear coming out of a record player's speaker. Lush strings, mellow woodwind and edgy brass, sounds of infinite beauty swirling around me, momentarily catching me up in its aesthetic power. And then the reality of performing within that realm, playing the tuba part that had its own voice, though often with another instrument. With my tuba, I sat in the middle of this explosive beauty with Maestro Carl Burkel leading its nuances. And when it was time for the tuba to play, he pointed at me. This was a musical experience like no other. The music I had a natural affinity for, and the instrument I love to play, all merging as one.

The Jefferson City Symphony, a semi-professional orchestra, represented higher performance standards and expectations, which, with Professor Penn's coaching, I managed to meet. Although, during the two years I was with the orchestra, it did not perform music that had particularly challenging tuba parts. But more important and unrecognized by me, this was the embryonic phase for my later change of musical focus.

I believe that Professor Penn's progressive deed was more than a near-term gesture. At that time (1957-59), most Black Americans with musical interests were aware that professional careers in classical music performance had only recently begun to open for African-Americans in the United States. Historical racist restrictions had made those paths off-limits for our hopes and dreams. Yes, opera's doors had been pushed slightly ajar with contralto Marian Anderson (1955), baritone Robert McFerrin (1955) and soprano Gloria Davy (1956) performing with the Metropolitan Opera. But professional American Symphony Orchestras were composed of white men, exclusively. So, perhaps Professor Penn thought that sometime in the near future that racial barrier should be challenged, interjecting a Black face among the white men, perhaps a tuba player named John Smith.

Continuing his nurturing efforts, Professor Penn invited me and two other music classmates to his nearby home for dinner during a four-day Thanksgiving holiday weekend when most university students went home. I looked forward to the home-cooked meal, but also to being around him in an informal setting, giving me the opportunity to learn more about his broader humanity.

When we arrived at his house that evening, Professor Penn directed us into his small neatly arranged, modestly furnished living room where we sat quietly on an L-shaped sofa around an old bass drum lying flat on its side, artistically adapted as a coffee table. With understated pride, he described how he transformed the instrument into this unique and decorative furnishing, combining art and function.

Taking care of host responsibilities, he pointed out where the bathroom was located, but that information came with an unexpected twist: "That's my reading room," he said with a little broader smile than usual, "it has a magazine rack, which provides undisturbed quiet where I get a lot of reading accomplished."

Huh? Did I hear what I thought I heard? The other students and I sat looking at each other, not knowing how to respond to our august teacher's declaration of private information, while he scampered off to finish dinner preparation. However, I must admit, today, I have a sizable assortment of reading material in my own water closet where undisturbed reading is indeed accomplished.

It was a wonderful informal evening with my teacher/mentor, mostly listening out of respect for his position, yet learning by osmosis from his random thoughts that casually rolled off of him and onto me. I learned about his limited social circle, which we had in common, his major home and caregiver responsibilities due to his wife's illness, and his brother, a Howard University music professor. On the way back to our dorm that night, me and my two cohorts laughed out loud rehashing Professor Penn's bathroom/reading room story.

"Okay. Let's consider your senior recital program," Professor Penn instructed as I settled in for my first senior-year lesson in August 1958. "We have lots of music to choose from, plus anything new we learn this semester," he continued. All of the solos performed the past three years were possibilities, and my lessons would involve perfecting them and testing my memory. Since the tuba was not considered a professional solo instrument, a full-length, one-hour memorized program was not required. Thirty minutes was a satisfactory length, according to the National Association of Schools of Music guidelines, and memorization was not necessary. Well, that was totally unacceptable. With Professor Penn steering my ship, I was not going to be a second-class seaman. No way. So, when Sunday, March 1, 1959, 8 p.m. rolled around, I stepped out on stage with Fred and performed well over an hour of music, all memorized, the result of four challenging years of rigorous study and mentoring with my august teacher.

Also, during my senior year, unanswered questions about "what's next" after graduation had become complex, graduate study had become an option. It was a seed planted by Mr. Baker, Professor Penn's sabbatical substitute, and since encouraged by him. Based on their endorsements, I applied and was accepted for the Master's degree study at Indiana University. This required the ownership of a specific type of tuba for studio study in the music school, generating a phone call to my parents who had only recently agreed to partially financing my graduate study. Not explaining their financial situation, they said "okay." Aided through the purchase process by Professor Penn, he and I picked up the instrument at the local music store the next week after my recital. When I saw it, my jaw dropped, mouth open, no words came forth. It was beautiful, laid out in its hard case: dark gold polished brass, four rotary valves and etched images around the outer bell. Designed and manufactured by Miraphone, a German company known for quality professional instruments. That was one of the happiest days of my life: owning my own tuba.

Years later after my parents' passing, I was going through their private papers and discovered the astonishing facts about how they paid for my tuba. Official documents indicate that my tuba was purchased on May 21, 1959, for $1,185.90 (approximately $10,570 today) through a *chattel mortgage* from the Exchange National Bank of Jefferson City. That means, my parents secured a loan from the Jefferson City bank, the location of the tuba purchase, agreeing to a delayed payment plan during which the bank holds ownership of the instrument. My mind reeled with that knowledge. I don't recall them ever borrowing money for anything. They worked so hard for every penny, paying cash for everything, so they would be beholden to no one, particularly white establishments. Yet, they did so to help their late-blooming son pursue his unusual passion, playing the tuba.

Unbelievable!

This discovery was truly overwhelming, and I will never get over the greatness of their sacrifice.

Lincoln's May 31, 1959 commencement was the last time I performed under Professor Penn's baton, a band transcription of the *finale* from Tchaikovsky's *Fourth Symphony*. Afterwards, back in the Fine Arts Building putting away our instruments, I thanked Professor Penn for teaching and encouraging my development at Lincoln, going beyond expectations, taking a personal interest in my growth. He reached out his hand, and while shaking mine said proudly, "Congratulations Mr.

Smith. You did well. And I wish you continued success at Indiana. Let me hear from you."

Over the ensuing years, I kept Professor Penn, informed of my academic pursuits and careers: completing the Master's degree at IU, a year of teaching at Grambling State University, four years of service in the Navy and six years in Oklahoma City performing and teaching. During that period, I married and had two children. I was aware of Mrs. Dorothy Penn's continuing struggle with a chronic illness until her death, and Professor Penn's retirement and subsequent remarriage. And during my professorship at the University of South Florida beginning in 1972, now remarried and a family of seven, I visited him and his new wife, Delores, twice in their home southeast of Lincoln's campus.

My first visit in the early 1980s was indeed very emotional for both of us: me, the somewhat accomplished student and he, the teacher and mentor I owed so much credit to for whatever success I achieved. Mrs. Penn met me at the door and escorted me to the classically fashioned dining room where Professor Penn momentarily joined us in business attire minus coat, moving somewhat slowly, but displaying that wonderful, genuine smile. We sat together at the dining table and began filling each other in on the significant events in our lives. My stories were designed to honor and impress him with examples of the impact of his teaching and mentoring on my life.

During the conversation, he admitted, "I worried when you went to Indiana University if I had prepared you well enough on the tuba, and in music history and conducting." I was astounded, completely surprised at his lack of confidence in how he influenced his student's learning, me particularly. All of that nurturing time, transferring knowledge and providing support. "Yes, you prepared me quite well, Mr. Penn," I responded, realizing I significantly understated his value. "I completed the Master's degree and was the first tuba player to receive the prestigious Performer's certificate. You had a lot to do with that."

He smiled and seemed to take pride in this revelation.

"You remember the Jefferson City Symphony? I'm still playing string bass, haven't missed a season," he proudly declared now in his early 70s. "And I attend music concerts and some social events at Lincoln. But the music program is no longer what it used to be." "Yes, I'm aware of that. That's so sad," I acknowledged. We talked about the old days, including interesting anecdotes about me and some of my music schoolmates, some humorous and others more sedate.

That evening, at Mr. and Mrs. Penn's invitation, I attended a special event with them at Lincoln where Mrs. Penn, a university professor, was a program participant. And I delightfully discovered that Bobby, one of my Lincoln music student schoolmates, was working there as a vice president, spending a few minutes talking with him before I had to leave. It was a lovely evening and memorable visit, including seeing the many campus changes.

Unfortunately, by the time of my second visit several years later, Mr. Penn was struggling with dementia. The symptoms, however, did not diminish the quality of that visit for either of us. When I entered their home this time, he was sitting in the living room's wingback chair dressed in business attire (minus the coat) as before, exhibiting that broad, congenial and affectionate trademark smile.

I am not at all sure that he recognized who I was, but his welcoming expression seemed genuine. Mrs. Penn left us to chat in the spacious, fashionably furnished room, which I tried to fill with my voice, as Professor Penn added an occasional "uh-huh." I talked about my student days, other music students and faculty he might remember, what they were doing, memorable music department events, and my career.

He probably did not understand much of what I said, and for me it didn't matter. Just spending time with him was most important, an emotional apex of my life—well-spent quality time with an influential mentor, role model and teacher. And, unknown to me then, this would be our last time together. Professor Penn died on November 24, 2000, age 79. Sadly, I did not know in time to attend his funeral.

But what he gave me, unselfishly, during those four crucial years at Lincoln University and beyond has significantly influenced each and every chapter of my life's trajectory since.

Chapter 11

Ever Present

Professor Penn's sabbatical my sophomore year at Lincoln University could have been a disaster for me. He had assisted and supported my 1955 transition into college and set me on a positive progressive path, academically and personally. Yet, the freshman year was grueling and full of anxiety. I recall walking out of my last final exam thinking aloud, "Wow! This year is finally ending. I can go home!" And, as if in confirmation, in the distance I heard another student crossing the campus hill-top quad yell loudly, "Wooooheeee! Thank God. It's over!" Later that afternoon, walking across the same now quiet quad on the way to my dorm, I was tempted to shout my jubilation again loud enough for the whole campus to hear, but couldn't find the courage.

However, there was one loose end that was bothering me greatly as I prepared to leave Lincoln, I didn't know who my tuba teacher was going to be my sophomore year, replacing Professor Penn. And no one could tell me, including Mr. Penn himself. Leaving Lincoln in two days, it seems I would not find out until I return in the fall, making for a very uneasy summer at home.

Still worried, I arrived back on campus in August 1956 to rumors flying around among my music cohorts, proclaiming, "Jim said Bobby saw someone on 'The Foot' carrying a large instrument case claiming to be a new Lincoln music teacher." The Foot was the two-block commercial sector on the western edge of our campus-hill where students enjoyed eating at greasy-spoon cafes and drinking cheap beer in dark, windowless bars. Places I visited infrequently.

"Bobby said he's a young-looking guy dressed in a pinkish-purplish street outfit, talking cool and jive to everybody; waitresses, bartenders, cooks, patrons. Anybody he sees."

"Impossible!" I said. "He can't be Mr. Penn's replacement. Lincoln faculty don't go to The Foot, or dress and talk like that."

But the animated chatter continued to spread like wildfire through the music-student grapevine, introducing the possibility of a fascinating and intriguing jolt to the music department's all too familiar and comfortable culture. Frustrated, I concluded I would not know exactly who my new tuba teacher was going to be until he or she actually showed up for class. My anxiety would just have to hang in there until then.

On the first day of classes, we looked up and there he was. Astonished, we saw him, the same guy described on The Foot. He walked into the Fine Arts Building, and promptly occupied Professor Penn's studio/classroom, much to everyone's amazement. "Wow. My new tuba teacher," I thought. "Incredible." At that moment everyone—music faculty, staff and students—realized that our music department, the small, intimate family as we knew it, was in for an abrupt cultural change. Though, at the time, we did not know to what extent. I soon learned his name was David Baker, and nervously realized: "I'm having weekly tuba lessons with him. What's that going to be like?"

On my first visit to Professor Baker's office to schedule my tuba lessons, I was met with "Hey man, come on in. How's it going?" an informal greeting I was not accustomed to. His attire was casual, unlike the more formal dress of our other faculty, but not quite as the earlier rumors had described. We quickly agreed on a time, but then he queried me about my performance background: how long have you been playing tuba, etc. And I responded with short concise answers.

He was young, that part of what I heard was right. Twenty-five, not much older than my senior schoolmates. At about five-foot ten, he had a thin stature, slightly receding hairline, and noticeable bowlegs. During that first brief visit, I didn't see or hear the other unique qualities I had heard about. However, my first tuba lessons over the following several weeks revealed someone very complex, who didn't fall into simple categories.

David Baker had just started Doctoral study at Indiana University (IU) in Bloomington after completing, in rapid succession, his Bachelors (1953) and Master (1954) degrees in music education, with trombone as his primary instrument. He had grown up in the culturally rich city of Indianapolis, Indiana, about 50 miles north of IU, which boasted well-established arts institutions. He spent much of his time there on Indiana Avenue, a thriving street for Black business and entertainment. Jazz greats Wes Montgomery, Freddie Hubbard, Larry Ridley, Lester Young and J. J. Johnson were regulars at Indy clubs and bars when David was young and attending prestigious Crispus Attucks High School, founded as a high school for Black students, and known for its advanced music programs.

Enrolling at IU in 1948, he majored in music education to teach high school, the most viable career option for Black music students, while also continuing his jazz interests in Indianapolis. However, under the aggressive leadership of the School of Music's new dean, Dr. Wilfred Bain (1947-1973), outstanding artists/teachers would also prepare him well for classical music performance.

When David completed his undergraduate degree, he was at the top of his game as a trombonist and musician, but discovered quickly that professional symphony orchestras were not hiring Black musicians. The same structure existed when I graduated from IU in 1961. Desperate to continue his musical pursuits, he entered the Master's degree program at IU and boosted his jazz performance efforts in Indianapolis, with the exception of teaching one year at Lincoln University where we would, thankfully, cross paths.

"Sit down. Show me some of the music you're playing," he said for my first lesson. I placed several solos on the music stand, he quickly thumbed through them and pointed saying, "play this one for me." And we were off to a year of intriguing collaboration. Professor Baker's youthful, urban traits by earlier descriptions played out in my lessons. But as the lessons evolved, I discovered that, while unexpected because of those traits, his depth of knowledge and scholarship was absolutely on par with my other music professors. What came to light as I got to know him was that he was a smart and complex young man that lived, worked, and communicated at multiple levels, a product of both the hip, urban jazz world and higher-education's traditions and expectations.

During my lessons, he could morph quickly, chameleon-like, from friendly hipster into dead-serious instructor, and back again. Sometimes, in an elongated sentence, he started in jive dialect and transitioned smoothly to in-depth intellectual discourse before the end —an ever-changing vocabulary leading the way.

"Look Brother John, you're movin' up the wrong alley, and ain't no way that's gonna fly," he once said. "You have to consider the intricate, intrinsic modules that define the composer's visionary intent."

And, as he was of my generation, discussions came easy, and contemporary subjects were more approachable. Although, with his keen intellect and wealth of musical knowledge, artistic talent and musicianship, the student and teacher roles were quite clear: he was the professor and I was the student.

My lessons were devoted to solo works, primarily, avoiding any pedagogy that might conflict with Professor Penn's approach. We explored the solos Professor Penn assigned previously, and ventured into a few new compositions. Professor Baker was often complimentary of my playing, making mostly stylistic suggestions, serving more as coach than instructor.

When I premiered one of fellow student-composer John Price's extremely difficult solo pieces in a performance seminar, Professor Baker provided critical advice regarding its contemporary characteristics. After the seminar, he passed me looking bemused, acknowledging that I had managed to pull off the intricate performance, perhaps, beyond expectations.

Professor Baker's office/studio was on the busy hall not far from the second-floor lobby, a busy section of the Fine Arts Building. He often kept his door open and in between, or when he didn't have classes, he sometimes stepped into the hall for informal chats with students, his youth bringing new energy to the music department's culture, and increasing the social banter. Even the weekly student performance seminar lost some of its reserved nature, resulting in less anxiety for performers. The faculty traditions of conservative dress and proper speech and manners were tested, and the interjection of jazz, R&B and gospel into conversations was no longer taboo.

Professor Baker embodied the coexistence of Euro/classical traditions and the new, improvisational jazz expression as equally valid—not often acknowledged during that time, in academia, particularly at Lincoln. However, he strongly encouraged students with jazz interests to pursue the genre and not be deterred by the music department's prohibition.

So, it was not a surprise when Professor Baker produced a special jazz performance during the spring semester that encouraged campus-wide participation, I assumed with Dr. Fuller's approval. He arranged a composition for an expanded jazz ensemble, augmented with assorted percussion instruments, necessitating the performers spilling off the small Page Auditorium stage into the first row of seats. He didn't write a tuba part, so I watched with curiosity and amusement from the auditorium's balcony, recalling my high school band director Mr. Strickland introducing us to jazz. The music was energized extensively by the Afro-Cuban rhythms arranged for the diverse percussion instruments played mostly by non-music students.

After a tuba lesson near the end of my sophomore year and his one-year appointment, I was sitting with my tuba resting on the floor putting my music away, when Professor Baker made an unexpected proposal.

"Why don't you transfer to Indiana University next year?" he asked.

"Uh, what?" I stuttered, stopping physical motions and looking over at him.

"You ought to go to IU next year. - your junior year."

"Well...I don't know," trying to figure what that means in speed-dial.

"You are competitive with the students there, and I think you would have a lot to gain."

I stared at him, curiously. Still wondering about the unknown, and not able to ask the right questions.

"Transferring won't be a problem. I'll help you," he continued. "And, IU has great graduate programs if you decide to continue studying."

Going to IU, or any other school, was something that had never come to mind. Lincoln's music department had become a deeply encouraging and nurturing home where I was growing musically and personally, building the confidence I needed as an individual and African-American. Plus, I was grooving along comfortably through my sophomore year, focused on completing my degree on schedule and teaching high school band, perhaps back in my home state of Louisiana.

But he was my teacher, and his proposal at least deserved consideration.

"Well, I appreciate the thought, Mr. Baker. Please let me think about it."

But what was there to think about? I knew my parents, the college-purse-string comptrollers, would quickly nix the idea with little or no thought. My mother's signature twisted-top-knot hair would surely fly loose from vigorous headshaking.

"No, no, no, no. No!" I could hear her saying. "Finish up where you are!"

A few days later, I approached Professor Baker in the hall.

"Well, about your suggestion to transfer, Mr. Baker. I don't believe it's a good idea for me right now. There are too many things that would make it difficult. But thanks a lot for your confidence."

Only seconds passed before he countered with, "Oh, that's okay. But you should seriously consider going to IU for your master's when you graduate from Lincoln. I think you would really want to do that."

Oh nooooo! I thought. *I am not getting off the hook easily. I must give blood! Continue school? Graduate study?*

I couldn't imagine that.

But now David Baker, the man who had arrived at Lincoln just months earlier under a suspicious cloud, had planted the idea of graduate study in my mind. It was a completely unanticipated and frightening proposition—one that I was inclined to provide a flippant response to like, "Maybe a few years later, somewhere down the road. I'll give you a call."

But at the very least, he deserved a diplomatic response.

"Oh my, well, that's an interesting thought," I dodged. "But graduation's a couple of years away, so I have time to think about it and see if that's what I want to do."

"Well, if you decide you want to attend IU, let me know," he said. "I can help make that happen."

I thought that would be the end of that subject. "Continuing school? Not me. Enough time in classrooms."

But the seed was now planted firmly under soil made fertile by my education-championing parents. And there was no escaping its presence in my subconscious, no matter how hard I tried. The idea continued to germinate during my junior year, and I discussed it with my parents that summer before returning to Lincoln for summer school before my senior year.

"Okay, sounds good, but hold on a minute," was their response. "Let's finish up the undergraduate degree. One step at a time. Let's not get ahead of ourselves."

The underlying message I heard was: late-bloomer son need not get too ambitious. One goal at a time. They were also cautious because, outside of music, my grades were just above average, not very impressive.

I was now juggling conflicting emotions. "That's a frightening unknown adventure, attending a large white university with escalated standards. But a Master's degree can possibly give me better school teaching options," I anxiously thought. I discussed graduate study with Professor Penn the fall of my senior year, receiving encouragement, and again with my parents during Christmas break. With no job prospects for after graduation, I cautiously suggested a solution: "I could go to St. Louis or Chicago where I'm told public school jobs are plentiful!" To which my protective parents replied: "Well, we don't think that's a good idea. So, if you really want to attend IU for working on your Master's degree, we'll assist you as best we can," visualizing the horrors of the big urban city.

Now there was no backing away from David Baker's proposal planted almost two years earlier; graduate study at IU had now become my new reality. Fear and anxiety would just have to roll on with me to this new adventure.

I phoned David Baker excited to report I was ready for graduate study at IU, if he was still willing to assist me.

"All right, I'll get right on it, get things rolling and contact some people here. You'll be getting information. Talk to you later." Application and subsequent admission quickly followed.

After graduation from Lincoln, and before I had a chance to hideout in Siberia, August 1959 found me on the beautiful Indiana University campus, welcomed graciously to the music school. I discovered David was no longer at IU, but in Indianapolis leading his own jazz band and pursuing professional opportunities. So, I didn't see him that first year, which was quite intense, adjusting to the new environment and increased demands. And although the degree I pursued was in music education, tuba performance increasingly dominated my focus (more on the IU experience in the next chapter).

My second year at IU included a wife, Janietta Robinson, the result of a whirlwind romance my senior year at Lincoln. We arrived on campus in a 1960 Chevrolet Corvair, a gift from my generous father. We agreed that he would make the monthly payments for one year, and after that it was my responsibility. The car was a major asset at IU, and for the next several years.

In a phone conversation with David early that year, he extended an invitation to visit him: "You have to come on up to Indianapolis so I can see you, man. And you can check out what I'm doing," Having a car, I jumped at the opportunity.

I scheduled my trip to include a visit to the prestigious Crispus Attucks High School to observe the extensive music program I heard so much about from David and others. It was indeed impressive. Late that afternoon found me excitedly sitting on the side of a small room of an Indiana Avenue nightclub where I watched David energetically exhort his jazz musicians through the intricate harmonic and rhythmic nuances of his new compositions. I recall one particular chart that entailed a fast scale pattern, starting with high trumpet notes down to the deepest notes on baritone sax and bass trombone, seamlessly incorporating the entire band. And I thought, "Wouldn't it be great to have ended that scale with a tuba," which, unfortunately, was not part of the instrumentation.

In late nineteenth-century jazz groups, the sousaphone or tuba was often part of the rhythm section, but used only occasionally in modern jazz arrangements. Three excellent examples recorded in 1949 are Denzil Best's *Move*, George Wallington's *Godchild*, and B. Powell/ Miles Davis' *Budo*, all performed by Miles Davis' nine-piece all-star ensemble with John Barber on tuba (The Best of Miles Davis: The Capitol/Blue Note Years, 1992).

It was revealing to observe the love and enthusiasm David poured into his music, demonstrating the embryonic stage of his personal style, characterizing his later jazz and classical compositions.

David's professional jazz exploits during the next several years included performances and recordings with George Russell, Wes Montgomery, and other bebop trailblazers. George Russell's album, *Outer Thoughts* (Milestone Records, 1975), probably best demonstrates David's remarkable trombone technique and artistry at its peak. But the longest and most stable part of his career occurred at IU, his alma mater.

North Texas State University (now University of North Texas) offered its first jazz course in 1947. A Jazz Studies degree program followed several years later, the first for a university. IU School of Music established its jazz studies department in August 1966, appointing David Baker as its Inaugural Chairman. Within two years, the Bachelor of Music Degree in Jazz Studies was approved, followed years later by

Master's and Doctorate degrees. During his long, productive tenure, he received numerous national awards and accolades, including the prestigious Kennedy Center for the Performing Arts' *Living Jazz Legend Award*. IU also recognized his academic achievements with designations as Distinguished Professor and Chair Emeritus.

After completing the Master's Degree at IU, I returned home to Bastrop for a couple of weeks before leaving for my first professional job as principal tuba player with the Aspen Music Festival Orchestra, lasting eleven-weeks in the beautiful Rocky Mountains (more on this in the next chapter). Initially thinking that my first teaching job would be at a high school, I secured a music faculty appointment at Grambling College (now Grambling State University), about an hour's drive from Bastrop. My parents were pleased with the close location, and I took advantage of the short drive.

During that year, I attended the Music Educators National Conference (Now the National Association for Music Education) Convention in Chicago. And as I was chowing down on barbecue pork ribs and collard greens for lunch at a popular Southside soul food restaurant, I looked up to see David Baker doing the same thing at a table across the room. I immediately set my bones aside and skirted around several tables to get to him.

"Hey, good to see you, man. It's been too long" he blurted out as we did the man-hug. "What are you doing in Chicago?"

We discovered that we were both there for the MENC convention. I quickly brought him up to date about where I was and what I was doing. He explained his convention presence: "I'm involved in several sessions on jazz education in secondary schools, trying to stress the importance." It was a short but delightful visit before we both had to finish lunch and hurry off to our next scheduled convention sessions. He seemed happy and content, but his usual personable self. Over the years, the MENC has certainly recognized him for his steadfast contributions to jazz education.

The year at Grambling ended with a military draft notice, which sent me to the nearest Navy recruiting station as the best option for my professional and personal future (more on this in a later chapter). Time seemed to pass slowly during this period. However, after being honorably discharged for four-years of service, I was appointed principal tuba player with the Oklahoma City Symphony. Responding to financial needs, I acquired a faculty position at Langston University, a historically Black institution established in 1897, only a one-hour drive north. I was promoted to music department chairman and director of the University's Lyceum Program for arranging campus professional arts and cultural events.

During those years, David Baker had been in an auto accident that caused a severe head injury, making him unable to play the trombone. But this did not alter his musical zeal. He quickly mastered the cello, performing jazz and classics, while more diligently composing new music. His classical music compositions were demonstrative of melding Euro/Western style and jazz concepts into one aesthetic expression.

During my five years as Langston's Lyceum Director, the artists I brought to campus included the great actress, Ruby Dee; pianist Sir Roland Hanna; the Modern Jazz Quartet; the Cannonball Adderley Quintet; The Fifth Dimension with my Lincoln schoolmate Ron Townsend; the Oklahoma City Symphony Orchestra featuring Black guest conductor, Paul Freeman and piano soloist, Eugene Haynes; and, of course, David Baker's touring IU Jazz Band. David and I spent brief but quality time together during their visit.

On the day of Cannonball Adderley's concert, I arrived at Langston to find him studying the music department's bulletin board in the hall next to my office. After discussing the logistics for his concert, I strengthened my nerves and blurted out: "Could you and the other members of your quintet spend some time with my students after the concert?"

"Okay. Be happy to," was the exuberant response.

The concert was spectacular, and the students were flipped out for weeks after their intimate late-night encounter with Cannonball and his quintet.

My tenure as music department chairman at Langston was remarkably life transforming. The time period, 1966-1972, was during the national thrust for Black identity, racial equality and social justice, a period some refer to as the "Black Revolution." Caught in the momentum, and interacting constantly with my racially sensitized and energized students, I was confronted with the conflict between my Western European musical, cultural and educational influences, and an identity that was inherently and ethnically African-American.

Related past experiences were contributing to my personal introspection and changing perspective. This included thoughts about racist experiences while growing up in the Deep South, and the progressive counter-activism I witnessed by family and mentors. I recalled Mr. Strickland's defiant introduction of jazz to his high school students, and the stealth racial equality tactics of Mr. Adams, my high school principal. Anger resurfaced while recalling the racism I experienced in the US Navy and experienced in pursuing a career as a symphony orchestra musician. And I continued facing racial hostilities in Oklahoma City where I lived, motivating me to cofound the Black Liberated Arts Center (BLAC, Inc.).

At Langston, a HBCU, those powerful prevailing circumstances forced me to open my ears to listen and absorb anew, the music loved by my students: blues, R&B, soul and gospel. This was music that profoundly expressed my Black heritage, but I had been taught to ignore and disparage most of my life.

Listening intently to the passionate voices of the explosive national Black movement required that I assess my identity to discover who I was behind the learned veneer of cultural denial. And facing the mirror now placed in front of me, I discovered that the monumental revolution was about me, my identity. My Black identity. My *ignored* identity. Consequently, the new image I faced in the mirror provoked me to defend, support and promote its values, my newly discovered African-American values, My Black values whenever and wherever possible. "Black power" had gained real meaning for me, demanding practical applications and an afro persona.

During that time, conversations with David, and observing his assertive leadership at IU in successfully developing the jazz studies program, led me to challenge Langston's music curricular. Jazz was a product of the Black American experience, and he was establishing a Jazz degree program at a white university. Yet, HBCU music curriculum, including at Langston, was mostly void of African-American history, culture and music. Every year, our Langston music department enrolled naturally-talented Black students into a Western-European focused music education program. But for the previous eighteen years of their lives, those freshmen were culturally grounded in Black popular, gospel and jazz music.

Their musical idols and performance models were Shirley Caesar, Aretha Franklin, James Brown, Diana Ross, Marvin Gaye, and Cannonball Adderley to name a few. Then, on their first day at Langston, we tell them that type of music was no good, not welcomed, and not worthy of serious study and performance. They were told to cast aside their cultural inheritance, disavow it, and quickly transform themselves into ideal models of Western classical music students and performers. At that point, many lost their enthusiasm, energy, and aspirations to study music, though some managed to continue on with their best effort to earn a school music teaching degree. This would at least provide them a respectable job and an upward mobile career.

I knew there was something terribly wrong with that picture, and as music department chairman with a rapidly evolving Black identity, I proclaimed, "This will not continue on my watch! Langston's music program will no longer deny the human richness inherent in the soul, culture and arts of Black people." (Reference: *The Souls of Black Folk, Du Bois, A. C. McClurg & Co., 1903*).

Changing the course requirements immediately, I added and taught an African American music history course using Eileen Southern's recently published book, *The Music of African Americans: A History* (New York: W. W. Norton & Company, 1971). And, I also established Langston Productions Unlimited, a mix-genre Black music student performance ensemble. Students were allowed to practice and perform Black music, along with classical music in teaching studios and for recitals. And I published *The Riff*, an occasional campus newsletter featuring current news and information about the music of Black Americans. I invited Oklahoma City jazz professionals as clinicians for course and curricular development, and to teach seminars.

Of course, those changes, done without university review, did not sit well with the university administration. And, although anecdotal evidence indicated heightened student enthusiasm and improved performance, things came to an abrupt halt when the university's president personally *ordered* me not to allow my studio trombone student to perform a blues number on his senior recital. In academic institutions, this is considered administrative overreach into faculty prerogative.

Well, the student performed the blues number as we planned, and at the end of the academic year I resigned as department chairman, anticipating being fired for insubordination. But since I was tenured, I would continue teaching for the foreseeable future. However, the following summer, I was recruited to teach at the University of South Florida (USF) in Tampa commencing that fall.

It was extremely emotional and difficult leaving behind my *Young, Gifted and Black* students. Through them and the occurring national Black struggle during six years at Langston, I discovered belatedly my Black identity, a major transformative experience. I acquired a new assertive self for pursuing Black justice.

Arriving at USF in August 1972, I soon learned that there was only one other Black faculty member in the music department of almost thirty professors, and a significant underrepresentation of Black students, as well. This was an abrupt racial and cultural change from the previous six years, as anticipated, but uneasy circumstances nevertheless. USF was a twelve-year-old, majority white, rapidly growing urban institution, and it was evident to me that the white faculty was uninterested in the musical contributions and influences of African-Americans, and could benefit from opportunities to confront this shortsightedness.

But to boldly attempt to rectify this racial and cultural shortcoming as a new untenured professor would have quickly ended my appointment, particularly since I was already becoming acutely aware of racist colleagues. And any aggressive effort of this sort would certainly receive defiant pushback from academic traditionalists; those who believed that Euro-Western music is the only music worth studying, teaching, and performing. In a way this was not unlike the Langston war.

However, not to be deterred, the fourth year of my tenure-earning probation I gambled on a less threatening, more stealth approach for faculty transformation, a three-to-five day visiting artist residency program for acclaimed African-American composers. The residency would include teaching classes, seminars and master classes, as well as performances of their music. Titled *The Black Composer-in-Residence Project*, I categorized it as an academic enhancement program and acquired financial support from non-music sources, avoiding possible department opposition. My secondary *unspoken* motive for the project was to motivate a student up-swell towards establishing a jazz studies program, making Black composers versed in jazz a priority. Although a jazz ensemble existed, led by faculty with limited jazz expertise, there were no plans to further develop the study of that genre. I also intended for the resident composers to serve as role models for Black students.

For the 1976 launch of my project, David Baker was ideal, having achieved national recognition for both jazz and classical music. He was followed over the next four years by Hale Smith, George Walker, Olly Wilson, T. J. Anderson, and George Russell.

"Hey David, I got this program going here at USF. Can't pay you much, but I'd sure like for you to come," was my initial phone call. "It's a three-day residency to teach and have your music performed." "Okay,

I'll do this for you," was his quick response, his residency establishing the program's model. Picking him up early mornings and shuttling him to each event, I was able to have some quality time with him. He lectured several classes, tutored student composers, presented a seminar on improvisation, rehearsed the jazz band, and coached and performed informally with a student jazz combo.

Later years we laughed (his more restrained) about how I kept him much too busy. "Hey man, can I go to the restroom?" he quipped once. A few white faculty members were accommodating, which was encouraging, but students were enthusiastic about his visit.

The major highlight of David's three-day residency was two priceless performances I arranged for him performing on cello with local professional jazz artists. The first was with John Lamb, bass (formally with Duke Ellington) and Al Downing, piano (local jazz leader and formally with the Air Force band) for an impromptu jam session for students. Familiar with David's reputation as a jazz arranger and bebop-era trombonist, they were excited about meeting and performing with him, gladly accepting my invitation. For years later they expressed their deep appreciation for the experience.

The second performance included David performing with drummer, Majid Shabazz and piano and trumpet players whose names I have since forgotten. Scheduling the performance at an East Tampa community center in the heart of the Black community was part of my continuing effort to share USF's valuable resources with Tampa's African-American community.

George Russell, David's close jazz colleague, was the last resident composer for my project, and was extremely important for his impact on increasing significantly student interest in jazz. But it took a herculean effort to convince him to accept my invitation.

"In the '50s, me and my quintet left Florida driving as fast as we could, chased by some white guys wanting us dead!" he explained anxiously over the phone. "I haven't been back since, and I'm still not interested in going back."

"I know what you're talking about," I responded. "I grew up in Louisiana. But things have changed. Look at me, I'm teaching at a white university in Tampa, and making the best of it. This Black composers' project I hope will make a difference, and bring jazz to the university."

After a short silence, with audible breathing heard through the phone, he continued, "Well, I don't care, I almost got killed."

I didn't give up, and after many phone conversations (glad he didn't stop taking my calls), he reluctantly agreed to place his safety in my hands. He later became so comfortable in Tampa that one evening at a local nightclub where we went to relax before dining, he strutted out on the dance floor and started swinging with a friendly, but unfamiliar, white female. He must have momentarily thought he was back in Boston. Or was he fraternizing with the white South's formerly forbidden fruit for Black men as an act of retribution.

Although George gave a lecture regarding his controversial Lydian music theory concept, he mostly rehearsed the fledgling jazz band, preparing one of his more ambitious compositions for a concert. The music was exceedingly difficult for the inexperienced students, causing George, the perfectionist, to display his temperamental side. He also insisted that we follow the music score's exact specifications: provide microphones for each instrument. This required a compatible mixing board for controlling balance, which we managed to acquire only hours before the concert, thanks to Associate Fine Arts Dean, John Coker.

The band performed superbly that night before a packed theater after only three rehearsal days. The students played beyond their capabilities and everyone's expectations. The major piece was last on the program, and had a highly charged-up and animated George dancing across the front of the stage clapping his hands above his head. The number brought down the house, and turned out to be the jazz event of the year for all of Tampa Bay. And my stealth effort worked. USF has one of the leading university jazz studies programs in the nation.

I managed to lure David back to USF on two other occasions in spite of his "overworked" resident-composer experience. One was for the university's Dr. Martin Luther King Jr. birthday celebration, which I produced, featuring the music of Black composers. David's composition, *Singers of Songs/Weavers of Dreams: Homage to my Friends*, written for cello and percussion was performed by music faculty cellist, Antony Cooke, and recent USF graduate Steven Brown, later resulting in the 1982 Golden Crest LP album (CRDG 4223).

The second occasion was a concert that included his composition, *The Black Experience*, for voice and piano, featuring our good friend, tenor William "Bill" Brown (1997 CD LISCIO LAS-11972). Both events, our collaborative efforts, allowed me close access to David's human qualities and musical genius. He always responded to my phone calls no matter the day or time, or how busy he was. Sometimes our conversations wandered back to the Lincoln University days, faculty and students, and the hilarious circumstances of his arrival on campus.

"I guess you all didn't know who that strange looking guy in pinkish-purplish getup was on The Foot, and what to expect, huh?" he would say with a chuckle.

While I was the USF Fine Arts Dean (1988-98), an unexpected appointment, my calls to him were often seeking references about African-Americans qualified for vacant music faculty positions. We eventually appointed one of his students who was not Black to our Jazz Studies Program where he has excelled.

When I resigned from the dean's position after eleven years, University President, Betty Castor, honored my service with a special gala reception and dinner. My second wife, Dr. Juel Smith, (more on her later) a USF Program Director, was greatly involved in its planning and implementation, particularly for its elegant qualities. The details for the event were kept from me.

Attendees included family from as far away as Minneapolis and Phoenix, faculty and staff colleagues, friends and neighbors, students, alumni, and major donors. The jazz quartet that performed during the reception was led by Robert Garcia, a talented Black harpist who I advised as a student. He was as happy to be part of the occasion as I was to see him joyously doing what he loved most. Sadly, he passed away only a few years later.

The program started with Rev. A. Leon Lowry's invocation (my pastor): "Let us bow our heads with closed eyes," which I did, noticing the chair across from me at the round table was vacant. At the end of the invocation, I raised my head, opened my eyes, and there sat a smiling David Baker in what had been the vacant chair.

"David! What in the world?! What a surprise!" I softly shouted, jumping up and racing around the table to embrace him, trying not to interrupt the program.

What an honor it was for my teacher and mentor of more than forty years to have taken time from his demanding schedule to celebrate the end of my college dean tenure. Juel had informed him of this milestone event, and he traveled from Bloomington, Indiana to be present. After the event, I spent some quality time with him in his hotel room, keeping it short since he had an early morning flight.

Almost a year later, I was appointed Fisk University president, another unanticipated life milestone. After starting my year's sabbatical before returning to the USF music faculty, a Fisk trustee phoned me for an informal chat, which led to several months of official discussions ending with my March 1999 appointment as the University's twelfth president. It was an incredible opportunity to serve as CEO of a highly regarded historically Black liberal arts university, directly impacting hundreds of young lives. And, it was a glorious way to conclude my academic journey, steering an entire university's ship.

One of the first important public events for new university presidents is the inauguration ceremony, a tradition that symbolizes the official assumption of institutional duties and responsibilities. The ceremony is one of much pomp and circumstance, with faculty in full academic regalia and the president receiving the institution's official medallion. Parts of the inauguration program, I learned, may be customized according to the new president's preference.

The program's music was of considerable interest to me, wanting an original composition specifically for the occasion. David

Baker immediately came to mind, but would he have time before the April 8, 2000 inauguration?

As I had done so often since 1958, I picked up the phone.

"Hi David, it's me. How's it going?" I asked, already uneasy about the request, aware of his extremely busy schedule.

"Doing good, and glad you called." Then he went on, "Hadn't had a chance to congratulate you on the incredible new job. Man, I'm so proud of you."

"Well, uh, thanks. It's a big job, but somebody's got to do it, right? Ha, ha, ha," trying to gain the courage for the big ask. "You know David; a university president gets to make some choices for the inauguration program. Mine is scheduled for April 8th. So, I would like for you to compose a special piece for the occasion, if possible."

Not even a second past before his response.

"Yes, no problem. I will be happy to."

Somewhere in the ensuing brief conversation, I managed to let him know the embarrassing fact that there were limited University funds for the commission, but I would provide the best stipend available. The dialogue continued as though he had not heard me.

"Do you have any ideas about the music you might want?" were his next words. "Style, subject reference, or anything?"

I had already invited our good friend Bill Brown to perform a recital as part of the annual Fisk Spring Arts Festival; scheduling the inauguration at the end of the week-long celebration, symbolizing a renewed commitment to the university's liberal arts mission. The University's historic Jubilee Singers came to mind.

"Could you consider writing a piece for Bill Brown and the Jubilee Singers?"

"That's an interesting idea. I've composed a lot for Bill," he jubilantly responded. "And the Jubilee Singers, they're known for singing spirituals, so maybe I'll consider that genre."

Greatly relieved, I thanked him profusely before ending our productive conversation.

Fisk University's inauguration ceremonies are held traditionally in the historic Memorial Chapel, constructed in 1892. It is the site of many famous speeches and performances, including Booker T. Washington, Frederick Douglass, Dr. Martin Luther King Jr., Thurgood Marshall, Duke Ellington, and Dr. John Hope Franklin, to name a few.

We had received David's composition, but by inauguration day he had not confirmed his attendance. Knowing the demands on his time I had steeled myself that he would not be there. But when turning to face the audience from the stage after the traditional academic procession into the chapel, one of the first faces I recognized sitting near front-center was David Baker and his lovely wife Lida. That was a powerful moment of honor and exhilaration prior to the official presidential installation.

Assuming the position of Fisk University president represented a level of personal achievement that had depended extensively on the presence of nurturing mentors throughout my life, certainly exemplified by David. And here he was, honoring me with his music and presence for my inauguration. His special composition, "My Lord, What a Morning," was a contemporary recasting of the Negro spiritual, and I presumed a spiritual blessing for my presidency. Well received by the audience, it garnered many accolades from the Arts community, and is archived with my presidential documents in the Fisk library special collection.

My Fisk University presidency ended May 2001, after an exceedingly challenging and productive two-years due to irreconcilable institutional views between me and the Trustees. They were focused on short-term survival and my goal was for the University to thrive once again, requiring long-term vision and tactics. After returning to Tampa for full retirement, compelling thoughts centered on the invaluable personal nurturing I received since birth that propelled me to success as a musician and educator (the motivation for this book). David Baker ranked high on the list, and with his continuing presence, I decided to reverse roles and honor him with a surprise appearance at a recognition event for him. I wanted to demonstrate my profound gratitude for his more than fifty years of support, encouragement, and counsel.

In a telephone conversation with Lida, I learned that David had absolutely no retirement plans. He was enjoying his academic and professional life thoroughly. So, honoring him at a retirement event, as he had done for me, was out.

However, she indicated that IU music faculty planned two concerts featuring his music the next academic year, honoring him as a revered composer and valued colleague. Given the esteem quality of the faculty, this was no ordinary event. The first concert was in fall 2001 on a Sunday evening, for which I decided to surprise David. My plan was to fly into Indianapolis on Saturday, rent a car for driving the 50 miles to Bloomington, and walk into the Sunday concert without his or Lida's prior knowledge. However, on the day of my trip, while standing at the Indianapolis Airport baggage claim turnstile waiting for my luggage...

"John, what are you doing here?!"

I recognized the voice, but refused to believe what was happening. What are the odds?

"Well, uh…" I said, turning toward the voice. "Hi David, uh…I'm on my way…uh, to Bloomington," being careful not to mention why.

Waiting for a reason and hearing none, David abruptly declared, "Lida is waiting outside to pick me up, why don't you ride with us?" an offer I couldn't justify turning down.

After delightful greetings, curiosity seeped into our conversation as we began our drive with David at the wheel.

"Why are you going to Bloomington?" David asked more insistently. "You're not involved with the music school's search for a new dean, are you?"

"No, no, no. Not part of any search. I'm finished with higher education," I said, realizing it was time for full disclosure. "Actually, David, I'm here to be part of honoring you at the special concert of your music on Sunday. This was supposed to be a surprise."

While giving the highway his undivided attention, my mentor, David Baker, managed a modest smile.

Discovering that I had no plans beyond attending the concert, he appointed himself the perfect host, assuring me transportation back to the Indianapolis airport. So, after dropping me off at my hotel, he returned later to take me out for a tasty meal and conversation.

The next morning, I attended church with him and Lida, followed by lunch with the entire Baker family, a Sunday tradition I learned. The afternoon included a tour of the campus, which I had not seen since 1973. Then a quick stop at their home where he shared several of his latest CDs with me. It was a beautiful house tucked neatly with others among rolling Indiana hills. His studio was home to a baby grand piano surrounded by shelves packed with CDs, books, and LPs. I heard that he left the house early most mornings for exercise-walks with a Walkman, listening to whatever CD fell off the shelf into his hand.

I notified Mrs. Beversdorf (Dr. Beversdorf had long passed) that I would be in Bloomington. She picked me up for dinner Sunday before the concert (more on this in the next chapter) which both of us later attended walking across the street from the popular student café.

The familiar smell, dark wood walls, hushed acoustics, and simple architectural stage backdrop of the recital hall, flooded my memory as I entered. I had performed and attended many concerts and recitals there during my IU studies, including my 1961 Master's degree and *Performer's Certificate* recitals. Walking towards the front where David and Lida were sitting, I noticed a sizable compliment of seemingly faculty, staff, students, and others from the Bloomington community, anxiously anticipating the concert. And after greeting David and Lida the program began.

Complex sounds, sculptured and uniquely layered with jazz nuances creatively spun by David's imagination, flowed through the darkened hall, performed by various instrumentalists ranging from accompanied solos to chamber ensembles. Distinct rhythmic, tonal and harmonic qualities kept me engrossed, connecting me with the progression of David's compositions since I'd known him. Others in the audience seemed emotionally and intellectually captivated as well, enthusiastically applauding after each work. And his performing colleagues appeared absolutely delighted to be deeply immersed in his compositions, honoring David with flawless renderings.

At the end of the program, they asked David to stand and be recognized, celebrating his exciting music and distinguished IU tenure. And with a slight smile he did, turning towards the audience to acknowledge their enthusiastic applause, applause, and more applause!

After David and Lida dropped me off at my hotel, scenes from the past two extraordinary days replayed in my memory before I surrendered to sleep: At church, David's head reverently bowed with eyes closed during the sermon, "not sleeping," he assured me; his humorous interactive husband and father roles played during the traditional after-church family lunch; David, serving as tour guide, reintroducing me to the IU campus, and urging me to sit next to the bronze statue of the popular former president, Herman B. Wells, reclining on a campus bench; And, David's expressed concern during Saturday evening's dinner, "You know, I'm really glad that you left Fisk when you did. It was taking a devastating toll on you. Seeing you now, and remembering you before, I can tell the struggle was difficult."

When I inquired about retirement that night during the drive back to the hotel, he responded half-jokingly, "There is this tendency that when people retire from IU, their earthly years are limited. And why should I retire anyway? I am enjoying teaching and performing. My colleagues ask me to compose music for them, and they perform the music I compose. The best of worlds for me, a composer." And demonstrated profoundly by the concert.

David and Lida arrived early Monday morning to drive me to the Indianapolis Airport.

"I'm sorry, man. I have classes this morning, but Lida will get you there," he said, which I found not surprising. "I really appreciate you coming for this special occasion. Hope we can get together again soon." As we dropped him off on campus, I was unsure when I would see him again.

My memories are replete with that powerful and meaningful weekend. David's long mentoring years were profoundly meaningful, intervening and available at important life-junctions. The suspicious man in a pinkish outfit who showed up on Lincoln's "Foot" as a new music professor offered the best of himself to me as teacher, counsel and friend for over fifty years.

But unfortunately, mortality reigns supreme. On March 26, 2016, while he was still academically and professionally engaged at Indiana University where he had been since 1966, David Baker passed away. He was 84.

And as promised, he never did retire.

Chapter 12

Unleashed Gift

The walls! The floor to ceiling, corner to corner solid vertical objects! They were closing in... coming at me from all sides. The closeted, windowless space I was in was suffocating; dark and glum descending all around. I felt warm tears trickling down my cheeks; depression creeping in. I wanted to scream, but refused.

Sitting there, cradling my tuba, late night in the dated Indiana University East Hall music practice room, I was starting to lose it. Frantically trying time and time again to make a sound, any credible sound, on my instrument, but it was resulting in a little more than whispers of air sputtering between my uncertain lips. This can't be happening after more than ten years of almost thoughtless effort.

Following my new teacher's precise instructions, I was trying to learn new techniques for improving my playing to become a professional tuba player. It was a complete makeover. But after weeks, I had nothing. Not even a single acceptable tone. I was devastated. It felt like the end of my tuba playing, the end of my greatest joy and major outlet for self-expression. The end of my world. And, Indiana University's School of Music, nationally eminent, was supposed to be the promise land for aspiring artists like me.

It wasn't working. Would I ever be able to play the tuba again?

From the beginning, studying at IU was an ordeal. Without a car at the time, getting to the campus in Bloomington, Indiana, from Bastrop, Louisiana in 1959 was no easy matter. There was no direct route. And, thanks to my loving parents, in addition to my regular luggage I had a brand-new professional-grade tuba in a giant hard case to contend with, the good and the challenging.

After considering all my travel options, the train was the only reasonable choice. Somehow, through various precarious connections, in late August I arrived in Bloomington on the regional Monon Railroad, which was closing out its final years of unique service to five Indiana universities. From the small limestone train station, I took a taxi northeast through the business district, peppered with store fronts, onto the beautiful tree-shrouded IU campus.

Wow! Majestic gothic buildings encased in Indiana limestone appeared, looming above the dense green trees and claiming their royal space as symbols of the institution's long academic history. From the taxi window I saw thick, colorful foliage concealing the meandering Jordan River, more of a creek I later discovered. I saw miles of intriguing trails and concrete walks that I later found essential for making my way to classes, activities in the Memorial Student Union, and my one-semester job placing music event posters on campus and downtown Bloomington. The picturesque campus view was calming after the grueling train ride.

My taxicab, now almost to my destination, was stuffed from top to bottom. I occupied the front passenger seat holding several items on my lap. The trunk was crammed with luggage and the hard case enclosed tuba demanded the entire back seat, already taking over my life, but nothing like the domination that was about to occur.

This was my first experience with the complexities of traveling with the recently acquired instrument. And I quickly learned that this was a love affair for which I was henceforth going to pay a significant penalty. Transporting it from place to place, walking with it cradled in my arms, and performing with arms embracing it while balanced on my thighs created an almost platonic relationship that demanded care and thoughtfulness. After all, it was the expressive voice for the quiet self I was. But why couldn't I have fallen in love with the flute?

Well, it seems love has its own criteria.

Years later as a professional musician, I paid half-fare to place my canvas-bagged tuba in the seat next to me on an airplane trip from Oklahoma City to an audition with the San Francisco Symphony. Checking instruments as baggage was unsafe, even when strapped tightly into hard-cases with cushioned form-fitting linings. Unfortunately, I witnessed this tragic occurrence when several musicians opened their cases to discover severely damaged instruments, needing to borrow a tuba for their audition.

But when I was invited back for the audition finals, our family-of-four budget could not accommodate the additional half-fare for my tuba, so I was unable to return. I was never sure if I missed winning the prestigious appointment to the San Francisco Symphony because of that financial shortfall. However, needless to say, physically carrying my tuba all these years is negligible considering the love, joy and benefits derived.

Finally, my taxi arrived at my campus destination, IU's graduate student residential complex northeast of campus, my home for the next year. The residential cluster consisted of several nondescript two-story buildings with a central multipurpose facility that included administrative offices, meeting rooms, dining services and a mailroom.

I was assigned a private first-floor, corner room. This was my first time living in a dorm room without a roommate, without close human contact and without the pressure to quickly make acquaintance and conversation with someone I didn't know—always a chore for me.

However, during the year, I got to know a few other resident grad students hanging out during study breaks in the common lounge, where the only television was located. I also went to a couple of campus cultural events with my next-door neighbor, whose aromatic pipe smoke penetrated the thin wall between us. And I got to know a few of the small number of other African-American graduate students at IU through the safe sanctuary of the informal "Black table" in the dining hall, a necessary survival tactic and security blanket for all of us attending the white institution.

After my required music theory and history exams and a writing skills test during orientation, I found myself asking the all-important question: "What am I doing here?" My anxiety, already heightened by the new experience and exams, was now escalating to a state of panic as I confronted the reality of the overwhelming white majority surrounding me, compared to the comforting Black majority I had lived among my whole life.

Further, I had been led to believe through enculturation that white people, in this case white students, were superior: they were smarter, better educated, more competent, more talented, more everything. Naturally, I thought: "Hey, I'm Black, from a small town in the Deep South, and graduated from a HBCU. I can't possibly qualify for graduate study at an all-white, Big Ten IU—in spite of what I was told. And these tests will show that."

Again, I asked, "What am I doing here?!" although recalling the influence and encouragement from Lincoln University professor and IU graduate, David Baker.

After the exams, disheartened and expecting the worst I hastily retreated to the sanctuary of my dorm room, set on packing up immediately and leaving. With no one to talk to except myself, "let's get out of here" was a very convincing argument, especially since the luggage storage room was conveniently just down the hall. "Pack up and get going!" my alter ego agreed. But as I stood looking out the window at the green grass and colorful, well-tended landscape between the clustered buildings, I thought about all the people back home, parents especially, and at Lincoln that I would disappoint by walking away, particularly before I knew the results of the exams.

"Wait a minute," a more objective voice interjected. "I'm already admitted to IU for Master's study based on university criteria; otherwise, I would not be here. And the orientation exams I took were for diagnostic and placement purposes only!"

And anyway, didn't I deserve to be here as much as anyone else? my home-grown and HBCU courage returning.

So, I reconsidered thoughts of taking off; "at least wait to see the results of the exams posted in the morning. And if they are as bad as I anticipate, leaving would be justified, right?"

Standing in front of the bulletin board early the next morning, extremely conscious of all the white faces around me, I nervously looked for my identification number, pleased that no one would know my exam results but me. Based on each exam score, deficiency survey courses, if required, were listed by the individual's ID number. Worse case would be four courses plus a writing lab, a full semester of remedial classes.

"What!?" I said to myself when I saw my ID. "Only two survey courses and no writing lab?" *How was that again? Let me double check!* After confirmation, I made a cursory review of the other listed student IDs, which showed that I was about middle of the spread. "I think I might stick around after all," I thought, greatly relieved. Feeling okay and relieved with the outcome, I quietly thanked my Lincoln University professors for preparing me so well, and set my mind on the last orientation hurdle: ensemble placement auditions scheduled for the afternoon.

Hours later, while waiting nervously in the lobby of the small theater for my audition call, a man suddenly charged out of the double doors and came towards me with an extended hand.

"I'm Dr. Beversdorf. Welcome to IU and the School of Music. I've been looking forward to meeting you," he said, all in one breath accompanied by a genuine smile. "David Baker told me all about you."

His greeting felt warm and hospitable, but it took me by surprise. *I had never shaken hands with a white person.* I hadn't anticipated that moment. But when it occurred unexpectedly, and not having time to think about it, it didn't seem to matter. The handshake, along with the intense sincerity of his eyes, seemed genuine and friendly.

"Thank you, I've been waiting to meet you also," I meekly responded.

As my tuba instructor, I knew that I would be spending a lot of close, individual time with him and hoped that our relationship would be as comfortable and compatible as I had experienced with Professor

Penn at Lincoln. But this was different. For the first time my teacher was white. But David Baker's relationship with Dr. B. (the title most student's use), along with his positive opinions of him, offered me a sense of comfort and confidence that I was welcomed, unconditionally and respectfully, as his student.

This was a critical juncture for me, as white men would become members of my growing list of nurturing male teacher/mentor/role models. From the outset, I had no justifiable reason to doubt that Dr. B. would be different from past Black teachers and mentors, offering me nothing less than the full benefit of their knowledge and wisdom. But I had no delusions that Indiana University, the venerable institution, and others, was somehow devoid or sanitized of racism.

And I would soon be proven right, when, needing a haircut, I ventured over to the Student Union barber shop.

"Sorry, we don't cut Black students' hair here," was my greeting. "There are places in the community."

I left, angry, of course, but the encounter sparked a memory: the aborted student protest I joined in high school when our team wasn't allowed to play a second championship game at Bastrop's all-white high school's stadium.

And even though I had just arrived and was recently concerned about my academic ability to stay, I rallied with several other Black male students and marched in front of the Student Union building with signs protesting racial discrimination, forcing the hiring of a Black barber. Just as insulting was my studio piano class long-tenured elder instructor who made it perfectly clear that she thought Black people were intellectually and artistically inferior to whites—in spite of evidence to the contrary.

Tactfully avoiding further social conversations, I completed the term and requested a different teacher for the spring semester.

After Dr. Beversdorf's gracious welcome in the theatre lobby, he escorted me inside for my audition, which I performed on my new instrument, not yet accustomed to its different traits. Consequently, I did not play well and was disappointed. After I finished, Dr. B followed me back out into the lobby.

"You did okay," were his first words, sounding unimpressed. "But you must use the double-C slide only in your tuba. Throw the B-flat one you used away," he continued in a straightforward manner. "This will require you to learn new fingering, including using the fourth valve for certain notes."

I stood there stunned hearing his abrupt instructions, stipulating major changes for my playing after hearing me play for the first time in the short audition.

"And there are a few other things we'll need to work on."

Well, that was about as direct and unsettling as one could get, and seeing my silent astonishment, he smiled.

"Well, we'll talk about all of this at your first lesson. Come by my studio Monday to set up a time."

And then he went back into the theater, perhaps disappointed from David Baker's assessment, while I stood there feeling totally deflated, not knowing that that was a mere whiff of what lay ahead for me.

The next day I checked the posted ensemble assignments. I was assigned to the concert band in the Department of Bands which resided in the basement of IU Auditorium, not the music building. I didn't think much about it until I later discovered from another student that the best performing students in the School of Music were usually assigned to one of several concert and opera orchestras and chamber ensembles under the direction of professionally trained and experienced faculty/conductors. But I had been assigned by the faculty, including Dr. B, to the band, and figured there was nothing I could do about it. Those feelings of not belonging at IU began to flow again. "Am I wading into where I'm not welcomed and over my head?" my mind cried out. "Since playing the tuba, I have never experienced such negative reactions to my playing."

On Monday, I attended my first band rehearsal and sat down with three other tuba players, which was a first, accustomed to being the only one in the band in high school and at Lincoln. During marching band season, the first semester each year, the concert band was composed of women and graduate students exclusively. The marching band was for undergraduate men only. I also discovered that I was not sitting first chair, which made me suspicious of the selection process since I was the only Black band member. Depressed by the circumstances, I knew I had to adjust to this new racial environment. It was too late to once again consider leaving.

For my first studio tuba lesson with Dr. B, he tried to offer me a glimmer of hope, probably realizing his earlier critique had been rather harsh.

"I really wasn't pleased with your ensemble assignment," he assured me, "but I was overruled by my colleagues." He was silent for a moment, and I waited. "There are a number of things needing change in order to improve your playing so we can place you in a better ensemble."

I sat listening, feeling my world crumbling around me. I knew I was a good tuba player before I came to IU, but was hearing negative feedback over-and over I hadn't heard before. This was new and heart wrenching territory. My self-esteem in free-fall.

Sensing my despair, Dr. B went on, "From what I've learned from David Baker and my short time with you, I believe you can make the necessary adjustments. It's just a matter of making some specific technical changes to the embouchure (lips and mouth), and how you use the tongue, lungs and lower abdomen, which will make a big difference in your playing." That covers almost everything involved in playing a brass instrument.

As he finished, I realized that the changes he described would be in addition to getting accustomed to the particulars of my new instrument, including rotary (rotating) valves and different fingerings that use the fourth valve.

"This is starting *all over*," I gravely thought.

Dr. B also acknowledged that making the changes while playing in the concert band would prove problematic, slowing the transition. "But you must follow my instructions and practice the specific new techniques as much as possible, doing your best in band rehearsals to navigate between the old and new," he explained before describing and demonstrating the embouchure adjustment.

I left my first lesson with my confidence shattered, one of the most uncertain periods in my life. "But if discipline and hard work was what was needed," I told myself, "I can do it." I brought that kind of work ethic and discipline with me, thanks to my father's Mr. Johnnie's Grocery Store and Smith Family, Inc. And through Lincoln's Professors Penn and Baker, I had tasted the solo and orchestral performance fruits, and was ready, and believed myself capable of, feasting from the tallest tree. But climbing that tree to acquire the sweeter fruit was apparently not going to be easy, or immediate.

"But that's why I'm here," I reminded myself. "That's why I'm at IU now."

The first two weeks were horrible, having to use my old playing method in band rehearsals, while individually practicing the new techniques, resulting in very little progress.

When I knocked on Dr. B's studio door despondently for my third weekly lesson, he opened the door with a gigantic triumphant smile on his face. He was the bearer of good news for his frustrated student. Smile continuing, he chimed, "You no longer need to attend concert band rehearsals. I've arranged for you to be dropped from the ensemble. And for the remainder of this semester, you will not be assigned to any ensemble at all. So, you can concentrate entirely on what I'm teaching you."

"What? Wow." That was a game changer that violated School of Music policy, which required all music students to enroll in at least one major ensemble each semester. Dr. B obviously had friends in high places, and pulled those strings on my behalf, an early indication of his sincere interest in me and my musical development.

Now, I was able to focus only on the new changes he introduced. Sounds simple enough. Then, that's when it happened... days in the practice room unable to produce a sound. Times when a few minutes were as long as I could tolerate the agony of sputtering sounds from my tuba, using Dr. B's altered embouchure. It didn't take long for me to realize: "I can't play the tuba any longer after all these years. My expressive voice silenced." Tears flowed as I leaned over the instrument wondering what's next, but knowing I must continue to try.

That's when Dr. B, whose studio was down the hall, started popping his head through the slightly ajar door after a quick knock: "You're doing okay. You're doing it right. Just keep at it. It's going to come around," encouraging my effort.

A difficult struggle ensued. In the private confines of a small windowless practice room, I spent agonizing times trying to reinvent myself as a competent tuba player. A process that involved mental and physical deconstruction of long-used methods, while at the same time reconstruction by adapting new techniques.

"I hope Dr. B knows what he's doing," I thought, trying to boost my confidence.

I heard one student scoff at his "my way or no way" teaching approach.

But who was I to doubt Dr. B?

The excruciating times in the practice room, with the walls seemingly turning dark and closing in, and where there was a continued mix of tears and fears, made me wonder whether I would ever reach the results Dr. B sought, or if I would be left with nothing. This "new start" or "reinvention" at IU had quickly become psychological trauma for me, completely crushing my already fragile confidence.

Dr. B's attentive and supportive presence was often the only thing that kept me going.

During those difficult weeks, my studio tuba lessons with him were short in duration, though poignant and intense, as he made sure his instructions were followed exactly. He was patient and persistent as I placed my tuba-playing future completely in his hands.

Born August 8, 1924, in Yoakum, Texas, to amateur musician parents, Dr. Thomas Beversdorf was musically gifted and highly intelligent. Graduating from high school at the age of sixteen, completing the Master's degree at twenty-two and the Doctorate in music theory and composition at the Eastman School of Music at the age of twenty-eight, he mastered the trombone and studied music composition with some of the top composers of his time.

After serving in World War II, Thomas Beversdorf taught high school band in his hometown, followed by teaching music at the University of Houston before coming to IU in August 1949, where, for a period, he was chairman of both the composition and brass instruments departments. As a professional trombonist, he performed with the Houston and Pittsburgh Symphonies.

Approximately five feet, ten inches tall, with handsome features, his character was all intention and purpose, his body animated by free-flowing movement and gestures. His personality exuded warmth and joy, including an occasional twinkle-eyed joke shared with colleagues. There was a hint of ego, which he backed up with knowledge and performance talent. He loved teaching, taking great pleasure in the growth and development of his students. And, he loved his family deeply, which included five children, one tragically lost very early. A devout Christian, he composed sacred music regularly.

In my studio lessons, Dr. B sometimes used dramatic effects to emphasize a specific technical detail to spur my progress. Once, when stressing the appropriate air control technique, he placed a stiff piercing finger against my abdomen slightly above the navel to stress the necessity for muscle contraction near the diaphragm to create pressure. Ouch! The pain of that jab followed me into my practice room and indeed hastened that technical development.

And on another occasion, he dramatically pulled out his tuba mouthpiece and placed it in my instrument, proclaiming, "I once studied tuba with Bill Bell in New York (referring to the famed New York Philharmonic's tuba player), so let me demonstrate the articulation technique and sound I've been describing." And he did. Whether the claim was true or not (based on his quizzical facial expression), it helped me understand that lesson.

Then, things started to happen, almost miraculously. The tone dramatically returned. And almost surreally, all the technical fixes were magically coming together like the final pieces of a difficult jigsaw puzzle. I was starting to match the performance qualities Dr. B wanted: a brighter tone capable of a brassy edge, the well-defined articulation of notes, and smoother delivery between notes, among other improvements. I was coming out of my despair, aware of the enormous changes taking place.

However, those inklings of progress only made Dr. B push me harder. There was no letting up. The studio lessons, which for weeks were less than fifteen minutes, now stretched beyond the scheduled one hour, accelerating my rate of progress and making permanent the new techniques. Sometimes, to encourage me, and perhaps satisfy his own ego as a teacher, he invited faculty colleagues into his studio to hear my progress.

"Bernhard," I heard him say outside his studio door once, referring to the prestigious composer Professor Heiden as he passed by. "Step inside a minute. I want you to hear someone perform."

"What? Oh no, listen to a tuba player?" I asked myself as I prepared to play. But Dr. B was like a proud father observing the incremental progress of his son and wanting to share it with others. It felt as though he had never witnessed such rapid progress by one of his students.

"Here is some music you need to learn," he abruptly interjected into one mid-semester lesson. "It's the tuba part for the Stage Orchestra for Verdi's opera, *Rigoletto*. It opens in two weeks."

There was no acceptable response but "Okay, I'll do my best Dr. B," as I braced myself to perform in my first School of Music ensemble, and what an ensemble that was.

The IU Opera Theatre, nationally recognized for exceptional performance standards, mounted four to six elaborate, fully staged productions each year, remarkable for a university.
Audiences filled East Hall Auditorium for consecutive weekend performances of each opera, and Dr. B had me playing in the first opera of the 1960-61 season.

For the small orchestra, playing behind the stage set was complicated by having to follow the conductor on a small video screen. The tuba part, originally scored for the cimbasso, a trombone-like brass instrument with piston valves, included rapid eighth-note octave intervals. I was anxious about playing with the new method, but without negative critique from the conductor, and encouraging remarks from Dr. B, my confidence got a boost.

For the spring semester, he assigned me to the Brass Choir and four Opera Theatre Orchestras including the massive pit orchestra for the Palm Sunday performance of Wagner's masterpiece, *Parsifal*, performed at IU annually for more than twenty years. The *Parsifal* performance tradition, which included a supper break after the first act, was discontinued in 1969, but reintroduced in 2019 for IU's Bicentennial.

Engulfed by Wagner's spellbinding, mystical and rapturous leitmotif-layered music from more than forty musicians packed into the semi-dark orchestra pit, it took tremendous discipline to focus on the tuba part in front of me initially, and make my appointed entrances. Powerful singers I could not see on the auditorium's massive, elaborately designed Memorial Auditorium stage set were projecting soaring lyrics over our heads into the audience—vocals that were intricately interwoven with the pit-orchestra instruments into the composer's passionate music. The result was a magical experience.

Now that the technical transformation was almost complete, Dr. B introduced me to the study of tuba excerpts from orchestra literature in preparation for future auditions for professional orchestras, which motivated me to attend and observe rehearsals of the IU Philharmonic Orchestra, the School of Music's preeminent instrumental ensemble, on the East Hall Auditorium stage.

Dr. B often attended the rehearsals to assess the trombone and tuba students' performances in the orchestra. On one occasion when I was there listening from the audience, he abruptly left the auditorium and returned shortly with his trombone in hand, evidently dissatisfied with how the trombones were performing in the Overture to Wagner's *Tannhauser.*

He replaced the first-chair student trombonist in the orchestra and requested Maestro Kozma to begin again at the section that featured the trombones prominently with a sustained and projected melody. "Wow! That was amazing," my musical ear told me, which gave me an excellent sense of what stylistic playing meant. Having made his point Dr. B left the stage, walked past us and out the auditorium exit, leaving with a cocky egotistical grin on his face.

"It was verrry clear!" We, his students, got the message.

By the end of my first academic year of tuba study at IU, deconstruction to reconstruction had succeeded, and now I was chasing perfection. From the depths of depression and lost confidence I had renewed hope that I could remaster the tuba. I was now in the mix of music students performing in major IU School of Music ensembles under distinguished faculty conductors.

When I arrived at IU, I was the only African-American among Dr. B's seven tuba students, which included another graduate student. And after the ensemble auditions that placed me in the concert band, the tuba student hierarchy probably felt that it was appropriate and didn't threaten their positions, particularly the student assigned to the Philharmonic Orchestra. However, during the spring semester, their nervous, concerned faces started appearing in the small window of my practice room door, listening to my rapid progress.

Meanwhile, Dr. B invited me to his home occasionally, where I met his lovely wife, Norma, a pianist, and their children. I don't recall what I anticipated before my first visit, after all I had never been in a white person's home before. But I felt entirely welcomed and comfortable, as I did when invited to his church, First Baptist of Bloomington, for performances of his sacred music.

Student musicians sometimes played with him for those concerts, other times performed under his baton. And as testament to the reverence Bloomington residents held for the esteemed Dr. B, an excerpt from his composition, *Three Epitaphs*, is permanently imprinted and preserved on the side of the downtown historic Smith-Holden building, a former music store.

The August 1960 second year of IU study found me on campus with a wife, Janietta, and car, 1960 Corvair, both acquired during the summer. She was a former music student at Lincoln. We were able to rent a studio apartment in married student housing. She quickly found work on campus, joining me during the year for attendance at concerts when I was not performing. I busied myself with class registration and other school-related formalities.

The day before classes started, while walking through the new circular-designed music building looking for Dr. B's studio, I noticed Professor Tibor Kozma, the maestro of the IU Philharmonic, coming toward me. "Oh wow" my nervous thoughts interjected, "It's him." Suddenly, he changed lanes and was standing in front of me. Given his reputation as a tyrant on the podium, perhaps with a little bullying mixed-in, I thought, "Uh, ooh! I am in trouble."

Without greetings or an attempt at personable formalities, but allowing a disarming smile, he said with his discernable foreign accent, "Mr. Smith, you are the tuba player this year for the IU Philharmonic." Then he stepped to the side and continued down the hall as if for him it was just another day. I didn't even know that he knew me.

But what did he just say? Did I hear him right? Did he say *I was the tuba player for the IU Philharmonic?*" Not sure because of the foreign accent and terrified of the prospect, I hastened my efforts to find Dr. B's studio, which was just a few doors further around the curving hallway, which meant that Professor Kozma may have just come from there. Dr. B opened the door after I knocked anxiously, and greeted me jubilantly.

"Guess what?"

I thought I might already know.

"You're the new tubist for the IU Philharmonic!"

The IU Philharmonic, considered the preeminent instrumental ensemble in the School of Music, and I was now its tuba player. I had not yet considered myself playing at that level, but who was I to make that judgment? Later, reflecting on my unexpected achievement, I realized that in one year, I did a complete makeover—going from the bottom to the top of the tuba-student hierarchy. Under Professor Kozma's baton that year, I performed five IU Philharmonic concerts, *The Nutcracker Ballet*, two operas, and including my classes, it was an extremely busy and productive year.

Maestro/Professor Tibor Kozma (1909-1976), born in Budapest, Hungary, studied piano and conducting in Europe, and became a U.S. citizen in 1945. He joined the New York Metropolitan Opera in 1951, after working in New York as a piano accompanist, vocal coach and conductor for Broadway shows.   He conducted more than eighty performances at the Met before joining the IU School of Music in 1957 as head of the opera and orchestra programs.

New to the IU School of Music, I was initially unfamiliar with Professor Kozma's background. But while performing under his baton, I quickly realized that I was in the presence of a musical genius. Extremely knowledgeable about all aspects of music, and meticulous and precise on the podium, he never missed anything in the score or on stage for opera—and all the time demanding perfection. But demanding may be an understatement. I thought of him as the long-lost brother of Arturo Toscanini, well known for his gesticulating rage on the podium.

Things got so intense in one IU Philharmonic rehearsal, two first-stand violinists sitting close to Maestro Kozma, stood-up and started punching each other. They couldn't fight the maestro, so that was the next worst option. I prepared well for rehearsals so as not to be singled out for his harsh critique. On a comical personal note, illustrating his somewhat eccentric nature, Maestro Kozma owned a three-wheel car, possibly a Berkeley T-60, which students picked up one day and turned perpendicular to his parking space as a prank, or as revenge to his "take no prisoners" attacks from the podium. From a safe distance, they laughed as they watched him trying to figure out how to move his car from the parking space. He finally found colleagues parked in adjacent spaces to move their cars so he could finally leave, looking really agitated.

Attending my first IU Philharmonic rehearsal, which included Tchaikovsky's *Fifth Symphony*, I felt comfortable and prepared. Peering around the orchestra from my seat on a platform near the back, while the musicians warmed up, I was amazed that I was among them. I took a deep breath knowing the expectations had never been higher. Tchaikovsky's symphony included an active and sometimes exposed tuba part with several quasi solos (i.e., tuba with bassoon and string bass) that required technical accuracy and musical sensitivity. And depending on the conductor's preference, the tuba could be the dominant voice.

When I played one of those musical lines, I noticed Maestro Kozma glance and smile in my direction. And at the end of the rehearsal Dr. B, who attended many rehearsals, rushed to catch me before I left.

"The solos were really musical. Keep it up!"

I congratulated myself on getting through the first rehearsal without mistakes. And later that year, during an opera performance, Maestro Kozma again extended kudos, this time by looking in my direction and taping his baton on the music stand after I executed rapid cadence arpeggios at the end of the First Act. "Wow, I must be doing things right," I mused. "But, no time to let down in my practice," which was at least five hours a day.

Sitting down for the Philharmonic's first rehearsal for the final concert of the fall semester (December 7, 1960), I glanced at the music on my stand and was completely surprised to see the title: *Symphony Number IV* composed by Thomas Beversdorf. "What? Can you believe this?" I got excited, thinking, "This is great, but why hadn't he said something about it." Recently completed, our orchestra would give the piece its premiere performance. And because he was one of our own faculty members, the maestro and orchestra members, especially me, gave our best effort in its preparation. It had an active and demanding tuba part, not unexpected. Dr. B was present at all rehearsals, offering suggestions for the difficult work.

The three-thousand seat IU Auditorium was completely full for the performance, university and community patrons attending with great expectations for Dr. B's new masterpiece. At the end of our Herculean effort, the audience erupted with an exuberant standing ovation, which continued as Dr. B was invited to the stage by Maestro Kozma. In his remarks, he graciously noted everyone who made the performance possible, including the IU Philharmonic. I felt especially proud to be a part of his composition's premiere.

A few weeks later, as I sat down for my lesson, Dr. B put a white-covered record album in my hand.

"Here's something for your record collection" he chirped. "Pull the record out."

I did, and my eyes lit up at the label inscription: "To John Lee Smith, a remarkable student of whom I am quite proud. Thomas Beversdorf."

Unknown to orchestra members, Dr. B had arranged for the performance of his symphony, including his remarks, to be recorded and pressed onto an LP, and I was holding the special recording. His gift to me. Each time I listen to it, his remarks at the end remind me of the voice, his voice, that pushed and coaxed me to unimagined heights.

In early spring, Dr. B surprised me again during a lesson. More of a *shock* this time.

"I have arranged for you to perform for Bill Bell, the tuba player for the New York Philharmonic, and perhaps meet Leonard Bernstein."

"Huh?! What?! No way."

"The orchestra is rehearsing that day," he continued, ignoring my incredulous response. "So, I asked Lenny if he could greet you after your session with Bill, which is all in the Carnegie Hall building."

I sat there paralyzed, unable to speak, understanding the incredible magnitude of what he'd arranged for me: meeting two internationally acclaimed, idolized musicians, and playing for one.

"I... I... I don't know what to say. This is beyond anything I could imagine," I coaxed out of my mouth. "Thank you so much. But...But... Am I ready for this?"

"Well, this is a great opportunity, and you're ready," he said, beaming. "So, keep practicing to do your best. We'll select what you'll play in your next lesson."

My appointment with Mr. Bell was arranged for the day after recent Eastman School of Music graduate and William Bell student, Roger Bobo, performed the first ever tuba recital in historic Carnegie Hall. The trip was scheduled so that I could attend. Three years later, he became the principal tuba player with the Los Angeles Philharmonic.

However, a horrific blizzard made the Pennsylvania turnpike treacherous the day of travel, as Janie and a schoolmate rode with me. The fine mist created by the sixteen-wheelers I was passing caused my air-cooled, rear-engine Corvair to choke intermittently, forcing stops for parts to dry out. This caused me to arrive too late for Bobo's recital. I managed only a few hours of sleep in my schoolmate's friend's packed Harlem apartment before my appointment with Mr. Bell in his Carnegie Hall studio.

Anxiously riding the Carnegie Hall Tower's ancient elevator up several floors, I discovered Mr. Bell's studio door open but empty. The waiting elevator operator suggested I leave my instrument in his room, and we descended to the first floor where he directed me to the Carnegie Hall Café/Bar. Walking in, I saw Mr. Bell on a bar stool, seemingly expecting my arrival, beckoning me to join him. A very large man, whose body virtually concealed the stool he sat on, swiveled around to greet me. I was at first fearful that he might fall off the stool like Humpty Dumpty, but quickly gathered my thoughts. As I approached, he hastily swallowed the last drop of beer from his mug, casually set it on the white marble counter and greeted me.

"Hello, hello, hello. I've been looking forward to meeting you. When did you arrive in New York?"

"Thanks so much for seeing me and being willing to hear me play," I responded, then briefly described my trip and disappointment in not arriving in time for Roger Bobo's recital.

Meanwhile, during our conversation, I noticed that without instructions or overt signal, the bartender refilled Mr. Bell's mug, and without so much as a glance, he picked it up and downed it during the final moments of our talk. This was my first encounter with a practicing professional musician, someone revered by all tuba players. But I was naive, not expecting alcoholic beverages, at least in the morning and while on the job. I had placed professional musicians on a high moral pedestal, along with preachers, teachers, and physicians. Now my standards were adjusting to reality.

We returned to Mr. Bell's studio, and I performed several pieces, receiving exceedingly positive comments. Dr. B had suggested to him that if he was impressed with my playing, and felt so inclined, a reference letter would be very appreciative as support for future professional orchestra auditions. Subsequently, I received his incredibly generous handwritten letter dated May 23, 1961. The most salient sentences were: "*I hereby recommend him [John Lee Smith] unhesitatingly as first-class material for any symphonic ensemble. In addition, he seems to me a very personable young man who should prove an asset to any organization he might become a member of.*"

The New York Philharmonic was rehearsing Mahler's *Third Symphony* in the Carnegie Hall Auditorium that morning, so when we were finished, Mr. Bell took me to a prearranged position in the hallway where Maestro Leonard Bernstein would pass on his way to rehearsal. The timing was perfect, and a very nervous John L. Smith Jr., me, was introduced to the very gracious Mr. Bernstein, standing with his music scores in hand. Appearing tall on television, I was immediately struck by his short stature. After the handshake and affable greetings, Mr. Bell gave him a brief assessment of my performance qualities while I stood in awe facing the Maestro.

"Where is your home?" he asked.

"Bastrop, Louisiana, a small town in the north of the state," I responded, talking faster than normal, and a little embarrassed about the southern location.

He seemed at a loss for words momentarily, but followed up with, "You should consider moving to New York City. This is where young artists like yourself come, develop and thrive. This is the city of the arts and artists."

Then he and the two companions with him signaled that they should continue on to rehearsal.

"It's such a pleasure to meet you, Maestro Bernstein," I said as he left. "And thanks very much for the advice."

For several years he had featured young artists performing with the Philharmonic on his nationally televised Sunday program, and I wondered if that was a hint from him of that possibility. But after my second visit to New York in five years, I could not imagine living in the huge, noisy and frighteningly fast-paced Big Apple.

Following the Carnegie Hall experience, my memory is totally blank, including the drive back to Bloomington, probably in shock from the astounding back-to-back Bell and Bernstein meetings. Nevertheless, it did not escape me how reassuring and supportive Mr. Bell was, and how Dr. B was calling on some powerful musicians in an attempt to thrust me into a professional career path compatible with my capability —but where African Americans are forbidden to tread.

"Congratulations! You're the tuba player for the *faculty* brass quintet," Dr. B happily proclaimed before I could sit down at my next lesson. "And we will be performing at the Indiana State Music Education Association convention in Indianapolis in two weeks."

I stood there cradling my tuba after yet another tremor producing announcement, trying to comprehend what he had just blurted out. Trying to understand the relationship between the words *"you"* and *"faculty."* Dr. B was the trombone professor who also taught tuba, and to organize a faculty quintet I was selected to fill the tuba role (William Bell would join the faculty the next year). Then I looked down at the music stand and saw the music we would perform under the title, *Sonatine for Brass*, composed by Eugene Bozza.

At that point I went into full-on shock, my heart racing as though trying to exit swiftly under the studio's acoustically sealed door. The chaotic and extreme notation I saw was far beyond any music I had played before. And then I thought about the *real* faculty I would be performing with, including Professor Philip Farkas, the newly arrived former principal French horn player with the Chicago Symphony. The standards and expectations for me had just leapt up several notches—again.

But, somehow, with Dr. B's methodical coaching, and my resolute practice and determination, the ensuing performance measured up. Sitting next to Dr. B in the quintet, I was able to make the audience believe momentarily that I was an IU faculty member, a gigantic hurdle. And afterwards, the real professors in the quintet expressed their complete satisfaction with my playing, raising my confidence to new heights. Although, I was just glad to not have embarrassed them and the university.

Taking note of my playing, Professor Farkas, along with percussion professor, George Gaber, both members of the Aspen, Colorado, summer Music Festival Orchestra, approached Dr. B. about my appointment to that orchestra for the upcoming 1961 festival. They had recently been informed of a newly created full-time tuba position with a request for recommendations.

"Of course," Dr. B instantly responded, and in my next lesson he told me, "You have a summer job as the tuba player for the Aspen Music Festival Orchestra."

And that was that, no questions asked, as usual.

Until that moment, I had not heard about the Aspen Music Festival, or the orchestra. But it became my first professional job as a tuba player, arguably with some of the world's greatest musicians. The major American Symphony Orchestra seasons ended late spring making it possible for the musicians to acquire summer positions. Consequently, that summer the Aspen Orchestra included Anshel Brusilow, concertmaster of the Philadelphia Orchestra; Ray Still, principal oboist of the Chicago Symphony; Keith Brown, principal trombonist of the Philadelphia Orchestra; Robert Nagel, first trumpet and leader of the famous New York Brass Quintet, and of course, IU's French horn player Professor Farkas and Professor Gaber, a former New York City professional percussionist, to name a few of the incredible musicians I performed with.

Coincidently, I discovered much later that my appointment made me the first Black principal tuba player for an American professional symphony orchestra, which may have become a permanent summer job, were it not for Uncle Sam's draft intervention the next year.

With my summer job secure, Dr. B pushed to the forefront my next two challenges: the Master's degree, and potentially, Performer's Certificate recitals. Since I was pursuing the Music Education degree, I had the option of performing a recital, or completing a public-school music-related practicum. I didn't ask. I knew that Dr. B had already determined that I would perform a recital.

We had been working on three solos during my studio lessons including Hindemith's *Sonata for Tuba and Piano* and Dr. B's *Sonata for Tuba and Piano*. The two sonatas had demanding piano parts, and somehow, Dr. B managed to persuade Sarah Carson, one of the music school's top student pianists, to join me in the quest for perfection.

Effectively masking the anxieties, I usually experienced for solo performances, the recital was almost flawless, before a small audience of faculty and students. And as I was walking through the backstage exit, Dr. B announced, "I'm nominating you for the Performance Certificate," and scampered off, presumably to do just that.

The Performer's Certificate is a prestigious honor bestowed on students who demonstrate exceptional solo performance qualities, and requires a recital before the entire school of music faculty who make the decision collectively. Later that day, Dr. B advised me that my certificate recital was in one week, on the last day of the semester.

"And by the way, no tuba player has ever received the award," he said casually as he left. "Oh my," were the only words I could mumble.

On the stage again, with intense lighting centered on me and Sarah, I did a repeat performance for perhaps the most critical audience possible: professional School of Music artists/teachers, many of them currently performing on major world stages. And some with specialties focused on research, theory and education. And who knew if some were even familiar with the tuba, or would even consider its solo potential. However, intently focused on preparation, the audience was the least of my concerns.

At the end of that performance, exhaustion descended on me like a hammer, compounded by two long years of intense, stressful circumstances. Slowly leaving the stage after applause that I could not gage, I wanted to get to my packed car parked nearby with waiting wife, Janie, and head home away from the School of Music's intense and competitive environment. But following instructions, I waited at the stage exit for the faculty decision.

A short time later, Dr. B was walking briskly toward me down the corridor smiling broadly.

"Congratulations!" he shouted. "You did a marvelous job! You are now the first tubist to receive the IU School of Music Performer's Certificate!"

Though exhausted, I managed to join the momentary jubilation with the few students standing there with us, thinking about how this accomplishment symbolized the tuba's acceptance as a legitimate solo instrument, an aspiration I had strived for since high school. Apparently, the faculty was not deterred by the musical source. But I also felt personal satisfaction in achieving this level of accomplishment as a young Black man of Southern heritage battling against the tide of systemic racism.

Dr. B was very proud of his protégé, and I was extremely pleased to honor him with this achievement for his steadfast confidence in me and my ability. He absolutely poured much of his time, thought and effort into my professional and personal development, more than I could have anticipated. And I was satisfied with the results of two years of hard work and struggle, but unsure of where it would lead. However, feeling drained, I felt it was now time for me to leave IU, only to discover that Dr. B wasn't done with me yet.

Unaware at the time, during the previous several months, he had tried unsuccessfully to acquire a university or orchestra appointment for me, positions he believed matched my competence and would continue to push my development. On my behalf, he pursued an advertised tuba teaching position for me at Youngstown State University, in Ohio, but found they were not ready for a Black faculty member—no matter how qualified, or who was making the recommendation.

So, as I started toward my car, Dr. B blocked my path.

"I've arranged for a doctorial assistantship for you here, in brass pedagogy, starting next year, so you can continue the great progress you've made. It's awaiting your return in August," he proudly announced, standing there as though waiting for an immediate affirmative answer.

But I was unable to respond with an "Okay, I'll do what you ask," as I had for two years. My mind was unable to function, deadened by the accumulation of stress from the back-to-back recitals, and the two years of unrelenting pressure at IU. I was tired.

"Thanks so much Dr. B. You have already done so much for me these two years," my mouth managed to mumble finally. "But I can't answer right now. I know this is an incredible opportunity you're offering, but there's so much to think about." He looked a bit deflated, but I went on. "I'm really appreciative of everything you've done for me. After I get home, I need to give it some thought. I'll call you real soon."

The disappointment registered fully on Dr. B's face, so accustomed was he to my following his every instruction and suggestion without question. He visualized his student performing and teaching in the highest ranks in the future, regardless of his race. And I did owe him a lot.

"Well, alright, but be sure and call me as soon as you can," he said. "I had to negotiate with my brass faculty colleagues to get this assistantship for next year."

IU had challenged my ability as an African-American to survive and succeed within a majority white institution, a highly ranked institution. With that silent, but passionate understanding, I said goodbye, picked up my tuba, walked to my waiting wife and car, stuffed the instrument inside and drove off—*the musician I never thought I could be, and the tuba player I would never be again, the impact of persistent racism.*

After a few days back home in Bastrop, trying to relax and clear my head for considering Dr. B's incredible offer, I discovered that I was indeed deeply in "burnout" mode, confirming earlier feelings. And while thinking about the opportunity, I recalled witnessing the extraordinary demands of doctorial study at IU with sometimes devastating consequences; some students leaving without completing the degree, and others simply freaking out.

If I returned for the offered doctoral assistantship, would I be able to survive in that environment? Even with the close and attentive support of Dr. B? And, in any case, did I currently have the energy and psychological stamina for doctoral study at IU, or anywhere for that matter? I thought not, particularly at the time.

So, I phoned Dr. B, and as diplomatically and apologetically as I could, told him that I needed to decline the offer, citing mental fatigue as justification. Again, I thanked him for all of his help, support, and encouragement. I could hear the disappointment in his voice, but I knew it was the right decision. Under the circumstances, I was convinced that attempting the doctorate could have meant failure and devastating disappointment for both of us.

Two weeks later, leaving Janie in Bastrop with my parents because my summer festival contract required that I share a room with another orchestra member, I began the drive to Aspen for my summer gig in my one-year-old Corvair. About 125 miles west of Denver my map showed two roads to Aspen, one more or less direct, the other considerably longer, going around northwest of Aspen to Glenwood Springs, then coming back southeast. Already tired, sleep deprived and tense from crossing 11,900-foot Loveland Pass, I wanted to get to my destination quickly, so I chose the direct route using Highway 82.

However, my map did not show the route traversed hazardous mountain terrain, including the 12,095-foot Independence Pass over the Continental Divide via a narrow, treacherous stretch of the road only recently reopened after being cleared of snow, ice, and rocks.

Alone and terrified after leaving the paved road, my little Corvair rattled violently at five miles per hour over rocks and boulders. I saw no cars going in either direction. Pressing the accelerator yielded little response making my heart pound faster and faster, worrying the engine would quit running altogether. I learned later in Aspen, it was because of the altitude's thin oxygen.

As if things couldn't get worse, the road narrowed at several points to one lane, where I could only see straight down for hundreds of feet on one side, straight up at cliffs on the other and completely blind as to what was around the next bend. And I'm thinking, "What if I meet a car? Then what? Who's going to back up?" although I hadn't seen another car or person since taking this route.

Driving around one sharp turn, my eyes widened seeing a stream from melting snow rushing across a freshly grated section of road. The ground looked really loose. "This doesn't look good," the inner voice cautioned as I slammed on the brakes, wondering if the road would support the weight of my car. I got out, took a closer look, walked across the section, and then, holding my breath and praying, slowly crept across. The road held up (or I wouldn't be writing this narrative), allowing me to breathe a sigh of relief, inhaling the cool refreshing, mountain air.

Periodically, I stopped to relieve the tension and take in the spectacular views of Mother Nature at her grandest. Though frazzled, I drank in the majestic snow-covered mountain peaks dominating the vista, separated by deep curving valleys in shades of green and gray, with roaring streams cascading between rock crevices and over ledges. It was there, on a dangerous and desolate Colorado mountain road, that I discovered I was not only partial to large bodies of water like the Gulf of Mexico, which I reveled in as a child at summertime Gulfside retreats. But I found that I was now enamored of those tall, evergreen-shrouded, snow-capped mountains. "This is simply spectacular," my eyes and senses drinking it all in.

Descending the western slope, my paramount concern was slowing my car without burning up the brakes. I could smell the telltale aroma. But when I finally spied the outline of Aspen appearing in the distance at 7800 feet above sea level, I began to relax. And when finally reaching the eastern city limits' flat terrain, it was like landing on solid ground after a slow-motion, anxiety-laden parachute jump.

It was a trip I vowed never to repeat, but unwisely did more than fifteen years later with Juel, my second wife, who has never forgiven me for the ordeal.

After a few days of altitude sickness, I began enjoying my eleven weeks of orchestra rehearsals and performances with professional musicians in the festival's signature open-sided tent. From my vantage point on a platform near the back of the orchestra, I could see past the conductor to the distant shape of Aspen Mountain, including fascinating, fleeting storms and showers popping up across the monumental landscape. Although this was a job, there was ample time for the badly needed relaxation after the stress of IU.

Izler Solomon was the orchestra's music director, and Walter Susskind and Darius Milhaud (the eminent composer) were visiting conductors. Adele Addison, Walter Trampler and George Gaber were renowned soloists. I also performed again with Phil Farkas in the festival brass quintet, and in a jazz band, led by George Gaber, where he discovered that I could not improvise.

Herbert Light, the newest member of the Philadelphia Orchestra's famed violin section, and only a few years older, was my roommate. Another first, I was rooming with a white person. I don't know how he felt about having a Black roommate, but our relationship worked out. Except for a fishing excursion he invited me to, we didn't hang out together. Anshel Brusilow, the orchestras' concert master, invited both of us for a delightful evening of food, wine and conversation at the house he and his wife were renting for the summer. They carried most of the conversation, but I enjoyed the evening.

During the first week of the festival, Brusilow introduced himself with a curious inquiry: "What position do you want to play on our softball team?" "Softball team?!" I responded. "We play softball?" I could not imagine professional musicians, whose critical body parts were worth millions, would risk injury playing softball. The image of that blew me away. But they did, and I joined them, playing center field, shielding my lips at all cost. Brusilow played second base with an oversized glove to protect his valuable violin-fingers.

That summer was memorable, not only for the softball, but for the broader experiences. Foremost, I played my first professional orchestra job that included eminent musicians from some of America's top symphonies. Later I discovered this made me the first African-American professional orchestra tuba player. The Aspen experience also broadened my horizons and exposed me to a life I never dreamed of as a young Deep South boy cutting meat in the back of my father's store. Thanks to Dr. B and the intense IU experience, it seems I had begun a promising future doing what I love most, playing the tuba.

However, a permanent professional orchestra position did not materialize, and having no other job offers, I accepted a teaching appointment at Grambling College. Later that year, I received a U.S. Army draft notice and decided to enlist for four-years in the U.S. Navy (1962-66. more on this period in the next chapter). For three of those years, I was assigned to the Great Lakes Navy Base band north of Chicago. While there I drove with a close bandmate to Bloomington for an overnight weekend visit with Dr. B and family. They were great hosts, doing their best to accommodate us while they were still raising children at home.

"So, what are we thinking after you leave the Navy?" Dr. B asked over breakfast, and then answered his own question. "To get you into a professional orchestra, perhaps we should look at minor orchestra positions to get some experience. However, I'm aware that the tuba position in the Royal Concertgebouw Orchestra of Amsterdam was recently vacated by Roger Bobo who joined the LA Philharmonic. I think we should apply for a two-year Fulbright Fellowship to that orchestra."

I couldn't imagine myself in another country, particularly one I knew nothing about. But with his encouragement and assistance, I applied, but made it no further than the second screening. And though Dr. B remained optimistic about my professional performance career, I was not. Meanwhile, the lack of performing challenging music in the Great Lakes band was continuing to take a toll on the quality of my playing and my morale.

Several weeks before my August 4, 1966, honorable discharge (extended one month because of the Vietnam War), I learned that the Oklahoma City Symphony was advertising to fill its principal tuba position. I contacted Dr. B immediately for advice. He phoned the orchestra's Maestro, Guy Frazier Harrison, following up with an official reference letter, and requested William Bell do the same.

Professional symphony orchestras usually hold open auditions for vacant positions, but based on my powerful references, including one from Arnold Jacobs, principal tubist with the Chicago Symphony, with whom I was currently taking lessons, Maestro Harrison appointed me to the position unseen and unheard. When I read the letter of offer and contract, I couldn't believe it.

"Dr. B, the Oklahoma Symphony job came through," I excitedly proclaimed in a phone call that day. "It's really happening. Thanks so much for your help and everything!"

"Well, you deserve it. You're talented and you've worked hard," he said. "So, go make us proud."

I could hear the joy in his voice through that sedate response, pleased and proud that his student/mentee had finally reached the full-time professional orchestra ranks, my dream coming true.

So, commencing in September 1966, I was the principal tuba player and first full-time Black musician with the Oklahoma City Symphony. Janie and I packed up and moved quickly so that I could make the first rehearsal of the orchestra for the season opener. A house and two children, Michael and Eva, and a dog soon followed along with my second job at Langston University, to help support it all.

This was all working quite well until it wasn't. Long work hours for the two jobs, the lack of challenging orchestra music for the tuba, and difficulty with Langston's administrators helped precipitate a failed marriage leading to a 1971 divorce.

Trying to distance myself from the calamity, I drove to Aspen that summer for a week's visit hoping that the beautiful, serene mountain landscape I had fallen in love with would provide relief. Riding the ski lifts, walking the trails and hearing the festival orchestra, as hoped, decreased the stress and cleared my mind significantly.

One afternoon, lying in bed enjoying the view of Aspen Mountain through my hotel room window, the phone rang.

"Sir, are you John Smith, the tuba player who studied at Indiana University during the early 1960s?" the voice on the other end pleaded.

Surprised and hesitant to respond as one might expect, I silently held the phone for a few seconds to determine my response.

"Well, yeeesss, I might be, who's calling?"

The voice on the other end instantly emitted a volcanic sigh of relief, and continued in a joyful laughing voice.

"Wow, am I happy to find you!" he said. "I've been calling every hotel in Aspen. I'm Don Owen, trumpet instructor at the University of South Florida in Tampa. We're developing a new tuba position in the music department. Don Kneeburg (1938-2020) and Lee Eubanks, Indiana University schoolmates of yours, recommended I call you to see if you're interested."

Was this for real? Someone I didn't know, calling from a school I had never heard of, in a state I'd never been to, offering a potential job without seeing me or hearing me play. And he referenced IU school mates I vaguely remembered, from ten years ago. This just didn't seem possible.

"Well, uh, I don't know...I..."

"We're just calling to see if you're available and interested as we finalize the position. It took some doing to find out that you were in Aspen, calling your Bastrop home, IU, the Oklahoma City Orchestra and all over Aspen," Don Owen continued happily, while I tried to weigh the reason he gave for his persistent effort to find me. "Almost all of the hotels had a John Smith. Ha, ha, ha. Some more than one!"

"Well, uh, sure I'm interested, particularly if IU schoolmates are there," I said, wondering why one of them was not calling.

"Okay, good. Give me a phone number where you can be reached and I'll be back in touch. Meanwhile, enjoy Aspen!"

It would take a year for the position to be confirmed, during which I received occasional updates. But the opportunity was timely, since my current personal and professional affairs strongly suggested the need for a change of location, distancing myself from the troubling circumstances.

As things at USF were developing, and still unsure of the position's prospects, I called Dr. B for his counsel. As usual, he was elated and responsive, sending the following reference letter to the University:

March 10, 1972

To whom it may concern:

Mr. John Lee Smith is a distinguished musician and educator. He has his Master of Music Education from Indiana University during which time he set a new standard for tuba playing, being the first person ever to win the coveted Indiana University Performer's Certificate on his instrument. In addition, he was the first tuba player with the Indiana University brass quintet (The National Brass Quintet). He was a student at the time, the only student ever to function in this capacity. Furthermore, he was one of the better instrumentalists in the group.

Since then, he has become one of the most respected solo performers with the Oklahoma City Symphony and the only black professional symphony tuba player in the world to my knowledge. He has been featured as soloist on a number of occasions. In addition, he has served as a teacher and in an administrative capacity at nearby Langston University.

Mr. Smith is a gentleman, kind, considerate, loyal, and responsible. He has encouraged many young students in the most idealistic and selfless way. He works well with people regardless of race, creed, or color, and I'm proud of my association with him.

Thomas Beversdorf

Professor of Music

The position was finalized in June 1972. And, in August of that year I started my USF job as tenure-track assistant professor of music, teaching tuba, music theory and advising students. The move included a new wife, Juel Shannon and five children (more on this later). In May '73, I was happy to return to IU for the first International Tuba Symposium-Workshop, and to see Dr. B. Driving all night with two of my students, we arrived too late for a special reception Dr. B hosted at his home. Unfortunately, I only saw him briefly during the busy event, chatting with him while sitting on the stairs of the concert hall lobby. I sensed he wasn't feeling well.

Almost eight years later, I learned that Dr. B had passed away on February 15, 1981, at the age of 57, a death hastened by complications involving asthma, a chronic condition he struggled with.

When I learned of his death, I felt a tremendous loss. He was my teacher, a white professor who inspired and prepared me for the professional world. Incessantly mentoring and encouraging me while trying to break down racial barriers so that I might perform and work at the level compatible with my competence. I had expected him to be there for unforeseen future challenges and opportunities, a steadfast and dependable pillar to lean on.

In November 2001, while back at IU attending the special concert of David Baker's music, described in the previous chapter, Mrs. Beversdorf picked me up at my hotel for dinner before the concert. We had exchanged notes and Christmas cards since Dr. B's death.

"Hi John, I'm so glad you let me know earlier that you were going to be here," She joyously chimed when I called her on arrival in Bloomington. "Tomorrow, I leave for international travel, so this is perfect timing." She picked me up, gave me a brief tour of the community, which included First Baptist Church, where I had attended premieres of Dr. B's sacred music, and a short stop at their home.

While Mrs. Beversdorf was in another part of the house, I stood in the familiar large but darkened living room, staring out of the drapery framed glass doors and beyond the balcony to the scenic view of tall oak, maple and hickory trees, as my mind quickly scrolled through the memorable times spent with Dr. B: The intense weekly lessons in his studio; his peeking into my practice room day and night providing critiques and encouragement; conducting and coaching brass section rehearsals for the IU Philharmonic; sitting next to me in the faculty brass quintet performance; hosting me at the family home; and seeing him on stage joyously acknowledging the noisy applause after the premier of his *Fourth Symphony*. This was an emotional and nostalgic moment, during which I felt and missed his powerful and persistent presence.

During the 1960s and 1970s, years of racial strife and aggressive protests against Black injustices in the U.S. (school desegregation battles, student sit-ins and freedom riders), Dr. Thomas Beversdorf used his own personal brand of *affirmative action* to make sure the talent and mind of this African American (me) did not go to waste, but would be of significant benefit to himself, his family, and unforeseen others.

Later, over dinner at the popular music student and faculty restaurant across the street from the School of Music where the David Baker concert would take place, Mrs. Beversdorf shared a remarkable comment Dr. B made to her during my student years at IU that left me speechless, and practically in tears.

He said, "I strongly believe that John Smith has an extraordinary future ahead of him."

PART III

They Enhanced My Career

Chapter 13

Avenue Opening

Grambling College the site of my first permanent teaching appointment. My mother's alma mater.

I felt really fortunate to have this job after leaving Aspen in the summer of 1961 without any other employment prospects. No symphony orchestra or major university offers materialized that Dr. Beversdorf had strongly advocated for. Nevertheless, the IU Master's degree was paying off, landing me the college position without any prior teaching experience. My expectations were to be teaching a high school band somewhere in Louisiana. However, I struggled greatly that year with the disparity between the exceptional musical standards at IU and those at Grambling, causing my disparate push for improvements. Unfortunately, some colleagues thought I was arrogant, overly influenced by my white university experience.

Janie and I were provided a temporary on-campus apartment in an old military style wood frame building complex. We laughed about seeing people approaching our front door through cracks in the walls. However, with a few friendly coworkers and my parents in Bastrop, only an hour's driving distance, we quickly settled in for the start of my college teaching career.

This resolve and commitment was going well until a letter arrived from the Morehouse Parish Draft Board. "What the...! This can't be what I think it is," I thought as I opened the envelope. But it was. "Greetings," it read. "You must report for examination and possible induction into the U.S. Army...." I couldn't believe what I was reading. I was shocked, and angry, but of course, knew I had to comply, requiring a one-hour drive to Shreveport.

After completing the physical and aptitude exams, which detected a slight arrhythmic heartbeat, a uniformed staff sergeant strode into the lounge where potential draftees were seated anxiously awaiting the outcome.

"John L. Smith! Identify yourself!" he shouted.

I waved my hand eagerly, anticipating an announcement of exemption, given my age, 23, and family deferment categories for which I believed I was eligible. And I was teaching full-time, as well.

But instead, to my horror, he bellowed, "Get your private matters in order, and expect an induction notice in the next few weeks!" What? Totally traumatized, I understood the message—as did everyone in the room. "Uncle Sam wants you. NOW!"

Thankfully, the drive back to Grambling that evening gave me the needed time and quiet space to calm down and contemplate possible options, if there were any. This was not supposed to be happening at this phase of my life. When I got home, Janie, and my parents on the receiving of my phone call, were as baffled as I was.

Early the next day, I hastily acquired Grambling College employment verification documents to request a teaching exemption. I express-mailed them to the Army. Several days later, I received a teaching deferment through the end of Grambling's nine-month contract. Then, I requested a summer teaching appointment with the hope of extending the deferment. But even after desperately pleading my case to the university administration, it was not approved. So, beginning June 1962, I was vulnerable for induction into the Army.

Apparently, with the Cold War heating up and the developing Vietnam crisis looming, the federal government was increasing military conscription, and my Bastrop/Morehouse Parish draft board was intent on Black men filling a disproportionate part of that need (evident by the disproportion of Black men serving in that war). But I did not fancy myself in a foxhole with munitions flying all around, wasting those six long, hard years invested in productive college music study. So, pushed by desperation, on July 5, 1962, I volunteered for the Navy, guaranteeing four years of service as a musician, the best option for me —and my country.

I inquired about the Navy's Officer Candidate School, but was informed that as a junior officer, I would not be assigned music duties. Dr. Beversdorf suggested I press for an assignment to the President's Navy Band in Washington, D.C., after boot camp, based on my performance and educational background. I got a verbal commitment, but no written guarantee.

The next week, I reported for induction in Little Rock, Arkansas, where I was treated to segregated meals in a private restaurant under Navy contract. The Black recruits were sent to the back door, where we ate in the kitchen, while our fellow white recruits were welcomed through the front entrance and ate in the main dining area. For overnight sleeping accommodations, the white recruits were quartered in private rooms at the nicely appointed YMCA. However, we recruits of color were dropped off at a rundown rooming house in the Black section of town, where four individuals slept with strangers on double bunk beds in small, poorly ventilated rooms. I was furious and emotionally deflated. "What happened to the integrated military service?" my mind shouted. When the induction formalities were concluded, I was given a date to report for boot camp at the Great Lakes Navy Base forty miles north of Chicago.

Those first experiences were rude awakening of what to expect in the U.S. Navy as a Black man—almost 14 years after President Harry S. Truman signed an Executive Order desegregating the nation's armed forces. Like school desegregation, progress was ultra-slow, both entities fighting the law and justice. I was *required* to serve in the military, and apparently also required to face embedded institutionalized racism. I later discovered the Navy staunchly held onto racist practices longer than the other service branches.

Janie and I packed up and drove to Chicago, where she stayed with a sister during my eleven weeks of basic training. Racial confrontation continued when a white racist recruit from Florida was selected as my boot camp troop leader, relegating me to flag bearer. Our paths crossed again two years later back at Great Lakes, where I heard him yell, "Kill the niggers!" while sitting in the band room lounge watching a televised newscast of Black students being beaten during a civil right protest. Superior ranked personnel heard him—but did nothing.

After the first three weeks of intense military grooming in boot camp, I was "thankfully" assigned to the recruit's marching band that practiced one hour each day and performed for weekly graduation ceremonies. Because of my university music background, I was chosen to lead my graduating class of over a thousand recruits in singing the Navy Hymn for that occasion. Standing on a tall ladder conducting them and the band in front of visiting relatives and recruit command officers, I had a momentary sense of honor and pride, even without Janie and her Chicago relatives in attendance, who were all unable to attend the ceremony due to work. Thanks to my Smith Family, Inc. home discipline and work ethic, I managed to avoid strict boot camp rule violations and castigation that so many suffered.

After boot camp, I was assigned to the Navy School of Music in Washington, D.C., as expected, across the Anacostia River from The Navy Yard where the President's Navy Band was stationed, hopefully my next move. Janie and I moved into an old, shoddy third-floor apartment with a bathroom at the top of the stairs, shared with an apartment across the hall, an anxious situation. Once affluent homes on tree-lined streets in northwest Washington, the buildings were retrofitted as apartments, and were in great disrepair as cheap rentals for desperate Blacks like myself. The area was later gentrified for Washington elites. It was a short distance from Howard University, where Janie found a clerical job, and an easy early morning drive to the base that took me in front of the Capital. There was also a berth provided for me on base for weekend duty and military emergencies.

During those first several weeks we at times wondered, "Where is our next meal coming from?" living off E2 military pay, less than $90 a month, before the housing allowance kicked in. This was all new to me having never lived in those conditions or felt the desperate want of anything. But I did not share this with my parents or ask for help. They had already given so much of themselves to me, college and support at Grambling, and not yet over the marriage surprise. We later moved into a more contemporary and safer apartment and were able to purchase weekly groceries rather than scraping money together daily for food.

The twenty-four-week music school curriculum was designed for high-school graduates, teaching basic music skills and preparation for performing at Navy ceremonial and entertainment events. Except for practicing band maneuvers for military rituals, there wasn't much new for me to learn. I continued the depressing analysis of how quickly my tuba performance qualities were deteriorating, and would continue unless I was transferred to a more challenging environment.

And knowing that the President's Navy Band was close by, and recalling the verbal promise, I applied for reassignment to the band --- twice, indicating a willingness to audition. Each time I was informed that there was no vacant tuba position.

Meanwhile, I learned the shocking news that following music school training, personnel were assigned immediately to eighteen months of sea duty, with only one rotation to a land base before returning to sea during the four years of service. For me, that frightening bit of information meant weeks on ships at sea without the ability to practice my tuba and perform challenging music, potentially losing entirely the professional skills I had spent years developing.

That spurred me to press urgently for a land Navy base assignment to the Annapolis Naval Academy Band or the School of Music teaching staff, where I had already been assigned to teach tuba temporarily as an adjunct. I had also performed in the school's staff jazz band for a piece that required the tuba (I have a LP recording of that concert performance). Informed that there were no tuba vacancies for the Annapolis band, I was ordered to the school Commander's office for consideration for a staff assignment. I reported, he saw me briefly, and that was the end of that request, regardless of my academic and performance credentials. What he saw was Black and unwelcomed. Seemingly the end of my options, I was desperate and devastated.

But the racist symbolism got worse. However, an honors band was formed representing the best student musicians, and I was selected as the tuba player, which provided a desired moment of excitement and the opportunity to perform demanding music. The conductor, a staff member, was also a composer and arranger, and programmed his latest composition for the concert. Sitting down for rehearsal and surveying the music in front of me my inner-anger exploded seeing his march with the title: *Stars and Bars.* Performing the composition again tested my personal dignity and self-discipline, leaving me crushed and helpless. The name of the march was, a tribute to the Confederate battle flag, and a counter to John Philip Sousa's *Stars and Stripes Forever,* considered the national march of the United States.

As the reassignments of students neared and my anxiety escalating, a new tuba teacher arrived at the school with the rank of Chief Petty Officer Musician, scheduled to stay only until his retirement papers were processed. During my first lesson with him, I learned he had just vacated the first chair position of the President's Navy Band, and that *another* tuba position had been vacant for over a year. After hearing me play, he encouraged me to apply again, which I did, immediately, for the third time. Days later, I received the same response: "There is no vacant tuba position." That lie made it obvious that the Navy's leadership had every intention of keeping the President's Navy Band all-white as it had been for its thirty-seven-year history.

Now I was running out of hope, feeling really desperate. Years of personal aspirations, intense and costly preparation for a professional orchestra career were in jeopardy. I could be sent to sea at any time.

The music school Commander again ordered me to his office. "Okay, this is it," bracing myself for the devastating orders as I stood at ease in front of his desk. "I'm about to lose everything." However, standing up and without preamble or explanation, he presented me two options for serving the remainder of my four-year Navy obligation. "One," he sternly announced, "assignment to the base band in

Anchorage, Alaska." A short pause. "Or two, assignment to the Naval Station Great Lakes Base band near Chicago" (where I had been for boot camp). What? I was startled and momentarily confused. Not a sea assignment? And before I could breathe a sigh of relief, the Commander continued his *order*: "I must have your choice now!" My mind was reeling, but quickly assessed my options, concluding, "That's a no-brainer. Who would volunteer for a three-year stay in Alaska?"

"I choose Great Lakes, Sir," speaking clearly, keeping my elation in check.

"Dismissed!"

"Yes Sir!"

I left feeling my life had been saved. No, it wasn't the preferred assignment to the President's Navy Band, but it was the next best thing. A land and *not* a sea assignment!

In later retrospect, why was I suddenly assigned to a land base rather than sent to sea? And why couldn't the Navy have done the lawful and right thing and sent me across the Anacostia River to fill one of the two vacant tuba positions in the President's Navy Band? Perhaps the Navy's high command—pressured by the recent March on Washington, President Kennedy's recently appointed Committee on Equal Opportunity in the Armed Forces, and the ongoing national Black protests—chose the middle ground that satisfied my anxiety over salvaging my career, *and* kept their premiere band, the Navy's national symbol of pride, completely white.

Two weeks later in late November, I reported to Great Lakes, after Janie and I quickly acquired a small basement apartment in an old house in Evanston, across the street from a scrap iron business, and only blocks from Northwestern University. For the first week, with one foot of frozen snow on the ground, I was ordered to stay home, the only thing a person could do under the circumstances.

Welcome to Chicago winters.

Looking back, my eleven-month assignment to the Washington, D.C., Navy Music School was not without some extraordinary and interesting experiences, two of national significance. Only days after I arrived, all U.S. military bases were placed on lockdown during the Cuban Missile Crisis (October 14-26, 1962). Though we were only a small standalone "music school" base, a threat to no one, I was ordered to strap a belt around my waist with a holstered pistol, minus live ammunition, and stand guard-duty at the entrance. Under the circumstances, I was a little scared and glad no Cuban or Russian hostiles showed up.

Additionally, the music school base was placed on high alert during President Kennedy's June 26, 1963, famous *"Ich bin ein Berliner"* speech in West Berlin; our government was unable to predict the Russian reaction. And for the August 28, 1963, historic March on Washington for Jobs and Freedom, where Dr. Martin Luther King, Jr. made his famous "I Have a Dream" speech, the music school was the camp and staging ground for hundreds of Army troops prepared to converge quickly on the mall to control the greatly anticipated riots that never materialized. Gazing over the rows of tents, I was amazed, but also angry that I was prevented from participating in the march.

My outrage escalated the morning of the march as I watched the Army troops sitting aboard trucks, riot gear ready, waiting for orders to deploy to the mall, which, of course, never happened. It was painfully theatrical, and I still carry that aggressive image with me today. Few people, I suspect, are aware of the level of military readiness ordered by

President Kennedy in anticipation of violent disorder, seemingly certain that Black people could not peacefully demonstrate their frustrations at the federal government's maddening inaction to protect their lawful rights as American citizens.

Joining the Great Lakes Naval Station band, I quickly experienced its busy schedule, performing base ceremonies and concerts, and traveling to events, large and small, in distant towns and cities, including Sioux City, Iowa; Sioux Falls, South Dakota; and Cheyenne, Wyoming. I was the only tuba player for the concert band, but joined by one or two others for marching duties, playing the sousaphone once again. We played for military rituals, special events, municipal parades, state and county fairs, and once playing for the Cheyenne, Wyoming national rodeo. In a small Iowa town, we led a parade to the county fair several miles out, and while enthusiastically playing I saw only stalks of corn on both sides of the road. Although the music was not demanding I was performing often and practiced occasionally in a small open space near the lounge, not ideal for concentration.

After my first year, the Navy scaled back its base-bands assignments, probably reducing expenses due to escalating Vietnam costs. Non-military-related requests were accepted if the host paid all expenses, which limited off-base engagements to military requirements, and community patriotic events and parades. Regular Great Lakes base performances included rousing marches in front of the base commander's residence and flag raising ceremonies each morning until it was too cold, and lunch-time concerts in a gazebo between the administration building and the base commander's residence, attended primarily by the local squirrels.

One annual off-base event I found amusing was the Lake Michigan nighttime Parade of Boats along the shore of Chicago Loop. The band played marches and show tunes from the aft deck of an anchored Coast Guard ship, while colorful lighted and decorated luxury yachts floated slowly between ship and shore. The on-shore gatherings were entertained by our music and the illuminated floating pageantry.

Choosing Great Lakes, I knew would provide the possibility for studying tuba with Arnold Jacobs, the celebrated principal tuba player with the Chicago Symphony Orchestra (CSO). The band's lighter schedule allowed time for me to explore that opportunity. However, I was not confident he would accept me as a student, not knowing me or having references touting my competence. Also, my performance quality had suffered significantly over the years since IU and Aspen, making me less appealing as a student. "But hey," I finally rationalized, "I won't know until I try." So, I made an uneasy cold call describing my background, and ending with expressing a strong desire for studying with him. Surprisingly, he graciously scheduled me for an exploratory lesson, an audition of sorts. Excited and anxiously looking forward to my first lesson, I needed to make sure I had the cash for his fee, which was a bit above expectation.

Arnold Jacobs was enjoying a remarkable international performance and teaching reputation, as his teaching expertise was not confined to the tuba. He taught all musical instruments that used human air for sound production, including voice. Consequently, professional musicians throughout the globe consulted him regarding certain performance issues, but most of his regular students were tuba players, like me.

A graduate of the prestigious Philadelphia Curtis Institute of Music, Jacobs was principal tubist with the Indianapolis and Pittsburgh

Symphony Orchestras before joining the Chicago Symphony Orchestra in 1944. The brass section of the orchestra, collectively and individually, was considered by many the best worldwide. Some, including me, conjectured that combining the brass and woodwind sections of the CSO with the luscious string section of the Philadelphia Orchestra would create the world's greatest symphony. Although, I'm sure the Berlin Philharmonic would take great exception to that assessment, and probably other orchestras, as well.

Arnold Jacobs taught in the basement of his home located in a Southwest Chicago working-class community, only a thirty-minute drive south of my Evanston apartment. Knocking tentatively at the modest one-story brick house, Gizella, Jacobs' wife, short figure, modestly dressed former dancer, greeted me graciously along with Schwepps, their friendly family dog. After a short wait in the quaint living room while he completed a lesson, Jacobs appeared in front of me with his hand out for a shake. "Hello, I'm Arnold Jacobs," the deep baritone voice rang-out. "Welcome. I hope you didn't have a difficult time finding my home." "No, not at all," I responded trying to sound confident. "You've met my wife and Schwepps, so let's go down to my studio. Follow me, but watch your step," he cautioned. "Wow," I thought following him. "This stairwell is tight for me and the tuba, and the stairs are steep. I wouldn't want to trip for my first lesson."

The studio I was entering was the subject of much speculation about scientific equipment Mr. Jacob's used for teaching. This, I would soon find out, was completely overblown.

"Why don't you tell me about yourself and how you learned to play the tuba," he said while sitting down next to me in the tight space. My briefing was short to make the best use of my lesson time. "Well, before you play for me, I need to measure your lung capacity with the spirometer," explaining the procedure, and announcing my capacity reading and its relevance. That was a new experience, indeed confirming the use of scientific equipment.

"Okay, let's hear you play something," he requested. All too aware of the diminished quality, I played a portion of a solo. Without direct criticism he made positive comments, but also suggestions for technical improvements based on his trademark "song and wind" approach: The musician must provide appropriate wind-lung support for tone production, "the respiration process," while concentrating on qualities demanded by the music. (See *Arnold Jacobs: Song and Wind*, by Brian Frederiksen, Edited by John Taylor, Windsong Press Limited, 1996).

At the end of my lesson, he commented, "You play very well. There are a few technical things we can work on, so let's schedule your next visit." I was very relieved and excited that he wanted to continue teaching me. Unfortunately, money was an issue that prevented me from immediately scheduling the next session. "Is it possible that I call you later to set up the appointment, given the Navy's unpredictable assignments?" I asked avoiding the embarrassing truth.

Living pay-check to pay-check, discretionary money was scarce. But getting into Jacobs' studio, studying with one of the country's tuba's "gods," was huge and demanded a special priority and sacrifice. So, I worked two part-time jobs, to earn extra cash for periodic lessons: Teaching music at the Firman Settlement House on Chicago's Southside one evening a week and Saturdays, and selling Mason Shoes door-to-door. This allowed for an average of two lessons per month.

Jacobs, along with William Bell, represented a paradigm for tuba performance that matched perfectly with my own intuitive approach since I had started playing the tuba and demonstrated at IU: that the tuba was simply another vehicle, though unique in tone and range, for conveying musical ideas and expressions. But he was where I wanted to be, the tubist with a top ten American orchestra. And perhaps studying with him could get me to that dream.

Not knowing what to expect initially, I found Jacobs amiable, and generous with his time and expertise. Many artists of his stature have strong egos and one must be careful of personal expressions. As an African American, I was always alert to possible racist slights from whites when meeting for the first time, even though this was a northern urban city. However, none of that applied to Mr. Jacobs who, over the course of our relationship, appeared genuinely interested in me and the development of my musical qualities.

Born June 11, 1915 and affectionately known as "Jake," Arnold Jacobs was approximately five-foot ten-inches tall with a barrel chest. Although it was mythically reported that he had the largest human lung-wind capacity possible, a tremendous asset for a tuba player, the truth was that he actually needed to breathe more frequently than normal while performing due to chronic struggles with lung disorders most of his life, which at one point required hospitalization. Perhaps because of this affliction, he became an expert on the efficient use of the respiratory system for wind instrumentalists and vocalists. This physical approach to playing the instrument varied from Beversdorf and Bell, but was useful as I continued to reverse the downward spiral of my performance.

Hearing Jake perform was exciting and instructional, which inspired me to attend Chicago Symphony concerts at Orchestra Hall on the Chicago Loop, and the Ravinia Summer Festival in Highland Park. Three interested Navy band cohorts and I, symbolizing a Chicago Symphony Orchestra groupie, often used our military IDs for free admissions to concerts, meeting Jake and other orchestra members at the stage entrance afterwards. They always seemed pleased to see us, and were gracious while responding to our questions as we slowed their walk to the parking garage. We also silently listened, taking mental notes, to their conversation about the concert they had just played. On Chicago winter nights, those were frigid walks, but talking with these venerated musicians, I hardly noticed, except after our meetings as I headed to my own car. The strong wind blowing across frozen Lake Michigan into the Loop was brutal, and nothing wrapped around your body could deter it from reaching straight through to your bones.

As I neared the end of my Navy commitment, not hopeful of finding a professional orchestra position, I asked Mr. Jacobs what he thought my prospects were as an African American—a question that surprised him. But after a brief moment of thought, he provided a diplomatic but sincere response.

It was late 1965, amid the civil rights and Vietnam War controversies that dominated America's sociopolitical fabric. In response, he acknowledged the context of my personal circumstances and dilemma, but nevertheless provided words of hope and encouragement.

"You are talented and perform extremely well," he said in his rich baritone voice. "Continue working hard and it's possible an avenue will open for you." Hearing the overall positive assessment, I thought, "Well, perhaps my performance mojo was starting to come back."

Several months later, he made one of the critical phone calls that led to my appointment with the Oklahoma City Symphony Orchestra. And just as important, I credit Arnold Jacobs with applying the final polish to my tuba performance capability. At that point, I was a really happy camper, a dream coming true after all.

However, while mustering out of the military joyfully anticipating my new job, the U.S. Navy, which I had served honorably for four years and one-month, hurled its final insult. The Pentagon proposed through my band Commanding Officer that in exchange for reenlisting for *six more years*, they would assign me to the President's Navy Band, presumably to integrate it, finally. And when I angrily rejected that affront, they quickly countered with an assignment to the Navy School of Music staff for the same reenlistment years.

I exploded, spewing an uncharacteristic profanity-laced rejection to that proposal, basically telling him where the Navy could put its offer, recalling the racist rejections four years earlier, and the lack of challenges since. Later I was thankful that my understanding Commanding Offer, the message bearer, did not communicate those exact words to the Pentagon, probably avoiding my court martial and a dishonorable discharge. August 5, 1966 marked the end of my military service for an "unequal justice under the Navy law", which I certainly didn't want interrupted.

Twenty-five years later in 1989, after six years with the Oklahoma City Symphony, and moving up through the ranks to become the fine arts dean at the University of South Florida in Tampa (more on USF experience later), I attempted to lure Arnold Jacobs to the university to fill the music school tuba position I had vacated to become dean. Recently retired from the Chicago Symphony, I reasoned that Florida, a state known for attracting retirees from frigid cities like Chicago, might appeal to him.

"Hi Jake. This is John Smith your former student calling to make you an offer you can't refuse," was my opening spiel. After appropriate re-acquaintance informalities, I continued, "I'd like you to accept a faculty position in the music school at USF and establish an international center for research and information dissemination of your "song and wind" performance concept. And by the way, the university is only an hour's drive to Sarasota where your son Dallas lives." Moments of silence, then, "Well, I don't know...I'll need to give that some thought and talk with Gizella." I felt like a super salesman. This was a big ask. At least he did not immediately reject the offer. But if I was successful, this would be a major coup for the USF School of Music, providing instant national notoriety.

He gave my offer considerable thought, but eventually declined because of long nurtured personal and professional ties to Chicago, which were much too deep for him and Gizella to leave. Yes, I was disappointed with their decision, but I also knew my offer was a long shot.

Two years later, Jake served as a consultant and panelist for a USF music school sponsored "Playing Less Hurt" conference at a Clearwater Gulf Coast resort hotel. Still USF Fine Arts Dean at the time, I shared a table with him during a luncheon, the only time my schedule allowed me to attend. Sitting two chairs over from him, we only managed brief personal interactions out of respect for the others around the table of eight, all wanting to converse with him.

Humble and gregarious, Jake welcomed the dialog, but during a break in the conversation he looked over and humored me by asking the big question: "Why on earth would anyone ever give up playing the tuba for academic administration?"

That has been difficult to explain to myself sometimes, but was exceedingly hard to justify to someone who had given his entire life to playing the instrument, and loving every minute of it! Unfortunately, not long afterwards, on October 7, 1998 Jake passed away, leaving a

powerful performance and teaching legacy for all of us who were lucky enough to experience his generous spirit and trademark "Song and Wind."

Chapter 14

Fateful Path

Let me take you back again to1972 in Oklahoma City, filling gaps that lead to and include Tampa, Florida. My life was in turmoil at the time, some of which you may recall: A collapsed marriage leading to a tragic unpleasant divorce. The loss of daily contact with my two young children, due to my former wife's custody. My discontent with the Oklahoma City Symphony and Langston University jobs. The orchestra music was not challenging enough to sustain my interest. And, Langston's president disagreed with the inclusion of Black music content in the curriculum.

Several months after the divorce was final, I was in a professionally unethical relationship with a Langston coed, unrelated to my marriage breakup. I convinced myself it was okay since she was a "mature" student with five children whose husband/father had passed away four years earlier. I taught her in a prior summer class, noticing her only when she complained about a presentation grade, the relationship later developing, casually. Yet, the way forward was unclear and unsettling.

"Oh man!" I shouted to myself now living alone in a small one-bedroom apartment. "This situation is stressful. Something's got to change."

Hope had appeared the previous summer from a phone call while I was vacationing in Aspen, Colorado. Although the call had offered the possibility of a teaching position at the University of South Florida, nothing definite had materialized during the year, though there were occasional updates. So, I determined that if change was indeed critical to my wellbeing, I needed to decide what, when and where sometime soon.

"Hey, wait a minute," my memory and forward thinking suddenly kicking-in one lonely night while lying on my water bed. "It's been ten years since completing my master's degree at IU, and much has changed in music and academics since then, including new tuba music and performance methodology. University professors often return to college to keep abreast of new developments. Perhaps that's what I should do this summer, get away and study. Also, from past experience, intense study and playing my tuba usually pushed problematic issues out of mind, temporarily."

So, I later proposed the idea to Juel Shannon, the young lady I was dating, while she set at her apartment's breakfast bar/desk busy studying spring semester course work. She managed an encouraging, "Yes, that sounds like a good idea," both of us immediately sensing the geographic distance that would create between us. The coming summer, she will complete the requirements for the Bachelor's in Elementary Education degree in only three years. Being away that summer was a difficult choice, but a beginning for resolving my dilemma.

After researching regional universities with credible graduate music programs, I selected the University of Missouri in Kansas City (UMKC) located 350 miles north, conveniently straight up I-35 from Oklahoma City and Langston. It offered highly regarded academic degree programs through the doctorate and was in the center of a large city, which was intriguing. Time being critical, I applied for summer admissions immediately as a non-degree seeking graduate student, receiving the affirmative response in just days.

Remembering my cousin Garland living in Bonner Springs near Kansas City, I called him for exploring staying with him for the eight weeks. Only 20 miles west of the UMKC campus, the distance was manageable. We agreed on terms for renting the basement, though cluttered and without modern conveniences. And, he and wife Ruby, welcomed me for meals with the family that included five children when my schedule permitted. After clearing a space for a twin bed and small study-table, it was perfect for my needs.

Garland and I had exchanged visits over the years since we were teens, and the small basement had been their first dwelling, building-out the house above it over time. With those things decided, it was time for me to make temporary relocation plans and begin my mental transition from teacher back to student.

However, just as I was preparing for relocation, I received a contract in the mail from the University of South Florida (USF) for a newly established tenure-earning assistant professor position to teach tuba, starting the last week of August. This had been the developing position at the university since last summer's Aspen phone call.

"Wow! This could not have been timelier," I thought, as I signed the document, deciding not to share the information with Juel immediately. But suddenly, the UMKC studies were more relevant and important as professional preparation for the large majority white institution. As an African-American entering a potentially racially hostile environment, I knew there would be challenges of my presence and qualifications. The UMKC setting and course work offered a bridge for success, and will also need to call on my IU experiences.

Absorbed intensely in summer classes, I rediscovered the excitement of learning, enhanced by the lack of pressure from a pending academic degree. It was gratifying to stay up past 2 a.m. each night exploring the subjects in depth. I was once again able to concentrate on practicing the tuba without multiple distractions, while studying with a teacher, a former student of Jacobs, who shared my performance methods.

Before leaving UMKC after a successful and absorbing summer, my music theory and history instructors advised me that the classes I had completed were actually the first of two-course sequences, and the second courses would be offered the next summer, if I was interested in covering the subjects entirely. Okaaaay, a very interesting thought, although I had no plans to return. However, I placed that bit of unsolicited information deep in my subconscious as I returned to Oklahoma City. Meanwhile, my plans to pack up quickly and relocate to Tampa, Florida had been complicated, significantly.

The year-long relationship with that "mature" Langston student, Juel, had further blossomed through weekend visits and letter exchanges, and when I stopped at Langston on the way to Oklahoma City, I told her about my new job in Tampa, Florida. She was surprised and obviously disappointed, not anticipating our relationship's end.

But then—what the heck—I proposed marriage, saying, "I really don't plan on leaving here without you and your children! I think we should get married." I was in love, and that was a powerful feeling and the passionate personal change I knew I truly needed and desired.

Beyond the deep romantic attraction, Juel embodied maturity and wisdom, traits I deeply wanted in a life partner and soul mate. And I wondered if they were the result of terrible personal loss, and her intense determination to prepare herself for a better future for herself and her children. I also detected a lingering sadness in her, from earlier experiences, that I thought I could help alleviate, while together securing a happy future for our new family.

But Juel Hickman Shannon was very reluctant to even consider the idea of marriage, not wanting to impose five young children on me and move them so far from their family roots. Completing her college degree that summer, she was intent on following through with her plan: acquiring a teaching job immediately to support her children and secure their future. Having grown up impoverished, she was determined on becoming a college graduate, and providing better standards for her family.

"I'm doing just fine," she said facing me across the kitchen bar/desk in her small campus apartment. "Adding another person to my life would only complicate things further."

But I was just as determined as she was, so I kept talking, trying to make sense of my marriage proposal for both of us.

Over the duration of our relationship, I had won the confidence of her children, Lisa, Gina, Angela, Babette and Kenneth, ages 6 through 12, and the Rev. Erma Coburn, her oldest and closest sister who was also working on her elementary education degree at Langston. These were very credible, important and persuasive endorsements, indeed. So finally, after a couple of days of meditating and talking with family while I was in Oklahoma City ending my lease, she decided to risk a future with me, and the new adventure that lay ahead for all seven of us in Tampa. I think of it as a blessing straight from heaven.

Married August 4, 1972, in a small family ceremony in a Tulsa hotel room by her church minister, Juel and I took a symbolic honeymoon road trip to Tampa for arranging living accommodations. And in late August, with the valuable assistance of Lawrence, Juel's youngest brother, our newly composed family relocated to an unfamiliar community of hope and promise, a trip that involved a caravan of two cars (one towed) and a U-Haul truck featuring a standard five-forward gear shift—a nightmare at first, but I managed.

With a one-night stop-over in Bastrop ("Hi Mom and Dad, this is my new family!" Mom, begrudgingly congenial. Daddy, gracious.), and an overnight stay in a Pensacola motel, we arrived at the newly constructed Barcelona Apartments and moved into our townhouse with barely enough money to buy groceries for the week ahead. The nearby large swimming pool was an instant hit with our children, and occupied them while me and Juel sorted out the various financial and residence issues, including arranging for a desperately needed loan from the USF Credit Union. A few days later, I started working at USF, my new academic institution, while Juel coordinated our children's schools and managed our residential affaires. After quickly finding out the number of additional college credits required for Florida teaching certification, she determined those credits were equal to requirements for the master's degree, and in January enrolled in the counseling education master's degree program at USF, taking advantage of free tuition for university employees and families. The degree focus was actually more in-tune with her passion and interest.

Surprisingly, my USF teaching assignment included freshmen music theory along with teaching tuba and student advising, giving urgent relevance to the UMKC summer class since I had never taught the subject before. Which also gave new meaning to my professor's "unsolicited" information about the theory course sequence completion during next summer. Again, fully aware of my Black professor status in a white institution, I felt compelled to acquire full expertise in this subject to be an effective teacher and assure positive evaluations. So, with Juel's support and encouragement, I returned to Kansas City that summer while she managed our newly established family and household, and continued her master's degree study.

During that summer at UMKC, an important introduction occurred.

"Professor Smith, I understand you just started work at the University of South Florida. Congratulations!" was a warm unfamiliar voice I heard while studying in the Music Conservatory lounge. I stood, curious to know the person that had this personal information. "Hi,'" he said with hand out for a shake. "Sorry to break your concentration. I'm Alexander Hamilton, conservatory associate dean. It's good to have you back this summer. How are your classes going?"

"Going well, thank you. I'm enjoying my professors," I responded still wondering about the breath of his knowledge about me. But that was just the beginning. Whenever our paths crossed or we were in close proximity that summer, he made it a point to engage me in brief, congenial and sometimes academic related conversations, more than casual. On the last day of the term as I was heading towards the music building's exit near where my packed car was parked for immediate departure for Tampa, Dean Hamilton stopped me.

"Professor Smith, Sorry to interrupt, but do you have plans for further graduate study after this summer?"

"Well, no I don't. These two summers here have been really great and beneficial, but now I must focus on gaining tenure at USF."

His facial expression and body language turned intense and serious suddenly, an unfamiliar stance from the brief period I had known him. Peering unblinking, directly into my eyes and speaking slowly with well-articulated words, he said, "You know, the classes you have completed these two summers are a significant portion of the core curriculum for the Doctor of Musical Arts (DMA) degree. And with your 3.8 GPA, positive assessments from your professors and exceptional academic standing, admissions for doctoral study are practically assured."

"What?" I blurted out, not sure of what he was talking about, or where this was going. My mind was on getting back to my family in Tampa. "Uh, sorry, could you repeat what you said?"

He did, and I stood there silently trying to decide how to react. That idea had not crossed my mind since Dr. Beversdorf's offer of a doctorial assistantship at IU over ten years earlier.

"Well, I'm not sure this is something I can consider right now. I must focus on tenure, the clock is ticking," I bemoaned while also recalling disturbing issues needing serious consideration regarding my just completed first year at USF.

"Why don't you give it some thought," he continued. "You only need to complete another summer of classes and pass an audition to qualify."

After absorbing that sobering message, I responded while turning toward the exit, "I appreciate the information Dean Hamilton, and I'll give it some thought."

"Please call me if you have questions," I heard him say, faintly, as I walked away.

During the long drive back to Tampa, I could not help but think about what Dean Hamilton had placed in front of me. It was obvious that he had monitored my matriculation closely since the first day of my enrollment, communicating with my professors and keeping apprised of my academic and financial standing. And he had also made his own personal evaluations of my intellect and character resulting from our conversations, concluding, it appears, that I was an excellent candidate for doctoral study. In a very subtle but carefully choreographed manner, Dean Hamilton had intervened in my life and challenged me to imagine a new possibility, one that could enhance my academic career.

Of course, discovering that I was near completion of the doctoral program's core curriculum was quite a surprise. "Wow! Can you imagine? Without intent, I was already vested significantly in a terminal degree," I thought, smiling to myself, which posed a question that begged for a timely answer: "What, if anything, should I do with this newly revealed information and opportunity?"

However, once back in Tampa, Juel and I commenced reviewing issues that may determine if I stay at USF long enough for tenure, leaving voluntarily before the five-year probation period was up. My first year at USF provided cause for concern at the university, and in the Tampa community. Incessant racism was evident on campus, including identifiable racist in the music department, people who were possible roadblocks for my tenure. A Black faculty and staff welcome-back gathering I attended offered evidence of a racially hostile institutional environment. Attendees were extremely cautious when discussing specific accounts of racism in their work environment, seemingly fearful of reprisal, if found out.

Surreptitiously acquired personnel and student data indicated Black faculty and students were in a revolving door: Black faculty appointed, one year later terminated; Black students admitted, and a semester later, gone. Each group officially recorded at USF just long enough to appear in federal equal access data and reports, providing skewed racial representation for the university. The data also indicated that there were no tenured and only five tenure-earning Black faculty, including me. And Black clerical and maintenance staff were all grouped at the bottom of their job categories.

Prevalent anecdotes shared within the University described white professors making racist remarks in classes that included Black students, and a Black male adjunct instructor abruptly fired for allegedly making inappropriate sexual remarks to a white female student, both situations either ignored by the university administration, or punitive decisions made without fair due process.

After Juel and I reviewed those critical factors and discussed their meaningful content, complaisantly standing by was not an option. Although without tenure and only one year at USF, and supporting a family of seven, my newly found Black identity, personal dignity, and aggressive activism meant pursuing racial and social justices for Black University constituents, immediately. The risks were real, including losing my job, but we agreed that some things are more important than personal security, and these represented those things.

The next week, I invited Black faculty and staff members to another informal gathering in a music department classroom, but only one tenure-earning faculty member attended, along with a large representation of clerical staff. They were the energy and enthusiasm for the group initially, covertly acquiring needed data for our strategic planning.

Officially designating ourselves the Black Faculty and Staff Caucus (later Council, and still later, Committee on Black Affairs), we met with President Cecil Mackey during my second year, the first time the administration acknowledged a collective Black presence, although small, on USF's campus. Over ensuing years, our relentless but constructive pressure led to meaningful accomplishments. They included increased Black faculty, staff and students, and eventual appointments of a Black provost, vice president and two academic deans. Newly established university programs included the Institute on Black Life, a program for bridging university resources with Tampa's Black community, and Project Thrust, a Black student counseling, tutorial and support service program. And, continued efforts led to building the Dr. Martin Luther King Jr. Plaza near the center of campus, featuring a large rectangle reflection pool with Dr. King's bust on one end and a granite stone inscribed with a portion of his "I Have a Dream" speech at the opposite end. (This is perhaps the only historically white American university with this powerful symbolic recognition of Dr. King).

Compounding the USF issues were living concerns for our family in the Tampa community. Racial tensions lingered from the 1967 Black rebellion against police violence, often referred to erroneously as a race riot. Whites were defensive and sensitive about Black presence almost everywhere in the city. This included recently desegregated schools where our children attended, situations sometimes demanding our presence. And, we were amazed that local Black leaders were not receptive to "professional outsiders" like me and Juel becoming directly involved with local organizations in confronting racial issues, perhaps believing we may supplant their leadership.

However, as unsettling as those things were, there were also important positive factors that could not be overlooked. My first-year annual evaluation by the department chairman and colleagues was "very good," securing a renewed contract, and signaling that my aggressive equal justice efforts were not detrimental. Don Kneeburg and I enjoyed performing together again in the faculty brass quintet, on campus and in public schools. He was one of my IU music schoolmates that recommended me for the USF position, and taught tuba before I arrived. The students were well prepared, respectful, talented and eager to learn.

And after understanding that the young Black guy with the huge afro and thick mustache standing in front erasing the green board was actually their professor, not the custodian, my freshmen music theory class became the most exceptional and exciting class I ever taught.

The prevailing racism that existed at USF and in Tampa was problematic and troubling and of great concern to me and Juel when considering our immediate future. We wondered if we were in the wrong place at the wrong time for our careers and raising a family, but quickly concluded it was too late for an immediate move. Racism was everywhere in the U.S.—where you were determined how pervasive. So, after careful thought and further discussion, we decided to give ourselves at least two more years for determining whether to stay or consider other options. However, the precarious situation gave more relevance and urgency to exploring Dean Hamilton's interesting and enticing proposal made as I was leaving UMKC, potentially influencing our future.

"I hadn't given doctoral study any thought until he brought it up," I confessed as we sat at our townhouse breakfast bar, the usual upstairs raucous from our kids floating down. "Obviously, he thinks it's something I can do. But I'm not sure…"

"Yes, I understand. But I don't believe it's something we can overlook," Juel responds thoughtfully. "The doctorate is the highest and most prestigious university degree, and may be necessary if you're going to stay in this field," she continues going to the heart of the matter, a trademark I discovered of my new wife. This forced me into reassessing my professional goals, realistically.

"Well, I've forever wanted to be the principal tuba player with a top-ten symphony orchestra, my dream job," I admitted remorsefully, "but I no longer perform at that level, and don't think I can achieve that standard again. So, maybe I should concentrate on what I'm actually involved in now and for the last several years, an academic career."

Prior to USF, I taught a total of seven years at two different universities, earning tenure and chairing a department at one. And I was also an adjunct teacher at two other institutions. Counting the year at USF, I thought, there is certainly a clear indication of an evolving career in higher education. However, if I wanted to build on that foundation and develop a successful higher education career, gaining tenure at USF was critical.

And the criteria for obtaining tenure in most higher education academic disciplines require a terminal degree, the doctorate or MFA, with some exceptions for meritorious experience. Hastily canvasing the music department, I discovered that most faculty members were without the doctorate, and those that had it were in research disciplines such as music history and theory, conveying encouraging information.

But what concerned me most was that African-Americans have too often found ourselves judged by a higher standard, a perceived "twice-as-good to be accepted" double standard that was often demanded of Blacks by white Americans in almost every profession, consciously or not. How will USF assess my value to the institution, fairly or otherwise?

My music department colleagues were highly qualified artistically, and very ambitious, with aspirations for making the department one of the top in the country, already very competitive in the state university system. Teaching and performance standards were quite remarkable, which meant the criteria, standards and qualifications for tenure and promotions were also exceptional. That created a tremendous challenge for me, but if judged "equally," I felt I could meet the department's benchmarks.

But I also had to consider the growing competition from a large number of well-trained and educated tuba players prepared for full-time university tuba faculty positions that were sprouting up at major academic institutions, a result of the "Tuba Renaissance" that was occurring. My colleagues might consider them at any time during my probation period, or while evaluating me for tenure.

Being able to talk with a tenured Black music faculty member about their USF experience while going through the process would have been very helpful, but there was no one, making it difficult to determine, with confidence, the best path for success. So, with all of the unknowns and threats staring me in the face, I concluded that I should try, as much as possible, to distinguish myself as the most qualified person for the position, and thereby, earn tenure and the connected promotion to associate professor, outright, based on the evaluation of my assigned duties. But for really distinguishing myself would require leaping over another hurdle.

"I think I need to follow up with Dean Hamilton and see where it's going to lead," I finally said with a tinge of dread as Juel began preparing dinner.

She countered with a logical thought, "Well, you know what may be said, it's certainly best to have the doctorate and not need it, then to need it and not have it."

"Yeah, and for sure," I said after allowing that thought to fully register, "If I should ever venture into higher education administration again, it would definitely be needed." And considering USF's racial climate, I added a final justification. "The doctorate would certainly eliminate one last-ditch rationale for racist colleagues to deny me tenure, because 'he doesn't have the academic qualifications!' perpetuating the racist double standard.

Telephoning Dean Hamilton the next day, I opened with, "Hi Dean Hamilton. I hope you remember me, John Smith at USF in Tampa." "Yes, of course I do," he responded as though expecting my call. "Well," I continued, "I decided to follow your suggestion and return this summer to complete the prerequisites for the doctorate, and submit the required application. With your support, I'm willing to give this my best effort."

"I'm so happy you made that decision. I don't think you will ever regret it," he responded cheerfully. "Come to my office when you arrive, and we'll get things rolling."

Arriving that summer (1964), I went directly to his office. "Okay. Great seeing you," after greeting me with a business-like hand shake. "Now, I'm going to get you started on completing the core requirements, and guide you through the doctoral application process for the Doctor of Musical Arts (DMA) in Tuba Performance." And with that, Dean Hamilton unexpectedly became my doctoral advisor, unusual for his administrative position. Already, I felt a sense of security knowing that I was in his hands as I started down the unknown path of doctorial study. Having the top academic administrator advising me and monitoring my progress is an enviable position for any graduate student, I mused.

I decided to live in a campus residence hall that summer due to the intense study and preparation that was required, providing fewer distractions from my cousin Garland and family, and more library access. But it resulted in periods of loneliness and more long-distance calls with Juel and the children. The multilevel building was noisy but the basement useful for tuba practice. I purchased a small hotplate for preparing meals, mostly boiled hot dogs, raw vegetables and fruit, a consequence of our tight budget. Juel's mother and sisters visited Tampa that summer to keep her company. And, I was delighted they were still there on my return, resulting in our first Caribbean cruise.

That summer went smoothly, and as planned, I completed the requisite requirements, including the audition recital, and was admitted into the DMA program. During my last advising session, Dean Hamilton summarized the substantial degree requirements, escalating my anxiety. Then, he dropped a bomb that exploded so loud that it brought everything to a screeching halt!

"Oh yes, there is a one-year residence requirement for all doctorial students," he said, casually igniting the blast.

"Huh? What? Residency requirement? What does that mean?" I asked. "Does it mean what I think it does? That I must be on campus for a full-year, twelve consecutive months, at UMKC, in Kansas City?"

"Well, yes, that's right, consecutive fall, spring and summer terms. More like eleven months," he responded somberly, not smiling. I stared unblinking at his emotionless face for an extended awkward silence. He met my stare still not smiling.

"What have I gotten myself into?" my troubled mind screamed.

My immediate unspoken knee-jerk reaction was, "Well, there goes the doctorate," my mind quickly scrolling the obstacles: How could I possibly spend a full-year at UMKC, needing to support my family who had just relocated to Tampa? The tenure clock was ticking for me at USF, and my on-campus presence was essential for my colleagues to evaluate me. And, as an untenured faculty, if I left for a year, there might not be a job to return to.

I concluded that possibly, the terminal degree itself might have to be *terminated* after an exceedingly short life.

"Well," I somehow managed to say disappointed, "I don't know if that's possible. There's family and finances involved which is making a yearlong residency near impossible. We'll see if we can figure something out, but it doesn't look good. I'll get back with you. However, I do thank you so much for this incredible opportunity."

The drive back to Tampa was long and disheartened.

Beginning my third year at USF after that dreadfully ending summer, I had all but given up on a doctorial study. A year's residency at UMKC was beyond our means. I concluded that I would just have to apply for tenure without it and depend on my academic and professional productivity. Checking my campus mailbox the first day on campus, I noticed an innocuous looking document from the Office of Academic Affairs. Still feeling despondent, I opened it prepared to drop it in the waste basket below. But what it said practically knocked me off my feet: *To applicable faculty, the Florida State University System Board of Regents offers Grants-in-Aid of annual salary plus $3,000 stipend for minority faculty who are currently enrolled for doctorial study for completing course and residency requirements, beginning current year.* I stood there, not sure if I read it right, and if it applied to me. I read it slowly twice more, each time my excitement escalating.

"Blessings to behold!" my mind yelled, "a glimmer of hope! That sounds like me!"

I called Juel immediately and read it to her, asking for her interpretation.

"This sounds like an exact response to our prayers!" she responded joyfully. "It's a miracle in the making for continuing the doctorate!"

But then reality set in as I recalled the information. "It starts this year. I've got to apply immediately if it's not already too late! See you when I get home." I hastily acquired an application, completed and hand-carried it to the provost office. One week later, I was awarded the State's Board of Regent's first grant.

"Hallelujah! Hallelujah!" Juel and I rejoiced. But there was no time to have a party and celebrate if I intended to use it. Time was critical.

In crisis mode, my first phone call was to Dean Hamilton describing the very timely grant allowing me to commence the residency immediately. "Wow! I'm so happy for you. This puts you on the road for success," was his response, even more elated than my own had been. But when he told me that UMKC was already one week into the fall semester, I thought the opportunity had already gone down the drain.

But in the typical "no brainer" non-perplexed manner that characterized his personality, Dean Hamilton simply said, "Get here as soon as you can, and I'll take care of enrollment and class attendance issues. This is an incredible opportunity for you. I'll make it work."

Get there as soon as you can? The complexity of that question caused us to wonder if it was possible, but only momentarily. Juel had just been employed by the USF student counseling center, after completing her Master's degree. But on request, she was provided a year's leave to go with me. They must have liked her work. So, we quickly tackled uprooting our family of seven for moving 1,200 miles to Kansas City, Missouri, which I estimated would take at least a week.

In four days, we were on the road, miraculously, huffing and puffing! We had stored our furniture, sold my beloved 1968 Karman Ghia, acquired the children's school records, loaded a small U-Haul trailer with personal items including my tuba, and all seven of us stuffed into our Buick sedan for the long two-day drive, thankful the children were small enough to fit. Our patience was tested with backseat arguments over contested space and the persistent "Are we there yet?" question.

Stopping at roadside parks to eat Juel's improvised sandwiches, and for an overnight hotel stay in Nashville, Tennessee, we left our children in Sapulpa, Oklahoma, with Juel's mother. She and I continued on to Kansas City to arrange living accommodations. Desperate, we signed a contract for a four-bedroom townhouse in Overland Park, Kansas, approximately fifteen miles from UMKC. The contract stipulated a maximum of four children, so we lied; hoping they never saw all five of them together. And there were excellent nearby public schools, resolving one of our major concerns.

With housing settled, we drove back to Sapulpa that night and returned the next day (day seven) with the children, moved in, and on day eight of our tight schedule I was at UMKC ready for classes—at least in body.

Dean Hamilton's office staff handed me my approved registration documents, and I rushed across campus to the cashier's office to pay my tuition and fees. After attending my classes that day, finding the professors accommodating with makeup information, I returned for an appointment with Dean Hamilton.

"We made it, and my professors were really wonderful, thanks to you," I said speaking faster than usual, my mind still racing from the previous seven days. "I have some catching up to do, but I'll get there."

"Well, glad you and your family made it safely," he responded happily. "And, oh yes, I have an assignment for you. We need a tuba instructor for our Community Music School division and a tuba player for the Kansas City Civic Orchestra. So, I have to set up an adjunct faculty position for you for those needs. My staff will work out the details with you."

Sitting there, tired but exuberant, I managed words of gratitude and appreciation for all of his help before leaving for desperately needed rest. I would soon be completely absorbed in the difficult challenges that lay ahead, the breadth and depth I could not possibly anticipate. But what I did appreciate considerably was Dean Hamilton's crucial assistance.

He had anticipated the enormous financial burden for my large family to relocate for the year-long residency and provided an adjunct faculty position to help with the expenses, a generous and hugely welcomed surprise. Every penny would be needed. Now, the ball was clearly in my court. It was up to me not to let my very kind and gracious advisor/mentor down.

A bespectacled gentleman of slender stature, Dean Alexander Hamilton was about five-foot eight inches tall with narrow features. A few more pounds of muscle on his frame would have been justified. His graying hairline had started to recede unevenly, demanding a slight comb-over. He wore long-sleeve, white shirts that appeared too large for his stature, narrow conservative ties, and pleated suit trousers with cuffs that draped over thin-soled dress shoes. His image was more that of an insurance salesman than an academic. He possessed a Doctor of Musical Arts degree from the University of Taxes, Austin, and held the UMKC academic rank of Associate Professor.

As Associate Dean, he was the Conservatory's chief administrative officer for academic and student affairs, and he always appeared to be on an important mission in the two-story main building, gliding smoothly over the vinyl floor with papers, a file folder or clip board in hand. His expression and disposition was always the same: relaxed, unassuming, genuinely personable and amicable. Each time our paths crossed before he became my doctoral advisor, he initiated brief conversation about my general welfare and academic progress, and occasionally, when there was time, we discussed issues regarding higher education.

I was so impressed with his administrative savvy and people skills that near the end of my second summer, I offered to recommend him for USF's vacant music department chairman's position. "Oh, well," beginning his laid-back response. "Sounds like a great opportunity. But with so much mildew around that gathers on shoes and clothes in closets and everywhere, I don't think I could cope. That's a miserable way to live." And he said that with a straight face. Of course, those were indeed the circumstances prior to air-conditioning in Florida, but nevertheless it was an intriguing joke that we shared for the duration of our relationship.

The residency year went exceedingly well, considering the extraordinary adjustments, demands and pressure. Fortunately, there were only limited public school and family issues, all of which Juel handled effectively while enrolled in a graduate level class that interested her at a nearby college. She loved learning, and staying home without an intellectual challenge was not an option.

It was tough on the children adjusting quickly to the new environment and circumstances. Juel involved them in the local Jack and Jill club as a constructive and safe social outlet. And with me, their still-new father, so intensely occupied and sometimes overreacting to their problems, I was not always helpful with their issues.

With the grant and my adjunct teaching assignment, we managed to stay just beyond financial crisis. I had excellent and sensitive teachers, but my study was practically 24/7. Fortunately, I only had to play one Kansas City Civic Orchestra concert: Saint-Saens' *Symphony No. 3*, a major masterwork that did not have a particularly demanding tuba part.

I enjoyed Kansas City's weather, with four distinct and dramatic seasons: The fall's yellow and rust-colored trees that dominated the flat landscape; The winter's bare foliage and white snowfalls that offered startling visual contrasts; The spring's plant-rebirths of shamrock-green leaves and rainbow flowers that reenergized and lifted spirits; And the summer's suffocating unyielding dry heat that made the outdoors unthinkable.

For diverting social activities, Juel drove the children to an extended weekend in Oklahoma, and her mother and several siblings visited us for a snow-blanketed, four-day Thanksgiving holiday celebration. We treated the children and ourselves to a drive-in movie.

One brightly lighted, full-moon winter night, while taking a break from my studies, I walked through eight inches of fresh, powdery snow blanketing a large vacant field next to our apartment building. It was clear and very cold with the stars brilliantly competing with the moon. And as far as I could see across the flat terrain, the pure white snow had not been trampled on by anyone other than myself.

The serenity of the scene was so beautiful and sensual. I was alone in its vast silent space, alone with my thoughts about where Juel and I had arrived so quickly. Three years after our marriage, I was now in residence at UMKC, performing an unanticipated, choreographed dance for the doctorate, pressured to accommodate one hurdle after another. It was all good. It had to be. A blessing that could not be explained.

In the final week of my residency, Dean Hamilton asked if I had selected a chairman and two associate faculty members for my dissertation committee.

"You should really do that before you leave, the chairman particularly, the person you will be working with very closely."

"I recall you mentioning it, but I hadn't gotten around to it," I said. "I'll get started right away."

Mentally inventorying faculty members who I enjoyed as teachers, had diverse musical interests (considered the tuba a valid musical instrument) and demonstrated a personal interest in me, I quickly narrowed the list for my dissertation committee chairman down to two professors. But unfortunately, neither could accept, due to the massive academic overloads they already had.

So, on the final day of classes, in desperation, I went to the studio of the last professor on my extended list, a wind instrument teacher who was an evaluator for my recitals and master class, knowing nothing more about him beyond that. His next private studio lesson student was anxiously waiting outside his door when I arrived. As the door opened, I barged in ahead of him to make my plea.

"Yes? Can I help you?" the obviously perturbed professor asked.

"Sorry to barge in between your students," I responded quickly, "but it's the last day of my residency and I need to identify the chairman for my dissertation committee. I would be honored if you agreed to serve in that role."

"Well, I don't know…I'm really busy…I don't know if I…"

"You will be very helpful," I interrupted, and trying to be convincing I added, "I could really use your knowledge and expertise."

Exasperated, with his student now sitting next to him anxious to get his lesson started, he committed. "Yes, yes, yes, okay!" came his frustrated answer, and I quickly departed his studio unaware of the devastating consequences of my hasty decision.

Whew! What a relief. Everything was finalized. After a brief "thank you" stop in Dean Hamilton's office, we were all on the road back to Tampa, exhausted. I was now ABD (All But Dissertation), the Doctorate in sight. What a blessing. Two years earlier, this stage of academic achievement was nowhere in our vision, not even a diminutive consideration. Dean Hamilton got the ball rolling by planting the seed, guiding me through, around and over the hurdles, and added much needed cash to our coffers.

We returned happily to recreate our lives in Tampa. Although we enjoyed the brief respite in Kansas City, the family was more than ready for social and financial stability. Unexpectedly, but to our great pleasure, this included the purchase of a new house, thanks to Herb, the wise Black realtor who advised me I was still eligible for a VA no-down-payment loan, even though I had used a similar one for my first house in Oklahoma City.

Unfortunately, the suburban location required our children to catch five different school buses for the first two years. This caused a logistical nightmare for me and Juel for making frequent visits to their newly desegregated schools to establish parent/teacher relationships and respond to racially-inspired issues. From us they learned not to accept racist slights, and I'm still learning from them untold incidences. We also attended many of their extracurricular activities, encouraging participation in school activities that excited them.

I rejoined my USF colleagues and commenced an exceedingly busy schedule, restarting the tenure clock. I was invited as tuba clinician for the state music education conference, performed occasionally with the local professional orchestra and launched the Black Composer-in-Residence project. I served on many university committees and councils, performed with the faculty brass quintet, and continued my aggressive leadership as chairman of the Black Faculty and Staff Council.

Meanwhile, my dissertation was not progressing as it should, due mostly to an absence of constructive guidance and follow-through from my chairman. Although I had been considering potential topics, I was unsure essentially of how to begin the process. So, with nothing to go on from my chairman, I selected my favorite subject, created a logical draft outline, and sent it to him to get the ball rolling, expecting it to generate dialogue and instructions on how to proceed. Instead, his response advised me to proceed with developing the document based on the outline I submitted without any questions, discussion, or specific guidelines. Believing that what I had submitted to him met UMKC DMA standards and guidelines, I began writing my dissertation—apprehensive and unsure. For preliminary discovery, I ordered a copy of a 1974 unpublished tuba dissertation by Stephen Brandon for information and guidance.

Richard Strauss is one of my favorite composers, and I thoroughly enjoy his motif-layered, wonderfully lush and beautiful, strategically placed melodies that dramatically symbolized Europe's Grand Romantic Era. The nine symphonic tone poems he composed for orchestra exemplified his poignant style, and each included at least one tuba. One included six! I was particularly interested in how Strauss used the instrument in creating the well-orchestrated masterpieces.

My submitted outline suggested an examination of the tone poems through an analysis of several orchestration characteristics that involved the tuba. I anticipated the need for brief footnoted opening chapters on the tuba's history and performance characteristics. But the preponderance of work would involve laborious, detailed analysis of the music and tuba parts, requiring several subcategories and the use of narrative, graphics, and illustrations.

Eventually, I was able to send my chairman a draft of the first chapter, but didn't receive a response for months. Puzzled, I tried to phone him without success. Over twelve-hundred miles apart, and predating the computer, the telephone, FAX and postal mail were my only means for communicating with him. And when the chapter was finally returned it was covered with red-pencil marks of edits and revisions. A little overly dramatic, I thought. But this was the pattern I struggled helplessly with for more than four years.

At some point, I found the slow turnaround time, non-responses to my phone calls and full-page exaggerated red-pencil marks hard to explain, and given my experiences as a Black man, I concluded his behavior was racially motivated. Unfortunately, I knew absolutely nothing about him beyond his faculty position. Nothing personally whatsoever. But he knew me from sight, having attended and evaluated my three recitals and the master class, and from my abrupt approach in his studio to request that he serve as my dissertation chairman. I didn't know how else to explain his unprofessional and insensitive actions.

Realizing that UMKC's seven-year deadline for completing the Doctorate was quickly approaching, I phoned Dean Hamilton with a desperate plea for help.

"I'm really anxious about completing my dissertation before the deadline," I said. "It has been extremely difficult getting my chairman to respond, almost as though he's deliberately delaying the dissertation's completion. And I'm not sure that the edits and revisions are always valid."

He listened patiently, asked a few pertinent questions, and at the end of our conversation simply said, "I'll look into it."

I don't know how he handled the issue, but suddenly I began receiving very timely responses from my chairman with very few red-pencil edits, corrections, and revisions. And with the greatly improved transaction rate, I was able to complete my dissertation, *The Use of the Tuba in the Symphonic Poems of Richard Strauss*, and receive the DMA degree in May 1979, seven years exactly after first setting foot on UMKC's campus.

However, it wasn't until much later that I discovered the extent of the injustice that occurred with the writing of my dissertation. And I accept my share of the blame for hastily selecting a chairman without appropriate vetting. The average length for DMA in Performance dissertations at the time was between 80 and 90 pages, the emphasis on "performance" requiring limited scope and research. My document was 194 pages with a broad multilayered scope requiring substantial analysis and documentation, the equivalent of a fully rendered research or Ph. D. dissertation. And although I was angry when I first discovered the unnecessary effort the chairman forced upon me for whatever reason, I was extremely proud and pleased that my dissertation provided new detailed knowledge about the tuba and its orchestral use.

The dissertation's completion and the doctorial hood lifted over my head at UMKC's 1979 commencement, witnessed by my parents, sister and extended family, was pure joy, enhancing my confidence and pride as a person and university professor. My parents were especially proud of their once slow-blooming son.

The timing of the Doctorate was perfect for acquiring USF tenure and promotion to Associate Professor, occurring simultaneously in the spring of 1979. Dr. Carl Riggs, university provost, although sincerely desiring my continued presence at the University, nevertheless, had indicated that I needed to complete the doctorate before he would sign the final approval. Knowing him as I did, his intent was to push me to finish the degree for my personal satisfaction and future academic success, aware of the dearth of fully credentialed African-Americans in higher education, and particularly at USF.

The last time Dean Hamilton and I were together was for a brief celebration in his office after I had successfully defended my dissertation. I thanked him for his persistent and enthusiastic support, encouragement, and assistance. And when I returned to UMKC in 1989 to receive the University's *Alumni Achievement Award*, he had retired. But I made everyone aware that he was the catalyst for me earning the DMA, and therefore, the subsequent achievements recognized by the award.

As a mentor, Dr. Alexander W. Hamilton pointed me toward the open door, encouraged me to enter, supported my stay, and assured my completion and exit, so I was prepared and credentialed to serve humanity through the arts and higher education.

Ultimately, that Doctorate allowed me to ascend through the ranks of academic administration to become the twelfth president of Fisk University.

Chapter 15

A Ladder

Juel and I were sitting there nervously, not knowing what to expect.

We were surrounded by Ivory-toned walls adorned with colorful contemporary art, modestly framed. Except, on our left, next to a door, were three floor-to-ceiling frosted windows with four small conceptual art sculptures in progressive design resting on short white pedestals at their base.

Our uneasiness was exacerbated, knowing we were inappropriately dressed for the unexpected meeting that was about to start. I was attired in a long pointed-collar open chest shirt and denim bell bottom slacks, and Juel was wearing a form fitting white pant set full of loose frills. We were models for the 1970s Black casual fashions.

One minute I'm checking-in with the University of South Florida music department chairman, my new boss whom I had not met, and the next minute we're ushered into the Dean's office for the College of Fine Arts without explanation.

Sitting in two identical black modern designed upholstered chairs, we are facing the Dean across an uncluttered wood grain, laminate desk exhibiting a quizzical expression that made the situation even more unsettling for us.

Steady eyes, lifted eyebrows, neutral uncommitted mouth and a head topped with unruly dark hair, he spoke: "I'm Don Saff. Nice to meet you. Please tell me about the interdisciplinary arts activity you created at your former institution," revealing a decidedly New York accent I had heard only on television. "Oh, uh, yes." I stumbled trying to recall the reference. "I think you are referring to the Langston student performance ensemble I started featuring several genres of Black music and culture that toured..." "That's fascinating," he interrupted, "but the music chair may have misunderstood my interest." Standing up, he continued, "But it was wonderful meeting the two of you. Welcome to USF and the college." Then he came around the desk revealing a body larger than it should be for his height, shook our hands and directed us to the door leading out of his office.

Juel and I hastily retreated through the reception area to a more comfortable zone in the courtyard just beyond his office, glade to be out of that setting.

"What was that all about?" I desperately but softly coaxed from my very dry mouth. "That certainly was not the best way to meet the dean, was it?" "Yeah," Juel whispered back. "I damn sure was not dressed for the occasion."

Distancing ourselves from that painful encounter, we hustled back to our hotel near Kennedy and North Boulevard picking up tantalizing fresh-fish takeout from the popular Mirabella restaurant on the way. We were in Tampa, Florida for arranging family housing for our relocation and enjoying a symbolic honeymoon. And as an afterthought, I scheduled a brief get acquainted visit with the USF music department chairman since I was appointed without the customary in-person interview. Into our discussion the chairman abruptly scheduled a meeting for me with the dean, which obviously didn't go well.

However, while driving back to Oklahoma the next day, after signing the contract for a four-bedroom townhouse, my thoughts wondered back to the strange meeting with Dean Saff, slowly realizing that the short, seemingly meaningless meeting might not be without its merits.

Since university faculty members seldom have the opportunity for personal interaction with high administrators, particularly new faculty, this was possibly an invaluable beginning for my USF venture. At the very least, the meeting provided Dean Saff a face for the appointment papers he recently signed that were now stashed away in an office personnel file. Maybe from my face and our short dialogue, his curiosity might be raised, eventually sending him to my file for a closer look at my curriculum vitae. "An excellent thought, or wish, but probably not likely," I finally reasoned

Dr. Saff was chairman of the USF Art Department for five years before becoming the first Dean of the newly established College of Fine Arts in 1971, a year before my appointment. Prior to USF, he held academic appointments at Queens College, State University of New York, Columbia University, and was a Fulbright recipient, studying in Italy.

A highly regarded international contemporary artist; Saff's works have been exhibited in major galleries and museums, including New York City's Museum of Modern Art. He earned his BA from Queens College, M.A. and Ed. D. from Columbia University, a MFA from Pratt Institute, and is considered an authority on printmaking and artistic collaboration. (See *Donald Saff: Art in Collaboration* by Marilyn Kushner.)

While Art Department Chairman, Saff established GraphicStudio, a printmaking atelier for collaboration with invited artists.

"The arts were not flourishing well in Tampa, and living in New York City most of my life, I was artistically lonely, felt somewhat deprived. So, with GraphicStudio, I could invite prominent artists to join me in creating new work. That was enjoyable and fun," was the rational he gave for founding the atelier. He invited some of America's greatest contemporary artists, including James Rosenquist, Robert Rauschenberg and Jim Dine, developing new limited-edition art prints, some using unique materials and employing new techniques. During its evolution, limited edition sculpture was added to its creative portfolio.

Select GraphicStudio works were later archived in the Smithsonian Institution's National Gallery of Art, the results of Saff's tenacity and persuasiveness, and a major coup for the university, while also validating his vision and political savvy.

My first year at USF witnessed political strife in the music department, which prompted Dean Saff to intervene and relieve the first-year chairmen of his administrative duties before the fall semester ended. The chairman and faculty disagreed intensely about the academic focus of the department, the chair wanting exclusive emphasis on music after Claude Debussy (1862-1918), and the faculty wanted to continue tradition, with complete historical coverage to the present. That was unsettling for me while trying to find my bearings in the department and prove my worth to my colleagues. Then in February, I received a message that the dean wished to meet with me.

"Ohooo Nooo! Not that office again!" my mind shouted recalling my earlier catastrophic encounter. Having intentionally avoided direct involvement in the department's dispute I couldn't help but wonder, "Why would the dean want to see me? That first visit to his office was enough." Very anxious, I found myself once again sitting in that oh-so-familiar chair across the desk from "the Dean," the man with the unruly hair, body a little bigger than it should be for his height, and the New York accent.

Entering his office this time was noticeably different. The Dean was smiling and convivial as we greeted each other, and the conversation less formal as he led into the reason I was there. "As you know, I relieved the music department chairman of his position last semester," he stated calmly.

"During his interview with me for the job, he expressed ideas about the arts in higher education that were very similar to mine, and that's why I appointed him. So, it was hard to ask him to step down. However," he went on, "I did not anticipate the faculty's forceful opposition."

Meanwhile, I'm sitting there anxiously thinking, "What's this got to do with me?"

"Well, I need to appoint an interim chairman to take his place until we find a permanent replacement, and I wonder if you would accept the position," he blurted out, leaning forward in his chair. "It would be through next year while we conduct a national search."

What? my mind responded, racing to comprehend. He can't be serious.

"I would like for you to serve as interim chairman of the music department," he paraphrased to make sure I understood. "I reviewed your cv. You have five years of administrative experience, more than anyone in the department."

Still speechless, I was trying to put his request into perspective. My experience was in a much smaller department and at a much smaller university; A HBCU at that.

"I don't know. This is a much larger department, and I'm new here. That's asking a lot," evading the proposition and suggesting in code "Hey, do you know what you're asking. I'm Black!"

"I believe you can do this, and sometimes being new to a situation helps," Dean Saff went on, pressing the issue.

My mind was racing, trying to determine the best way to handle his proposal, not knowing if he understood the coded message. But he's the Dean and believes I'm the best choice. How can I refute that, or disappoint him, which, as a new faculty may not be the wisest thing?

"Well, uh, if you think I can do the job, okay, I'll try to do my best," I said immediately thinking that before committing I should have discussed it with Juel and the three colleagues who recommended me for the faculty position.

"Thank you, thank you. I know you will do an excellent job," he said with relief. "But it's not official, I'll need to get the approval of Dr. Riggs, the provost. I'll let you know soon."

I left his office especially concerned about how my new music department colleagues would respond to this, many probably still upset about the dean's earlier choice for chairman. How would they react to a new, Black, junior faculty member being appointed chairman without their consultation? This wasn't feeling right, and Juel agreed when I called her, but as expected a bit angry about my commitment without discussion. This led to some unsettling hours of contemplation.

Two days later, Dean Saff again requested I meet with him, but this time I knew the reason, and the dreaded possibility.

"I'm sorry, but I have to tell you that the provost didn't approve my request," he said as I was sitting down. "And, I must say, I understand and agree with his reason."

He explained that the provost was concerned that as an untenured faculty member, I would be unprotected from colleagues blocking my tenure who disagreed with decisions I made while interim chairman, putting my future at USF in jeopardy. He felt the interim appointment was unwise. I sat listening quietly, greatly relieved.

However, Dean Saff was not finished. He did not like having to appoint someone else to the interim position with less administrative experience than I had, regardless of the reason. And since he had built up my expectations, he had another plan.

"I'm going to appoint you as assistant chairman for the department, starting immediately," he said, without giving me a choice.

"Well, uh, thank you," was all I could mumble before leaving his office, apprised that the assignment was part-time and without teaching load reduction or stipend. And, as I later discovered, the appointment was without precedent and a position description. But I appreciated his "affirmative action" effort, whether he thought of it as that or not.

However, the arrangement did not sit well with the interim chairman Dean Saff appointed a few days later. If there was going to be an assistant chairman, he would have preferred making the selection himself. And to demonstrate his displeasure, he completely ignored me in defiance of the Dean's decision, and I soon learned, because I was Black.

After concluding that his action was racist (not the first or last by him and certain colleagues), I decided to identify several areas that I believed crucial for improving and advancing the department, something positive that would enhance its profile. After discussing them with several trusted colleagues, I selected one—*develop a student recruitment brochure*—and began its design. Of course, it was never published for lack of funds. But he got the message.

I wasn't going to relinquish the administrative position quietly.

But he wasn't giving up on putting me in my place, either. One day early the next academic year, he stopped me in the hall near his office.

"Excuse me, John," he said, surprising me with his greeting. "I'm going to miss the next scheduled department faculty meeting. I want you to chair the meeting for me. The agenda will be prepared for you, so you'll just need to steer the meeting."

I found the request rather odd, since he had yet to acknowledge my assistant chairman appointment. And, although I was suspicious of his motive, I told him I'd be happy to.

I prepared myself mentally for the usual challenge of university faculty meetings, which can be contentious. I also knew that there would be those colleagues wondering if a Black man could provide the requisite leadership for such a provocative setting of strong-willed professors. As the meeting approached, my confidence was bolstered by my past leadership experiences, and the strength I drew from my newly absorbed Black identity.

Following the agenda, the meeting was going quite smoothly; until I saw the door opening at the back of the room, where the interim chairman was slipping inside and positioning himself against the wall.

He's not supposed to be here, I thought. What's going on?

Soon after his stealth-like entrance, a faculty member near me at the front of the room suddenly began to object loudly and vociferously about how I was handling an agenda item, unusually volatile and confrontational, even for a faculty meeting. I recognized quickly that this was a scene set up to test my ability to control the meeting on the assumption that I would fail, at which point the interim chairman would jump in and save the day, rendering me incompetent.

And indeed, the meeting could have erupted into chaos, with some perhaps already thinking (and hoping) that I had lost control.

However, the interim chairman wasn't the first, or the last, to be fooled by my normally modest, soft spoken non-confrontational demeanor. Standing tall and firm over the belligerent faculty member seated in front of me, the image of an angry Black militant with a large afro and newly grown beard suddenly made his presence known. With forceful voice and jabbing finger gestures, I called for order in the room, and declared that the meeting would adhere strictly to *Robert's Rules of Order.*

"No one is to speak without my recognition," I bellowed, and managed not to raise a defiant "Black power" fist into the air, although it was tempting.

Surprised by my vociferous and aggressive tone and action, there was immediate quiet in the room. Maintaining my forceful persona, I continued the agenda, never recognizing the disruptive faculty member's hand to speak, and ending the meeting as orderly as it had begun. The interim chairman was the first to leave the room, as quietly as he had entered.

But it wasn't quite over, yet.

While walking back to my office, stressed-out but proud, the embarrassed disruptive faculty member walked up close beside me, loudly protesting that I didn't recognize him to speak in the meeting, using belligerent, hostile, and disrespectful words. Feeling very tired and angry from navigating the "setup," I could not tolerate his harassment, telling him in clear, profane terms where he could go and what he could do to himself, using a four-letter word I never use in public. My explosive reaction and profanity-laced words along with a combative stance caused him to back off quickly, allowing me to continue unassaulted to my office for the quiet solitude and peaceful environment I desperately needed.

However, someone who witnessed the meeting and the confrontation reported the details to Dean Saff, and the next day I was invited, again, to his office.

"I understand you chaired a rather interesting meeting yesterday," he said, with a slight smile that I could not easily read.

"Yes, it was a little contentious, but not unlike most faculty meetings," I said, not wanting to divulge the details.

"Well, seems as though you kept control of what could have been a much worse outcome. Good job. But I also understand that you had a confrontation with a faculty member afterwards. Tell me about that."

Now I was getting uneasy, unsure of why we were meeting and where this was going. Did I violate a professional protocol?

I nervously described the scenario; except I could not bring myself to reiterate the exact words I used. But he interrupted me at that point, with laughter.

"Didn't you say, 'Get the fuck out of my way! Go fuck yourself'?"

What? Oh no, he didn't just say that, did he?

"Uh, Yes, I guess that's about right," was all I could manage, wondering what was next.

With laughter subsiding, but his face still brightly lit-up, he continued, "I must commend you on how you handled both situations. You demonstrated tremendous courage and tactical skills in the faculty meeting, given what looked like a setup. And you certainly displayed tremendous personal strength with the faculty member afterward. But you can't repeat those words, can you?" he said, laughing again.

At that point I started laughing with him, slowly at first, but wholeheartedly, as I realized the hilariousness of my reticence to repeat the profanity—words I rarely use, unless provoked! And it was a relief to know he understood and supported my reaction to the circumstances.

Although dabbling in unacknowledged administrative work, teaching and performing were the main focus of my assigned duties. But advising instrumental and composition majors, about half the music students, was a responsibility I loved and took quite seriously. I wanted all of them to successfully graduate, and did what I could to assist them, working with the college's advising coordinator, a senior art professor. However, in July1975 the coordinator retired and Dean Saff appointed me to the half-time administrative position. I requested release from only one course, music theory, being sure my assigned duties met tenure requirements. Therefore, in reality, the administrative and faculty responsibilities constituted two full-time jobs, requiring long intense hours to perform both at the highest level, and meet the standards for achieving tenure and promotion to associate professor.

The coordinator of advising reports directly to the dean, and was responsible for student matriculation from admissions through graduation, offering me opportunities for directly supporting the unique needs of Black students.   But most significant, the position was a member of the college's Executive Council (EC) headed by the Dean and included department chairs, directors and the assistant dean. The EC's scope included the dean's vision and agenda, college policies and procedures, curricular and personnel issues. The coordinator position also placed me on several university committees and councils providing valuable insight into institutional-wide management and operations.

In one of my first EC meetings, a student matriculation issue occurred in the theater department and Dean Saff asked me to assess the situation and send a memo to the chairperson recommending a solution, which prompted a poignant professional protocol lesson. Naively, the memorandum I subsequently sent the chair did not express the appropriate collegial, professional and deferential language for communications from a new "program coordinator" to an academic full professor "department chair." Rightfully, the chairperson was angry after reading the rather authoritative communiqué from a low-level administrative novice in the college.

She immediately registered her dissatisfaction with Dean Saff, who requested my appearance in his office. Fortunately for me, he understood the root of the problem and viewed the situation as a "learn and grow" opportunity for his new wet-behind-the-ears junior administrator. But rather than telling me how to fix it specifically, he suggested that I figure out a strategy for repairing my fractured relationship with the theater chair, thereby affirming my ability to serve as an effective leader and respectful colleague.

After considerable thought, I telephoned the chairperson and apologized, sent an appropriately worded memo addressing the issue, and visited her to apologize in person, establishing a convivial relationship moving forward. It worked. She and I became close colleagues for the duration of my USF tenure, including a brief period when I was her dean. Dean Saff marveled at how well I handled the situation, and I learned the value of interpersonal relationships in leadership roles.

Observing Dean Saff that year, I discovered his passionate belief in the power of a distinct and recognizable "brand" for marketing meritorious programs. This meant establishing an intriguing symbol that garners public attention and generates excitement and potential national and global attention. These are often powerful marketable trademarks that are based on a unique "big idea."

The name, GraphicStudio, its unique typeset, at first fulfilled the big idea purpose for his administration, identifying what was rapidly becoming an internationally acclaimed printmaking atelier and fine arts college symbol. But he wanted an even more dramatic brand that would make a larger global splash for USF and the Tampa Bay community. A dramatic brand with a capital "D."

Through exclusive connections, Dean Saff acquired the construction rights and details for Pablo Picasso's "Bust of a Woman," a massive 102 foot high 50-foot base outdoor concrete sculpture, if built to specifications. His plan was to fabricate the work as originally specified and position it on a specially built pedestal-plaza within an expanded arts section of the campus. There, due to the region's flat topography, the classic work would be visible for miles.

Artistically unique, and created and designed by Picasso, the internationally acclaimed artist, the massive structure would garner international recognition, and become a focal point for Tampa Bay tourism. And of course, it would bring major recognition for USF and the arts. But he was unable to raise the funds required for the ambitious construction design, despite local community enthusiasm for the project. Not accustom to failures, Donald Saff sadly abandoned the idea and rededicated himself to the artists and artisans that gave GraphicStudio its premier status.

During his final weeks as dean, Saff served as Marshall for the University's Honor's Convocation. As advising coordinator, I went to the auditorium early to assist with registering and lining-up the fine arts honor students. Academic regalia was required for faculty participating in the formal event. But not a program participant, I dressed in dark business attire.

While assuring the platform was setup properly and prepared for the ceremony, Dean Saff, dressed in crisp white shirt and dark tie before donning his robe, saw me standing over to the side of the auditorium waiting for students to arrive. He came over, spoke, and setting his eyes directly on mine commented: "This is like preparing for your Bar Mitzvah. Are you ready?" What? Huh? I was stunned. I did not know what to say…or how to respond. He smiled broadly, turned, and headed back to the stage. I was looking for a "just kidding" look-back over his shoulder, but it never came.

His Jewish identity was common knowledge; mine was not. In fact, my Jewish heritage had not been shared by me with anyone, formally or informally, and was a subject to which I gave very little thought. Both parents had informed my sister and me that we were the benefactors of Jewish lineage on both sides of the family, but they, nor we, never researched that particular ancestry. We were Negro, colored, African-American and Black, as the references changed, but had not given serious consideration to our Jewish identity.

However, several years later, when I was fine arts dean, inexplicably, this was "hushed" knowledge fostered and shared among the college's Jewish patrons, who were some of my most avid and staunchest supporters and donors, exemplified by the unique African Art Endowed Chair established by Roberta Golding. But sadly, after my 1999 retirement, the chair was inexplicably dissolved and the funds generated by the endowment reallocated to regular art faculty positions, allegedly because "it didn't fit the art department's Western focused academic program." But that was exactly the point; students deserve diverse knowledge and a more expansive global exposure, one of the objectives of Mrs. Golding's gift. This was very disturbing for me, given Roberta's vision for the endowed chair and the time she and I shared in its development.

Juel and I attended many Jewish events during my time as dean, including Roberta's grandson's Bar Mitzvah. And a Jewish elder, I often saw at those and other events, with gentlemanly subtlety, let me know that he was available if I ever wanted to learn about the Jewish faith.

Harrison Covington succeeded Saff as dean in 1977. Considered *the father of the college of fine arts* after establishing it through curriculum transfers from the College of Arts and Sciences, he became its second dean. Meeting him for the first time during his interview for the position, he was now my new boss. After reviewing my responsibilities, which had increased over the last several years to include overseeing human resources, payroll data input and equal opportunity/affirmation action, he promoted me to assistant dean. And under his sensitive guidance, I learned the value of liberal arts education, a passion for him and a new academic priority for me. Five years later he resigned after confronting the president over redirecting construction funds from the fine arts college for building the basketball coliseum. The succeeding dean, the college's third, was terminated for cause after less than two years. Meanwhile, I'm continuing two fulltime jobs as assistant dean and music faculty, but joyfully achieved the rank of full professor.

As Provost Gregory O'Brien prepared to begin a national search for the fourth arts dean in December 1986, he met with fine arts college department chairs for their recommendation for an interim appointment. They opposed the associate dean, the logical choice, recommending me instead, the reason I would soon discover. That night the provost called my home. "Professor Smith, based on the recommendation of your leadership colleagues, I'm asking you to serve as the college's interim dean during the national search for a permanent replacement." "What?" I sat stunned. "I'll need your response now so we can move ahead with the search immediately," he continued. "Well, uh, I'm completely surprised and flattered, but I will need to discuss this with my wife before I can respond." "Okay, please call me back as soon as you can. I believe you are the best choice."

Juel and I deliberated over two hours about the precedent setting opportunity, the first Black USF dean, although interim. There were powerful symbolic elements for considering, but also negative reactions that were certain to occur, including the reaction of the associate dean. I knew from fourteen years' experience in the college, and at the university, there were many sharks in the water. But the internal and external representation as USF's first Black dean was a message we felt worth personal risks, and represented opportunities I had been pushing for since my university appointment. So, I called the provost back and accepted the leadership role, but my racial anxieties were quickly confirmed.

At my first college executive council meeting, January 1987, I faced an unexpected confrontation. "We will be meeting regularly as the executive council to give you directions for running the college," the group's spokesman proclaimed. "All important decisions should be discussed with us before any actions." The direct unspoken message was, "We, the fine arts department chairmen, intend to administer the college ourselves as the executive council, making day-to-day decisions, and expect you to execute our decisions as the executive officer." Apparently, they had decided that I was incapable of providing the decisive, insightful leadership for the college, and I assume had recommended me to the provost simply to prevent the associate dean's appointment, the obvious choice.

I listened to that opening barrage, astonished, not believing what I was hearing, thinking, "This can't be real." And to have the audacity to believe that I would actually agree to their arrogant, or perhaps racist, terms.

"Here we go again," I thought, "My Blackness is being tested."

"Excuse me!" I said. "Excuse me! For your information, and contrary to your wishes, I intend to assume the fullest authority that's extended the dean's position, just as the provost has authorized. I will provide the direct leadership officially expected of a dean, without exceptions! There is no compromise or abdication of that authority. I would not have accepted the position otherwise."

Stunned into silence by my sharp rebuke of their unscrupulous plan, the chairs were unable to respond. And sensing their inability to back down from their position without discussion amongst themselves, I continued, "I suggest you all take some time to talk this over, overnight, and let's meet again in the morning. And if you still wish to proceed with your plan, I will step down from the dean's position, giving you the opportunity to work something else out with the provost." I was angry. The position was something I hadn't asked for, did not need, and was a burden I could very well live without.

In our meeting the next morning, the chairmen agreed reluctantly to my assuming the full authority of the dean's position, working in the usual collaborative spirit with them individually, and as the executive council. But that was the beginning of a rather contentious relationship with the chairs and the associate dean that lasted for months, although improved over time as I demonstrated my ability to effectively lead the college and win general faculty approval.

After the national search to fill the permanent dean's position, I was selected and appointed in 1988 after being encouraged by many faculty members to apply for the position. That made me USF's first African American permanent Dean.

By then Don Saff had extended GraphicStudio's title to *GraphicStudio/Institute for Research in Art*, and the unit had been relocated to the Office of the Provost as a university research institute, receiving direct line-item funding from Florida's State Department. Those paramount changes were a result of GraphicStudio's international prominence and Dr. Saff's astute lobbying, which significantly augmented its artistic capability, geographic reach and preeminence. The artist's, exploratory mission and elevated profile also increased the value of its art.

But since GraphicStudio's institutional mission also required continuing programmatic ties to the fine arts college's museum and art department, I was involved in managing those personal and programmatic relationships. The strong personalities of the three leaders tested my diplomatic skills, considerably. Policy required that one replica of each work produced by GraphicStudio is archived into the museum's collection, and GraphicStudio was obligated to offer art students learning opportunities through its collaborative and professional printmaking process. My responsibility was to assure the policies were followed.

For his part, Don Saff kept me apprised of GraphicStudio's activities, often inviting me to observe the use of innovative technology and techniques in creating unique works of art. As a musician, experiencing the creative elements of visual artistic expression was fascinating. Occasionally, he introduced me to the acclaimed artists he invited for collaboration.

In November 1989, my second year as dean, Don Saff requested that I join him on a trip to Russia for GraphicStudio business. His wife, Ruth, was accompanying him, so he suggested that Juel also join us. By then, Juel had earned her PhD in counseling psychology, and was founding executive director of USF's Institute on Black Life, doing an incredible job of bridging the University's resources with Tampa's Black community. He referenced awarding a USF Honorary Doctor of Arts to a distinguished international figure while there, and as fine arts dean my presence was important.

After consulting Juel, we enthusiastically accepted the invitation and began preparations, since the scheduled departure was only weeks away, a close timeline for acquiring Russian visas. And if everything went according to plans, we would receive them at the Kennedy International

Airport's International Terminal only hours prior to departure, hand delivered by Brenda, Don Saff's ingenious chief administrative assistant.

Prompted by Brenda, Juel and I excitedly made preparation, acquiring thick, wool clothes for the anticipated frigid weather, and purchasing cartons of cigarettes and other personal items that were invaluable for transactions with the Russians. This promised to be an extraordinary opportunity for us to expand our sense of the world and experience a decidedly different culture as the Soviet Union was collapsing.

Unfortunately, only days before our scheduled departure, my father died peacefully at home at the age of 97. Needless to say, we were all devastated by his passing, but I was also disheartened by what the last-minute change of plans meant for Don. Of course, he was quite disappointed, as we all were that we would not be able to make the trip, but he assured me that the appropriate choice was obvious. Juel and I went to Louisiana for my father's funeral, and the Saffs went on to Russia.

I later learned their trip was quite successful, but the painfully cold weather froze their camera's shutter preventing a photo album, which Juel and I would have enjoyed viewing even without being in the pictures.

In 1991, the Smithsonian Institution's National Gallery of Art organized its first exhibit of GraphicStudio art and, as customary, hosted a formal gala the evening before the official opening. Don Saff extended a special invitation to me and Juel to attend, including a VIP reception later that evening at the historic Willard Hotel. We felt honored to be among the many national dignitaries, esteemed guests, distinguished artists, and major contributors to the arts. Don took the time to introduce us to many of them, continuing to mentor and expand his protégé's professional contacts.

In a later effort to expand the marketing and sales of GraphicStudio works, Saff opened a gallery with a residential loft in a restored and modified historic building that was once a 19th-century carriage house in mid-Manhattan, New York. He invited me to visit him there when I was in the city on college business. Exquisitely designed and elegantly fashioned, the retrofitted, high-ceiling interior exhibited two- and three-dimensional GraphicStudio art with matching contemporary furniture. It was very impressive.

After a brief tour of the gallery that included several works of art I had not seen before, Don took me to lunch at a wonderful Italian restaurant within walking distance. The wooden door inside a larger gate opened directly onto the busy sidewalk and the noisy Manhattan traffic beyond. Over savory cuisine, we talked about his evolving GraphicStudio strategy, including the New York City entrepreneurial endeavor, and my fine arts dean exploits that included an arts and technology laboratory, a new dance education degree program, three endowed chairs and a weekly television production. This was an incredible meeting, and yet for me another mentoring session where I continued to learn about the business of art, and political and tactical leadership strategies from this complex multitalented genius.

Although GraphicStudio achieved significant international recognition, Don Saff realized that there were still huge segments of the global population that had not yet been exposed to its remarkable art. So, to reach some of those communities, he and Robert Rauschenberg established the Rauschenberg Overseas Cultural Interchange (ROCI), targeting non-Western and developing countries. They arranged exhibits in countries that included China, Tibet, Malaysia, and Cuba, where exposure to American contemporary art was practically nonexistent, but where they believed the vibrancy of Rauschenberg's art would resonate. At the very least, they rationalized, it would probably motivate broad questions among the viewers on "what is art, and what is its purpose?" the kind of questions that new and unfamiliar artistic expressions often generate, regardless of global or demographic context.

During the years I was fine arts dean, Don often invited me and Juel to GraphicStudio related social events, particularly those that involved his loyal community patrons, placing me in contact with them for future involvement. He used those occasions to promote, market and push GraphicStudio's mission, and encourage its patrons to continue their support. I embraced the events as an opportunity to cultivate potential donors for the fine arts college, eventually raising over $120 million dollars.

At one particular elegant, Saturday-evening dinner party hosted at a prominent lawyer's beautiful home in Old Tampa Bay, guests included USF's newly appointed president, Francis T. Borkowski, and some of Tampa's most avid arts advocates. Don Saff had recently completed a major partnership contract for GraphicStudio that needed the new president's signature, so he staged a surprise mini-signing ceremony during the event.

In the midst of the gala's excitement, Don got the attention of the guests, ceremoniously explained the gist of the contract, and led the president to a small, round, fashionably decorated table where the document was displayed, placed a pen in his hand and showed him the exact line for his signature. The president, laughing in the spirit of the moment, and registering no apprehension, did exactly as instructed.

However, later that evening, President Borkowski cornered me in a quiet section of the house. Because his academic discipline was music, I had already commenced cultivating a relationship that I hoped might be beneficial to my college. I thought: "This is good!" But that was far from his more urgent focus. Embarrassed, he confided, "You know, I knew absolutely nothing about the content of the document I signed. I wasn't even informed that I would be requested to sign something this evening. Were you aware?" "No, I wasn't told about it. But I assure you that Don Saff has always acted in the best interest of the University. And what you signed is probably a win-win for GraphicStudio, the University, and all involved," I said trying to ease his anxiety.

Juel and I laugh when we remember that night and how Don, facing a deadline, cleverly used the event to get the results he wanted, without the usual formal meeting. For me, it was another political and tactical lesson indirectly taught, and learned.

In June 1999, USF's President Betty Caster hosted a special banquet in recognition of my resignation as Dean of the College of Fine Arts after serving eleven years, the longest for a dean at the time. The program and participants were kept secret, and I would not know the details until they unfolded during the event. Much to my surprise and delight, at the special invitation of Juel, Don Saff, no longer at USF, was one of the program's participants. He made a remarkable, delightful and straight-face humorous presentation that evening about me and the tuba, which required diligent in-depth research.

His remarks were based on his experience while USF Fine Arts Dean and writing his book on printmaking (*Printmaking: History and Process* with Deli Sacilotto, 1978). Much of his writing took place in a small room next to his office, which happened to adjoin my tuba teaching and practice studio. Unfortunately, his research and writing often coincided with my practice schedule, during which the sound of my tuba too easily penetrated the wall that separated our rooms.

Don Saff had carefully researched the acoustic design and decibel properties of the tuba, and dramatically presented the details of his findings to the attentive audience. He also researched the acoustical sound transference capacity of cement block, the building material that separated our rooms; both were engineering investigations of the highest order. Then, he brought the two fact-loaded subjects together.

According to Don, the wall between our rooms offered excruciatingly little filtering of the long wavelength frequencies of the tuba. No matter how beautiful and musical (self-critique) my playing was, the amplified sound filled his room and wreaked havoc on his concentration. And as a perfectionist, my prolific repetitions during practice only intensified the exacerbating misery, all of which I was completely unaware. This was quite stressful and aggravating at the time for Dean Saff, but for the banquet he treated this calamity with abundant and imaginative humor.

By the conclusion of his episodic presentation, the audience, including me, was hysterical, some with tears streaming down their cheeks. It was absolutely hilarious! And the fact that he dedicated so much of his time to research the information for the presentation was very humbling. But in retrospect, I was also thankful that, as the Dean, he did not banish me to a maintenance closet in a building on the other side of our sprawling campus.

I felt honored that Don Saff, my mentor and career enhancer, and now manager of multiple major projects from his home near Washington, D.C., took time from his extremely busy schedule to attend the culminating event of my USF deanship, a job he prepared, nurtured and positioned me for starting the first year of my USF appointment, over twenty-five years earlier. It was so wonderful to see him again, and as it turned out, that was the last time we were in each other's presence.

All of the university administrative positions I have assumed over the course of my academic career since coming to USF began when Don Saff appointed me Coordinator of Advising for the College of Fine Arts. And, over succeeding years, through our working and collegial relationships, I acquired many personal and organizational leadership qualities from him that were beneficial all the way through to my ultimate appointment as university president.

However, during a phone conversation Juel and I had with him after my Fisk University presidency, I pointed out, "You know Don, all those academic jobs you mentored and prepared me for were extremely stressful, and took an enormous toll on my mind and body, causing dire mental and physical afflictions I experience daily? They're all your fault, Don, right?!"

We all laughed together, and Juel and I signed-off, with "Thanks for everything, Don."

And we meant—everything.

PART IV

He Taught Me Grace

Chapter 16

Blessed Assurance

"Hallelujah!"

"Hallelujah! Praise the Lord!"

"Hallelujah!"

The worshipers, feeling the powerful moving spirit, forcefully urged on by thundering rifts from the full-volume organ, energetically praised God their savior.

"Hallelujah! Rump! Praise God! Rump! Rump! Hallelujah!"

The church was packed, many standing. Their piercing shouts from the joyous celebration was captured by the sanctuaries high angled ceiling and slammed back down like a rumbling avalanche; the sound embellishing the emotional responses inspired by the devout sermon just delivered and they had just heard.

Its compelling message was profoundly based on an ancient Christian gospel, expressed in contemporary narrative. It referenced human stories enhanced by relevant metaphor, touching the depth of the congregants welcoming souls. The sermon was powerfully delivered by the exhausted black-robed preacher, now retreating from the light oak-wood pulpit where he had saintly stood, to the stately chair directly behind. He seemed content that perhaps he had succeeded in his noble mission: to spread the word of God.

I sat there with Juel and our children near the back of the chandelier-lit sanctuary, mesmerized and thinking: Finally! Perhaps this is the church I am seeking. One with a pastor whose sermons were as intellectually provocative as the spiritual message they conveyed. And, judging by the organ prelude I heard before the sermon, a church with music that balanced emotion and musicality. Perhaps, I thought, if Juel agrees, we need not look any further for a church home for our family. Later that day, I discovered happily, she was already on board.

Almost a year earlier, August1972, we had arrived in Tampa, Florida, with our five young children knowing absolutely nothing about the city's social life, particularly for African-Americans. Having accepted an assistant professor position at the University of South Florida (USF), and visited Tampa for three days earlier to secure living accommodations, Juel and I did not have a sense of the area's ambiance. After seeking information in advance from local Black organizations without success, we relocated from Sapulpa, Oklahoma to Tampa with guarded optimism about our future, knowing that learning the new community would be left to our own intuitive exploration.

Accustomed to attending Sunday worship service, and eager to continue our children's religious education, we commenced visiting Black churches immediately. Juel was a well-entrenched Baptist, but I was Episcopalian, after growing up Methodist with a brief Catholic interlude. So, for me it was less about religious doctrine and more about the worship experience, primarily the sermon and music. Initially, Juel was more methodical and persistent than I in the search for our family church home. Each Sunday she identified and visited a church with or without me; sometimes a different church, other times a repeat visit, but all were Baptist—her comfort zone of theology and worship traditions.

On this particular Sunday, the church we visited was Beulah Baptist Institutional, and the inspiring sermon we heard was delivered by the Rev. A. Leon Lowry, Sr. The beautiful soul-wrenching organ performance was by Wayne Leonard, the minister of music. I felt that together, they would compel me to wake up Sunday mornings looking forward to attending church.

Beulah, which attracted a considerable number of Tampa's Black professionals, was an excellent compromise for us, a decision greatly influenced by the well-organized religious education program for children. Not attracted to the highly spirited services of most Black Baptist churches, I found Beulah's worship services comparatively moderate; closely aligned with the ethos and reserved nature of the Methodist Church that was still deeply embedded in my spiritual DNA, thanks to my mother's impassioned beliefs.

Rev. Lowry, Beulah's pastor, was a 1939 honors graduate of historically Black, all-male Morehouse College in Atlanta, arguably one of the most prestigious liberal arts institutions in the nation. He completed theology studies in Massachusetts at Andover-Newton and later attended Harvard and Boston Universities before returning to Morehouse as theology professor, dean of students and assistant football coach. One of his students was Dr. Martin Luther King Jr., who he described as, "not particularly distinguishable at the time." Following Morehouse, he entered a life-long career dedicated to the Baptist ministry, and the pursuit of social justice and equality for African-Americans.

Accompanied by wife Claudia, and two sons, A. Leon II and Benjamin, Rev. Lowry assumed the pastoral leadership at Beulah in 1956, a church founded by freed slaves and Tampa's oldest Black Baptist church. He went on to serve an extensive tenure overseeing remarkable growth and development. As a progressive racial justice activist, he courageously led civil rights battles in Tampa, and served as Florida's NAACP president. But my introduction to him occurred in 1973 while sitting with my family on a back pew at Beulah, experiencing the power of his spiritual essence.

His sermons, often laced with intellectual ideology and perspectives that required critical thought, wove in metaphor and illustrations from the arts and humanities to clarify and emphasize theological precepts. Referencing western philosophy, literature, world history, psychology, geography, and music, he preached that Christian belief is firmly rooted in sound intellectual understanding and reasoning, as well as unquestioned faith. And that Christian living functions in the context of real-world humanity that encompasses the mind, body, and soul daily. I left church each Sunday with much to ponder, life adjustments to consider, and a moral imperative to act on.

Some of Rev. Lowry's sermons were rooted in Black liberation theology focused on biblical assertions that Jesus came to liberate the oppressed, which meant fighting for freedom, justice, and equality for Black Americans, and not accepting the white-supremacy interpretations and practices of Christianity (See *Black Theology and Black Power*, James Hal Cone, 1969). Never one to cast African-Americans as victims, he used biblical parables to urge his parishioners to confront the vestiges of racism and inequality in Tampa—or wherever found.

Strategically, many of those carefully worded sermons occurred as important elections approached, particularly those that had racial consequences. This was his way of being political without compromising the apolitical requirement of churches as a non-taxed entity. However, by the end of his sermon, you not only knew that you were expected to go to the polls and vote, but you also had a good idea for whom or what you should vote for or against.

For clarity and impact, Rev. Lowry crafted his sermons thoughtfully, structuring them like classical music's ABA "Sonata" compositional form with his prose replacing the music. As a student of classical music, I readily identified this approach. The main subject was introduced, followed by a brief supportive rationale, counter thoughts, and clarification. A development section ensued, using present-day anecdotes, metaphor and related topics often emotionally charged by repetition of phrases and extreme inflections in volume, before ending the sermon by restating his subject or theme, and closing. Sometimes a short, passionately expressed section (*coda*) was added, extending the repetitive phrases and volume inflections, a style typical of the Black ministry. But for Rev. Lowry, this was usually the result of him yielding to his own overpowering emotions.

Stepping back from the podium during those impassioned moments, head tilted up, arms waving, deep baritone voice challenging the inner sanctuary walls and generating comparable responses from aroused deacons and deaconess standing in front of him, his passion was laid bare. But hearing the ever-increasing antiphonal response from the congregants seemed to remind him of his own lost composure, whereby he returned to the podium to cool down and gather himself, bringing his praising parishioners back to a quieter state.

I recall one profound Easter Sunday sermon. After the usual inspirational organ prelude by Wayne, Rev. Lowry entered the pulpit from stage left, suddenly, surprising everyone. He was usually seated on the podium already. While striding purposely across the platform, looking toward the congregation, he began his sermon dramatically.

"He's alive! He lives! He lives!" he proclaimed, punctuating the air with his right hand for emphasis. "Do you know that? He's alive!"

Reaching the lectern, he turned to the congregation abruptly, and slammed the loose pages of his sermon down with one last, "HE'S ALIVE!"

Then he dove into a multilayered text about the meaning of The Resurrection. It covered, made relevant and tied together disparate subjects, including restoration, resuscitation, Hinduism, overcoming tragedy and the trap of mislabeling people. He spoke of Christ as the center of history, that truth is stronger than a lie, that death cannot destroy God's purposes, Calvary was a setback and Easter was a comeback. All of this was followed by a brief reference to the popular sci-fi blockbuster movie, *E.T.* He ended the sermon with a dramatic restatement of his opening proclamation.

"He's alive! He lives! He is Alive!"

It was thought provoking and emotional. A powerful moving message.

Gifted with a powerfully resonant bass-baritone voice, a quality not unlike the famous singer, Paul Robeson, Rev. Lowry, though not a competent singer, was more than capable of filling the church sanctuary with the spoken word. Sometimes his booming voice, caroming off the church walls, gave the mystical sense that God was there, talking to us.

Over six feet tall, muscular, with dark complexion and strong African facial features, Rev. Lowry was bald, except for extended sideburns that seemed to appear out of nowhere. A man of impeccable taste, he dressed in fashionable business attire tailored for a perfect fit. Once, when I informed him that I would be traveling to London, he referred me to Burberry's for my shopping pleasure, one of his favorite clothiers. His sense of style and interest in durability led him to choose the diesel-engine Mercedes-Benz sedan for his mode of transportation. I made a similar choice for the same reason, but a less expensive model initially.

Wayne Leonard's organ preludes that preceded Rev. Lowry's sermons set the tone for his message. But because of Wayne's powerful expressive musical renderings, I thought of the preludes as "the sermon before the sermon." They were as electrifying in their aesthetic and emotional features as were the informative and passionate qualities of Rev. Lowry's sermons that followed.

However, unmistakably, Rev. Lowry managed to surmount Wayne's passionate challenge, greatly inspiring the hearts and minds of worshipers. But I sometimes left church laughing to myself, wondering, "Are those two guys competing with each other? And in so doing, pushing each other to excel beyond their individual capability?" Regardless, my spiritual needs were being well served at Beulah.

However, I learned that there was much more to Rev. Lowry than his ministry; much more to influence my life. When the 1960s national sit-in movement eventually motivated Tampa's Black youths to action, Rev. Lowry stepped forward as advisor and protector, placing his life in considerable danger. Positioning himself within the nearby downtown Woolworth drug store, where the students sat courageously at the lunch counter, he was prepared to protect them against the worst instances of physical hostility. Violent threats and actions were made on his life, during that time, including gun shots fired into his home endangering his family. He did not request special police protection, but men from the community guarded his house each night, voluntarily.

Persistent pressure from the students' courageous actions, aided by behind-the-scenes negotiations involving Rev. Lowry, Mayor Julian Lane, and the city's Community Relations Board, peacefully desegregated the drugstore lunch counter and other businesses and public accommodations. In1961, Rev. Lowry was among a small group of Black leaders who met with President John F. Kennedy at the White House to persuade him to use his considerable powers and personal influence to eliminate America's racial inequalities.

In an effort to alleviate the persistent financial constraints imposed on African-Americans by Jim Crow segregation, Rev. Lowry co-founded with other Black leaders the Community Federal Savings and Loan Bank in 1967, one of the few African American owned and operated banks in the country. Serving as chairman and president of an uncompensated board, the bank offered routine financial services, and access to capital for purchasing homes, building churches, opening small businesses, and acquiring education and emergency loans. However, it was not easy to establish and maintain.

According to Rev. Lowry, "It was 10 years before we got into the black.... the founders had to borrow money to help take care of the federal requirements." (From *Leon Lowry, Sr.: A Warrior in the Vineyard*, Free Press Publishing Company, Tampa, 1995)

In the early 1980s, the bank's assets had declined significantly due to white financial institutions opening services to African-Americans and hiring them as employees. In a final heroic effort to save the bank, Rev. Lowry, speaking from Beulah's pulpit one Sunday: " Beulah, I come to you today asking that you consider buying bonds from Community Federal Savings and Loan. They are safe and guaranteed, and would help continue the financial services the bank offers our community," he urged. Indeed, the bank desperately needed investors for its solvency.

But, unfortunately, insufficient response forced the bank to close September 1990. Juel and I, feeling extremely guilty, had declined the investment opportunity because we believed the bank had already reached irreversible insolvency. It appears we weren't the only ones that reached that conclusion. However, again according to Rev. Lowry, "Every depositor received his money, plus interest." (*Leon Lowry, Sr.: A Warrior in the Vineyard*) Was he implying, perhaps, that the founders, again, privately-sourced the final payout?

As Rev. Lowry continued to push for racial justice and equality through direct and legal actions, he decided that perhaps he could fight discrimination more effectively as a law- or policymaker to help craft laws/policies that prevent racial inequities. Perhaps, he concluded, having a seat at the table would eliminate the need for protests and litigation, as we've had to do. "After all," his rational continuing, "that's how democracy works, we just need to make it work for everyone."

So, in 1976, four years after I arrived in Tampa, Rev. Lowry entered and won an election to the Hillsborough County School Board, becoming the first African American on the board, and the first Black person to win a county-wide elected position. It was an eye-opening political achievement for the Black community, motivating others to run for elected positions to gain political influence for improving their lives.

I was certainly impressed by Rev. Lowry's audacity and evolving longevity. He was reelected to the board until his retirement in 1992, serving several times as chairman. During his tenure, the board managed the difficult issues of school desegregation and explosive growth. When he retired, board colleagues spoke of him as *the voice of fairness, reason, compromise, and compassion, always able to gain their attention.*

Impressed with Rev, Lowry's professionalism, political savvy and dedication to community development, several white leaders invited him to invest in a new Tampa-based telecommunications company that established a television station serving one of the largest viewing areas in the country, an investment that made him modestly wealthy. Using the new financial resources, he built a modern brick house not far from Beulah, ending years of living in the parsonage next to the church. He also contributed significantly to community programs, civil rights initiatives, and his beloved church, often anonymously.

Meanwhile, for seven years I had been religiously (no pun intended) attending Beulah and enjoying the Sunday service and growing spiritually from Rev. Lowry's sermons. And due mostly to our children's involvement I was developing warm, genuine relationships with several members. However, I was not a member of Beulah, and had begun to feel that I was outside the church's celestial windows looking in, seeing my family intimately involved—without me.

Not eager to commit myself to organized religion again, including the complexities of church governance and politics, I was nevertheless uncomfortable enjoying the spiritual benefits without putting some skin in the game directly. So, one Sunday morning, without alerting anyone, I walked to the front of the church and made my commitment to become Baptist and an official member of Beulah Baptist Institutional Church. Everyone was elated that day, Juel particularly, but nonverbal language by certain deacons as they congratulated me, proclaimed, "What took you so long, brother!?"

In preparation for baptism, I attended required religious sessions with Rev. Lowry to explore the source and strength of my convictions, and learn the basic precepts underlying Baptist theology. Since I was the only participant, the sessions were one-on-one, allowing me the incredible opportunity to intimately know Rev. Lowry as a minister, and man.

Aided in those sessions extensively by my knowledge of prior denominations to which I had belonged, noting differences and similarities, I listened mostly, only requesting clarifications as needed. However, after each session ended, I hung around to chat about non-religious topics to understand "Rev. Lowry, the man."

My earlier more distant assessments of him were confirmed: He was indeed the humble, sincere, spiritual, and liberally, educated intellect I judged him to be. He was also a minister who staunchly attempted to live his faith, even under the most difficult and dangerous political and social circumstances.

After the education sessions were completed, Rev. Lowry submerged me in water during a baptismal ceremony in the church, behind the dais, in the presence of my family just before Sunday service —to symbolize my rebirth and new transcendent Christian status. I am not sure that a rebirth and transcendence actually occurred, but I knew that at that moment Rev. Lowry was my spiritual leader officially, in addition to role model for which he was already serving unwittingly. Up until then, there were only two other religious leaders I had known personally, my Uncle Jap and Rev. Norris, who appeared to make a sincere attempt to practice their faith and walk the values they preached. I welcomed him eagerly to my small select family of ethical and morals-driven role models, and the courageous leader for social justice.

With my new Beulah membership came a sense of responsibility to become involved in church programs. I could no longer simply attend and enjoy Sunday service without feeling guilty of underserving my religious commitment. So, when Rev. Lowry requested that I serve as Minister of Music (Wayne moved to Florida's east coast), I accepted eagerly. Then he promptly provided me a copy of the *Baptist Church Music Guide* to make sure I got it right.

He greatly enjoyed the stately protestant anthems with their poetic texts, supported by the powerful organ. The music's text was extremely important to him, as he wanted it to relate to the theme of his sermons. An occasional Negro spiritual inserted in Sunday service was acceptable, but Black gospel music, though tolerated, was not his favorite, a little too progressive. The musicians attempted to honor the diverse church membership with a genre mix that did not too often upset the Reverend. But gospel music was gradually becoming the congregation's favorite, his acceptance or not. As a classical music musician and professor, I stayed out of the fray, allowing the choir directors to take their calculated risks.

Occasionally, Rev. Lowry appeared unannounced at choir rehearsals and committee meetings, sometimes early enough to provide the opening prayer, which were cherished moments. His prayers lifted the spirits of those present and set the appropriate spiritual tone for the task at hand, somehow managing to connect directly with the power that provides positive energy to face present challenges. Often poetic and metaphorically punctuated, his prayers left you at once serene, peaceful, searching and reaching, but never questioning faith, human capacity, and capability.

One evening, Rev. Lowry arrived at the close of a committee meeting I was attending wearing less the pastoral, and more the ordinary human hat: *Rev. Lowry the man*. He was jovial and initiated casual conversation about secular subjects with the few of us who remained after the meeting. He loved to talk about football, especially the Tampa Bay Buccaneers. Although, he never rushed through Sunday worship service when the Bucs were playing in town so that congregants, including himself, could rush home and catch the opening kickoff. And he sometimes jokingly teased church members regarding the peculiar quirks of their social sororities and fraternities, while indirectly poking fun at himself as a fervent fraternity member as well, having joined in college.

But on this particular night, underneath Rev. Lowry's jovial exterior was a person who seemed lonely, needing to temporarily shed the formal and serious "reverend" constraints, and enjoy a moment of secular levity while relaxing in the company of a few loyal congregants.

Not too long before, he had experienced the tragic deaths of his wife, Claudia, and youngest son, Benjamin, which affected him greatly. For the sake of his beloved church, he continued carrying out his pastoral duties valiantly without grieving noticeably. They had an older son living elsewhere in the state, so there was no family member at home for intimate interactions, which may have accounted for the unusual moment we were experiencing.

Then, much to our surprise: "Excuse me," he announced, "I'll be right back," leaving the room abruptly and quickly reappearing from his nearby office with a popcorn popper. "Just a minute, I'll have this set up and we can enjoy some popcorn." And while it was popping he left the room again this time returning with a portable record player and several vinyl albums. With the aroma of freshly popped popcorn swirling in the air, he commenced playing the music of Duke Ellington, Count Basie and Ella Fitzgerald, his favorite jazz greats, while talking about them and their artistic styles, short descriptive sentences. I was just glad, for obvious reasons, he didn't pull out a Bessie Smith deep-down blues album.

It was apparent that he really loved and enjoyed jazz and did not condemn the genre because of the "low down dirty" blues roots underlying its creation and early performance venues that included juke joints and night clubs. Some conservative Baptist clergy and parishioners would have thought this was sacrilegious and unbecoming of a minister. But Rev. Lowry, for a brief moment anyway, allowed himself the freedom to enjoy, along with us, the small pleasure of listening to globally treasured music that was the product of our African-American culture, while eating popcorn. It was also obvious that he was indeed lonely, and just needed a brief break to loosen up and enjoy a little social camaraderie.

Initially, we did not know exactly how to respond to this unfamiliar pastoral persona. But we adjusted quickly and joined in creating a safe environment for him to expose his authentic humanity. We ate popcorn, listened with him to music, talked about the jazz greats, and laughed with each other. However, before very long, things gradually began to return to normal, and the old roles restored. When we departed that night, our pastor had returned to the formal-self we were accustomed to, and we his devoted parishioners.

As I drove home, I realized that my trust and belief in Rev. Lowry as my spiritual leader and role model had not diminished because of his momentary escape from the minster-self, but were actually elevated. The secular side of him I witnessed during that short period was sensitive, authentic, and vulnerable, reflecting the greater humanity underneath his high moral aspirations. It illustrated that he also struggled each day, as all of us do, to fend off powerful immoral and unethical temptations in order to follow what we believe and espouse as true Christian values, often unsuccessfully. Sometimes it takes experiencing our vulnerable side to realize the strength of our faith and convictions.

The public image of a dedicated minister, Rev. Lowry's comportment made sure interpersonal relationships were not too casual and informal. Handshakes, nothing beyond, were the norm when greeting someone, regardless of familiarity. I was pointedly reminded of this personal protocol when I attempted a compassionate consoling gesture one Sunday morning.

On that particular Sunday, his sermon seemed intensely personal and anxious, as though he was extremely troubled by something traumatic. But he did not share the reason for his anguish.

So, at the end of service as we filed into the vestibule where he greeted exiting congregants, I decided that Rev. Lowry needed a compassionate, consoling embrace. Hugs, or an air-kiss near the cheek, were not unusual among friends and members of the congregation. I walked up to him and said, "We all love you Reverend" while reaching up to his robed six-foot frame. Well, he was totally unresponsive, like hugging a telephone pole.

"Oops!" I thought, "No man-hug for the Reverend."

I had crossed an invisible line and knew immediately that it was a huge mistake. I withdrew quickly, feeling embarrassed and disappointed, having offered a gesture of human compassion, but was summarily rejected. Back then, it was not easy for me to demonstrate my own feelings in that way, a compassionate gesture I was learning from my wife gradually. In her world, hugs are the norm.

Later, as I reflected on the incident, it dawned on me that I had never seen Rev. Lowry embrace another person, female or male, which is probably a safe practice for a church pastor. My doing so as a man was probably extremely intimidating for him. However, from another perspective, maintaining personal distance from others may have been an innate trait, as well as professional choice, not unlike my grandfather, Jasper Scott and great uncle, Dr. Julius Scott. A trait I may have picked up from them. Thankfully and more importantly, Rev. Lowry's sermons strongly advocated the demonstration of human warmth, love, and compassion for others, as Christianity teaches.

As my relationship with Rev. Lowry evolved, I became more and more impressed with his vast knowledge, oratorical power, and sociopolitical contributions. From my perspective, as a USF professor and assistant college dean, those were exceptional qualities and deserved appropriate recognition. And I'm quite certain that if achieving the PhD had been a personal goal, he would have accomplished it with incredible ease, aplomb, and honor, probably from Harvard, where he attended briefly.

So, while vigorously pursuing my aggressive equal-opportunity/affirmative-action efforts at USF, I discovered that the University had not awarded an honorary doctorate to an African-American in its twenty-year, fifty-commencement history of honorific presentations. And with Rev. Lowry in mind, I thought it was time to change that racial imbalance.

For the nomination process, I teamed with Dr. Melvin Stith, my Black assistant dean counterpart in the College of Business Administration, and a Beulah church member, to nominate Rev. Lowry for the Honorary Doctor of Humane Letters. The nomination was approved without question, based solely on its merits. I didn't need to make one phone call. The degree was awarded during the University's spring 1981 commencement.

Melvin, Juel and I enjoyed being with Rev. Lowry in the dressing room backstage in the Sun Dome that day before commencement started. He tried concealing his personal pride as he donned the special black robe for the hooding ceremony. Over six thousand graduating seniors, family members and faculty would witness the occasion.

During the regal ritual, he stood center stage, tall and impressive, as the hood was placed over his head and adjusted by Provost Gregory O'Brian, followed by a congratulatory handshake from President John Lott Brown. As commencement speaker, the Reverend Doctor Lowry made short and compelling remarks offering encouragement and hope for the graduating seniors who responded with enthusiastic applause.

Everyone attending commencement who knew Rev. Lowry was happy for him, knowing that he was truly deserving. However, for the Beulah church members who were unable to attend, Melvin Stith and I staged a mock hooding ceremony during Sunday worship service a week later. Rev. Doctor A. Leon Lowry was genuinely humble and appreciative for the in-church recognition, and the congregants were proud of their pastor, appreciative of the opportunity to witness the honorific ritual.

Following the success of that worthwhile effort, I decided to pursue another challenging initiative at USF the following year that involved Rev. Lowry, recommending him for an adjunct lecture appointment in the religious studies department. Using the influence of my assistant dean position (whatever power that represented), I made the proposal to the department chairman directly. Aware that the department did not have Black faculty, or a professor with expertise in Black theology and religious practices, an obvious deficit, I thought the chairman might jump at the opportunity. He requested Rev. Lowry's application and curriculum vitae eventually, which was encouraging. Later that summer, I bumped into the Reverend leaving the campus library excited about the potential to teach college again. He was delivering a Black theology course syllabus to the department chairman for consideration.

However, near the beginning of the fall semester, the chairman informed me that the department decided not to appoint Rev. Lowry, vaguely alluding to his lack of documented research. I was greatly angered by that decision, and the feeble excuse, given that it was an adjunct "teaching" appointment we had discussed, not a professorship. But well aware that most academic disciplines at USF were still unwilling to appoint Black professionals, or validate African-American culture and history in department curricular and course offerings, I was not surprised.

However, for me, the most regrettable aspect of their decision was how the rejection would crush Rev. Lowry's hopes and excitement for being in the university classroom again, expecting to teach African American culture, religious beliefs and practices to curious students. In a phone call to him, I attempted to apologize for the University's shortsighted decision, but I am sure that the longtime "social justice warrior" knew better than I the real underlying reason for the appointment's denial: white racism.

Beulah Baptist Church continued to grow and expand under Rev. Dr. Lowry's astute leadership. Every Sunday I witnessed new individuals and families joining the church and participating in the various ministries and activities. Christian education and social service programs were augmented to serve the growing congregation and surrounding west Tampa residents. Our children thrived under sensitive and dedicated teachers and program directors, and we were deeply embedded in the church's loving spirit.

On one Thanksgiving holiday weekend, encouraged by Rev. Lowry's spiritual humility, Juel and I loaded the trunk of our car with turkeys from the Tampa food bank and distributed them to Beulah's elder and infirm members, some, who from previous visits, had adopted us as godchildren and care-friends. One mother, living many years in public housing, was raising several children while confined completely to a bed. Those were cherished visits for us.

Invariably, when it came election time, whether national, state or local, white politicians sought Rev. Lowry's support as a means to acquire the Black vote. Illustrating savvy political diplomacy, he permitted a select few, the more liberal leaning and racially accommodating, to make brief presentations during the eleven o'clock worship service, some even staying for the entire program. For Black people, it was always choosing the lesser of none beneficial options.

On such occasions, his message to the congregation was: "Be sure to express your personal freedom by voting, and urge others to do so, as well. Voting was a hard-earned right that many African-Americans and others sacrificed and died for, and we should not abuse or take for granted that privilege."

Beulah's modern church building was constructed in 1969 with a thirty-year bank mortgage, still very new when I started attending. But with Rev. Lowry's strong leadership and personal contributions, the mortgage was retired in 1983, sixteen-years early, an occasion celebrated joyously with a special Mortgage Burning Service. However, only months had passed before plans were developed to build an education and fellowship center adjacent to the sanctuary that included a children's nursery targeting the surrounding community. When completed, the building was aptly named the *A. Leon Lowry Family Center*.

Thoroughly enjoying Rev. Lowry's sermons each Sunday, Juel sometimes complimented him on their quality and urged him to select and publish a few for sharing with an expanded audience. His response initially was to politely ignore her, until one day he proclaimed modestly, "The sermons only represent a preacher's humble attempt on Sundays to inspire human goodness through the word of God," implying they did not merit preservation for future reading.

However, one Sunday after church service in 1999, a few weeks before Juel and I left for my Fisk University presidential appointment in Nashville, he handed her original copies of several sermons without any comment. Just placed them in her hands and walked away, while she stood there dumfounded. Today, we feel privileged to possess those profound well-thought-out spiritual testaments, and intend to explore their publication in his honor and memory.

In the early 1990s, Juel, the director of the USF Institute on Black Life (IBL), sponsored and coordinated the publication of *Leon Lowry, Sr.: A Warrior in the Vineyard* (Free Press Publishing Company, Tampa, 1995), an abbreviated biography of Rev. Lowry that includes substantial oral history. He was a member of the Black community advisory committee, which along with the Black Faculty and Staff Council, persuaded USF's administration to establish the IBL. The late Peggy Peterman, editorial writer/columnist for the *St. Petersburg Times* (now the *Tampa Bay Times*), researched and wrote the book, a modest effort to pay homage to our Tampa icon and beloved spiritual leader.

But there were occasions when Juel and I experienced a more personal relationship with Rev. Lowry. In 1988, when I was offered the USF College of Fine Arts dean's position, I requested a meeting with him for counsel and advice before making a final decision. After serving over a year as interim, I knew that the position was difficult, extremely complex, and stressful, and I needed spiritual assurance that I would make the right decision for me, my family, and the institution. And that if I was to accept the offer, I wanted to know that I would not be alone, but guided and protected by God, my spiritual source.

Rev. Lowry agreed that the offered position was indeed challenging, but also a significant opportunity for me, and for others whose lives I would impact. He provided calming words of encouragement and confidence in that soothing and compelling baritone voice of his. And then he prayed with me that from the decision-making struggle the right path would reveal itself with clarity and assurance. He prayed that if I chose to accept the position, I would have the strength, courage, and wisdom to persevere and be successful. Standing holding hands while we prayed in the solitude of his small church office was a spiritual experience that sustained and empowered me throughout my tenure as dean, and beyond.

Ten years later, for the banquet celebrating the end of my dean's appointment, Rev. Lowry provided the opening convocation and closing benediction symbolizing the Alpha and the Omega of my tenure. In reserved but profound prayers, his eloquent words gave thanks to God for the occasion, and for everyone who shared in my success. It was fitting that he began and ended the program that celebrated my appointment, for it was the power of his prayers and Sunday sermons that helped sustain me throughout those demanding years.

After Rev. Lowery retired as Beulah's pastor, Juel and I invited him out for a Saturday evening dinner to demonstrate our love and appreciation for the many years of his counsel and friendship, and to just enjoy some quiet quality time with him.

We choose Armani's, a five-star restaurant on the top floor of the Grand Hyatt hotel overlooking Old Tampa Bay (now closed). Known for its fine dining, featuring Northern Italian cuisine, it was arguably the best formal restaurant in Tampa Bay, chosen by us to reflect Rev. Lowry's refined tastes. But to further emphasize the special nature of the event, we chauffeured him that evening, picking up and returning him to his home.

Dressed as dapper as ever, in one of his Burberry suits, he appeared to relish the social nature and elegant ambiance of the evening. Due to his deep respect and high regard for individuals with earned doctorates, he always addressed me and Juel affectionately as "Doc." However, when we turned the table and called him "Reverend Doctor," he gracefully declined the honorific title because the doctorate was honorary. Of course, we called him Reverend Doctor anyway.

From the restaurant's position high atop the hotel, with floor-to-ceiling windows offering panoramic views, we watched the sun dip beyond Old Tampa Bay that evening as we teased our appetizers, picked through our salads, allowed refreshing sorbet to cleanse our pallets, and devoured our scrumptious main course, while discussing various topics ranging from education and politics to local socioeconomic issues.

We touched lightly on family and personal subjects during which I noted hints of Rev. Lowry's continuing sadness over the loss of Claudia and Benjamin, his wife and youngest son. However, he was excited to hear about our foreign travel to Africa and Europe. We shared a few humorous stories about church and community, and discussed how to improve the plight of African-Americans.

It was a delightful and very personable evening, one that Juel and I will long cherish and treasure. And, for me, it was an absorbing experience with my most valued mentor and role model.

On April 8, 2000, while scanning the audience during my Fisk University President's inauguration, much to my surprise and joy, I recognized Rev. Lowry sitting in the audience. His presence was so meaningful to me, symbolizing that his powerful prayers were for my wisdom and strength to effectively lead the institution. After the ceremony, prodded by Juel, he briefly joined me in the Jubilee Hall reception line, but left unnoticed for the return flight to Tampa before I had an opportunity to thank him for coming. I later learned that he made the one-day round trip not feeling well, and I felt bad for his personal sacrifice to support me.

While we were at Fisk, Rev. Lowry remarried, much to our surprise. We didn't have a hint that was coming. And when we next saw him after returning to Tampa, he appeared energized, experiencing a newly revitalized phase in his life. Juel teased him unmercifully for marrying without getting her permission, and each time he would smile, give her a brief silent stare and continue on his way. But after marrying Shirley, who was much younger, he appeared more relaxed and happier than I had seen him in years. She provided a sense of security as he aged, but also a more guarded privacy, perhaps a little too extreme for longtime church members who were accustomed to easy access to the Reverend.

For Rev. Lowry's 80th birthday, Shirley invited me and Juel to a special celebration at a local restaurant that also included several other Beulah and Tampa community representatives, a small group. Requested to make remarks, I referenced his sermons: "Rev. Doctor Lowry often structured his powerful sermons in the musical *sonata* ABA form, subject introduction, development and recapitulation, sometimes with coda, and effectively used the organ prelude before his sermon as an emotional transition for his message," which motivated a broad twinkle-eyed smile and slight nod of his head from him indicating our mutual understanding of the artistry he applied to crafting his sermons. But he had to help me recall the organist, Wayne Lenard's, name. Although much older than I, his memory was sharper.

During Rev. Lowry' retirement, I saw him for Sunday services at Beulah when he attended, and once a year he was invited to deliver the sermon. I observed his health and aging struggles, though they appeared modest. However, feeling a strong urge to spend personal time with him, I phoned Shirley and arranged to visit at their new home, now in the northern suburbs. When I arrived that day, she cheerfully invited me in directing me to the living room sofa. Moments later, I was joined by the Reverend Doctor who slowly made his way into the room and sat next to me.

"Welcome Doc, I'm so glad for your visit. It's really good to see you," he said sincerely while sitting down. As usual, he was dressed impeccably in business attire, minus coat.

Shirley came through moments later, made sure we were comfortable, kissed him and excused herself to run errands. I started the conversation by bringing him up to date on my recent activities, starting with my Fisk University experience. W. E. B. Du Bois, a Fisk graduate and one of his heroes, intrigued him.

"Can you imagine? I walked the same grounds he did?" I said with astonishment.

"Yes, he was a great man," he responded haltingly.

I went on to describe the historic buildings that grace the campus and talked about the academic excellence that continues to characterize the university, in spite of its continuing financial struggles.

"You know, Reverend Doctor, Juel and I visited John Hope Franklin, another distinguished Fisk graduate, at his home in Durham, North Carolina," I said, happily recalling the memory. "He showed us his orchid nursery, his pride and joy."

Then I noticed that his responses were limited. So, I began saying things to pull him into the conversation, but his speech was unusually slow and tentative.

Finally, he looked over at me with a sad expression, one that I will never forget, and said in a slow, labored voice: "Doc, I apologize for being unable to express myself as normal," his face registering intense frustration. "My current health conditions prevent me from readily articulating my thoughts."

This caught me off guard. I wasn't prepared for his mental decline, wanting him to be his usual quick-thinking articulate self. But not having spoken with him for nine years since his 80th birthday, I should have anticipated and been prepared for his possible decline.

So, frozen in place, I mentally kicked myself, heartbroken for him, seeing the monumental disappointment in his eyes. I was unable to respond appropriately, and the passing of time suddenly hit me at warp speed, revealing that my spiritual leader and friend for over twenty-five years, now in his late-eighties, was succumbing to advanced age, and I suppose, like him, I wanted to reverse the clock, if only by a few years.

At the end of our visit, Rev. Lowry walked me to the door and out onto the small porch. Two of his young sons, inherited with his second marriage, were throwing a football on the front lawn. Standing on the porch, he surprised me by yelling, "Throw me the ball!" And one of them responded with a respectful gentle lob accurate enough for Rev. Lowry to catch without moving. Then he yelled again, "Go out for a pass!" and he flung the ball on target to the running youngster with surprising zip.

"Wow," I thought, "so much for the need to reverse the clock." My 89-year-old mentor/role model just demonstrated that certain parts of his life were working just fine, thank you very much.

Rev. Dr. A. Leon Lowry personified all that I consider essential and important in a spiritual leader and man. His influential presence in my life and my family's was considerable, and truly inspiring. The carefully crafted sermons served as a source for spiritual guidance as I attempted to understand life's meaning, react to its demands, and chart courses that would embrace the challenges and opportunities that inevitably occurred. His life and humanity served as a model exemplifying the epitome of high moral standards, human compassion, and incredible courage. And his presence in my life has provided me spiritual confidence and social convictions and encouragement to continue the fight for Black justice and equality.

On August 20, 2005, Rev. Lowry's earthly presence ended at the age of 92. Attending his funeral at Beulah, the church he loved, with hundreds of others was an incredibly sad moment in my life. WEDU, the local PBS television station, on whose board of directors Rev. Lowry had served, interviewed attendees leaving the church, including me and my solemn ramblings. I was unable to express the depths of my feelings. However, I suppose that if I were following the exactness of his teachings, I would have, at least in part, felt joy for his transition to the heavenly world.

But I didn't. I felt only a great sense of loss.

Now, years later, whenever Juel and I reflect on the life and teachings of The Reverend Doctor A. Leon Lowry Sr., and the cherished relationship we shared with him, we feel an abundance of joy, happiness, and inspiration. For, along with all of the important, influential, and "intrusive" mentors throughout my life, Rev. Lowry's spiritual essence continues to guide our paths and counsel our hearts, even though we continue to deeply miss his physical presence and moral example of how a true Christian life can, and should, be lived.

EPILOGUE

Are we missing the opportunity to influence another person simply because of the common every day relationship? Or, are we actually mentoring without knowing it? Mentoring is the noble giving of one's self to another for their personal enhancement and enrichment; it doesn't matter the relationship. Sometimes all we need to do is understand our role in a relationship, as potentially beneficial to the other person and take it seriously.

Nothing is more satisfying than recognizing the positive influence made on another life, whether minor or major. And often it's hard to tell. But more importantly, you know when you've made the effort and that makes it worthwhile.

Unknowingly, the nurturing experiences I encountered, encouraged my own instinct for mentoring and providing an ideal role model for others. And I hope, if nothing else, this book inspires others to honor everyday common relationships as opportunities for influencing another life. Just take the relationship seriously. I did!

Mr. Smith,

This letter's intent may never be fulfilled for it is one of gratitude and appreciation; and with words I couldn't commend you adequately for your service to me in obtaining my B.A. degree in Music.

You, in many instances, bent over backwards to ensure me proper finance and academic support. In addition to that, your words of encouragement served as a source of inspiration to me in times of hardships and depression. Without prognosticating my own future, you've again offered aid. On many and various occasions, you ignited initiatives within me by providing a prime example of what the Black man's role is. I will not hesitate nor procrastinate when saying you have contributed more than my own family toward my college education and I admire and appreciate every single thing you've done. I only wish that I could in some way repay you. I'm gratefully indebted to you. "Thanks man."

Musically yours,

Dennis Grant, Langston University '72

(Former student and mentee)

ABOUT THE AUTHOR

John L. Smith, Jr. was the twelfth president of Fisk University and the first Black principal tuba player for an American Symphony Orchestra.

He's the first tuba player to earn the coveted Indiana University Performer's Certificate. His Doctorate is from the University of Missouri-Kansas City, Master's from Indiana University, Bachelor's from Lincoln University, MO, and postdoctoral study at Harvard. He was the first Black president of the International Council of Fine Arts Deans and the first Black Dean at the University of South Florida. He served on numerous arts, civic, education and community organization boards in Tampa, FL and Nashville, TN, as well as, co-founded Oklahoma City's Black Liberated Arts Center and was recognized for professional and community service.

He also served honorably in the U.S. Navy (see www.smithjuniorliteraryworks.com for additional information).

Dr. Smith lives in Tampa, Florida.

www.ingramcontent.com/pod-product-compliance
Lightning Source LLC
Chambersburg PA
CBHW050733150726
48196CB00038B/910/J